PENGUIN BOOKS

THE END OF THE THIRD WORLD

Nigel Harris lives in London with his wife and two grown-up children. He is a member of a small unit specializing in developing countries at University College London and works extensively in developing countries. He has lived in Malaysia, Nigeria and India, and frequently visits Mexico and East Asia. A former editor of *International Socialism*, his previous works include *Beliefs in Society* (1967), *Competition and the Corporate Society* (1972), *India–China: Underdevelopment and Revolution* (1974), *The Mandate of Heaven: Marx and Mao in Modern China* (1978), *Economic Development, Cities and Planning* (1978) and *Of Bread and Guns: The World Economy in Crisis* (Penguin, 1983).

D1341218

Nigel Harris

The End of the Third World

Newly Industrializing Countries
and the Decline of an Ideology

Penguin Books

PENGUIN BOOKS

Published by the Penguin Group
Penguin Books Ltd, 27 Wrights Lane, London W8 5TZ, England
Penguin Books USA Inc., 375 Hudson Street, New York, New York 10014, USA
Penguin Books Australia Ltd, Ringwood, Victoria, Australia
Penguin Books Canada Ltd, 2801 John Street, Markham, Ontario, Canada L3R 1B4
Penguin Books (NZ) Ltd, 182–190 Wairau Road, Auckland 10, New Zealand

Penguin Books Ltd, Registered Offices: Harmondsworth, Middlesex, England

First published by I. B. Tauris & Co. Ltd 1986
Published in Pelican Books 1987
Reprinted in Penguin Books 1990
10 9 8 7 6 5 4 3 2

Copyright © Nigel Harris, 1986
All rights reserved

Printed in England by Clays Ltd, St Ives plc
Filmset in Monophoto Times

Contents

List of Figures

Preface

In the late 1940s and early 1950s, the idea of a Third World was beginning to emerge. At that time it did not refer merely to a group of countries, those territories for so long concealed within the European and American empires, but rather to a political idea. After the terrible deprivations and destruction of the Second World War, the globe had become divided between two apparently terrifying alternatives, Washington and Moscow, capitalism and what many people supposed was socialism, the first and second worlds. The Third World, newly created from the wreckage of the old, offered a different path for humanity, a third alternative.

The semantic history of politics is full of ideas that begin life as a radical indictment of the existing social order, but over the years pass neutered into the everyday lexicon. So it was with 'democracy', the rule of the majority, that concept that was once known to terrify comfortable citizens in their beds, but ended its life as no more than the governmental conventions prevailing in some countries. So it was with 'liberalism', with its heady promise of universal freedom, in the early nineteenth century, and 'socialism' later in the same century, both, in the fullness of time, fading into a vague kindliness (or, for socialism, the name of an official status quo). In our own times, the same thing is happening to 'women's liberation'. Thus does the established order subvert the ideas of its critics, robbing them of the conceptual means to express opposition, without conceding the substance nor permitting recourse to battle.

The same thing happened to the 'Third World'. By now, few ask where the first and second worlds are. The contrast has disappeared. The 'Third World' is no longer seen as a political alternative and merely denotes a group of countries – referred to more pompously as the less developed countries.

This book is about the idea of the Third World, the social-science theories to which the idea gave rise, and, above all, development economics. The idea presented a picture of how the world had arrived where it was in the 1950s, where it was likely to go, and where governments in the Third World could take it. We shall attempt to identify what actually happened, and to explain the divergence between theory and practice. In the process, we shall look at the roots of the ideology of Third Worldism, at how its protagonists came to employ the new states of the Third World (which now came to include the independent states of Latin America as well as the ex-colonies of Asia and Africa) and at the social basis for this new type of society.

The book is not directly about economic development. If it were, we should have to consider many more factors. Nor does it do any kind of justice to the many preoccupations of what are known as development studies. Nor is it concerned directly with contemporary world development as a whole; that is the preoccupation of an earlier work, *Of Bread and Guns: the World Economy in Crisis* (Penguin Books, 1983). It is a work about the central ideas guiding those who tried to launch economic development in the Third World in the fifties and sixties. It is mainly about economic questions, but it is not written for economists and is in the main non-technical (even though one person's technicalities are another's everyday usage). But there is relatively little attention to politics, society, culture or colour. This is not because these things are not important, but because the underlying evolution of economies has to be identified clearly first, before we can see at what points other factors influence the process. It is a deliberate attempt to identify the economic process, since far too often the intentions of political leaders are confused with what happens economically, when, in reality, economic changes are often the *cause* of the political intentions. The approach is frustrating for those for whom politics is always in the foreground. It turns everyday assumptions on their head. Indeed, any account of the modern history of Brazil or Indonesia which omits politics appears wilfully perverse.

Nomenclature is a problem. The definitions of groups of countries (of which the Third World is one) are inevitably arbitrary, or rather, the several definitions reflect many different purposes. We deal with a group of countries known as the Third World, but also: the less developed (the main term used here), developing, underdeveloped, the non-industrialized, the poor, the backward, the South. They are contrasted with the First World, the more developed, the developed, the industrialized, the rich, the advanced, the market economies (the industrial market economies), the North, the OECD Group (that is, the twenty-four members of the Organization for Economic Cooperation and Development, the twenty-two richest western countries with Japan, and two others, Turkey and Greece). Of the 180 or so established states of the world, the World Bank classifies the 126 largest (covering the overwhelming majority of the world's population) as including ninety-four less developed countries, five 'high-income oil exporters', eighteen 'industrial market economies' and seven 'East European non-market economies'. There are arbitrary elements throughout. For example, some 'non-market economies' – China, Vietnam, North Korea – are included with the less developed. Ireland (per capita income $5,150) and Spain $5,430) are included in the 'industrial market economies' presumably because they are in Western Europe, but Trinidad and Tobago ($6,840) and Singapore ($5,190) are in the less developed.

Among the less developed, we occasionally employ the World Bank's subdivisions: (i) 'low-income countries' which had in 1980 an income per head below $490 per year (covering thirty-three countries, including China and India, with 49 per cent of the world's population); and (ii) 'middle-income countries' with a 1980 income per head of between $410 and $4,500 (sixty-three countries, 26 per cent of the world's population). By contrast, the industrial market economies had per capita incomes over $4,500 in 1980 (and 16 per cent of the world's population). By and large, this account does not pay attention to the 'high-income oil exporters' since they have a very small share of the world's population; and omits the 'East European non-market economies' for lack of comparable data; this inevitably distorts the global figures, but the need for simplicity takes priority over strict accuracy.

Within the less developed countries there are many other subgroups, but one in particular concerns us here: the newly industrializing countries. These are countries which are said to have experienced high growth of output in the sixties and seventies, sometimes but not invariably on the basis of expanded manufacturing exports. The members are variously identified, depending upon the author, but in most accounts they include: Hong Kong, Singapore, Taiwan, South Korea, India, Argentina, Brazil and Mexico. Also, often included are Spain (in other accounts, an 'industrialized market economy'), Portugal, Greece, Yugoslavia. Sometimes included are: Iran, Malaysia, Pakistan,

Colombia, Philippines, Thailand and others. The lack of a clearcut boundary is not vital for this account, and the countries included in the group are identified as we proceed.

The heart of the book is a test of the theses of the Third World case (presented in the first chapter). This is done in relationship to four countries of east and south-east Asia – South Korea, Taiwan, Hong Kong and Singapore (in the second chapter). The third chapter looks at a different kind of development in two Latin American countries, Brazil and Mexico. Chapter 4 then seeks to determine how far these six cases are peculiar by looking at the less developed countries as a whole, and at what is happening to the manufacturing industries of the more developed countries. The fifth chapter summarizes the implications of what has happened for Third Worldism. Chapter 6 examines the peculiar role of the state and of governments in the pattern of rapid growth, and looks at the origins of the belief that states could direct the market. If Third Worldism was an ideology, Chapter 7 seeks to suggest the social interests that might have been embodied in it. The final chapter then summarizes the argument and draws a few speculative conclusions.

As always, the errors of fact, language and judgement are exclusively my own, and not to be attributed to those who have very kindly laboured in the arduous task of trying to turn this into a readable work (not always with success). They include, pre-eminently, despite our disagreements, Alasdair McAuley; and Duncan Hallas, Rakesh Mohan, Tirril Harris, Desmond McNeil, Dilip Mukerjee, Michael Safier and John Lindsay. It is a thankless task, but nonetheless my thanks.

NH

NOTE. Dollars are always those of the United States unless otherwise specified (Singapore as S, etc.) and 'billions' means thousand millions, not million millions.

1 = Third Worldism

What can we do? We can do much! We can inject the voice of reason into world affairs. We can mobilize all the spiritual, all the moral, all the political strength of Asia and Africa on the side of peace. Yes, we! we, the peoples of Asia and Africa, 1,400,000,000 strong, far more than half the human population of the world, we can mobilize what I have called the 'Moral Violence of Nations' in favour of peace.

President Sukarno of Indonesia, Opening Address to the
Asia–Africa Conference, Bandung (Indonesia), 18 April 1955.

In April 1985, the government of Indonesia celebrated the thirtieth anniversary of the holding of the Asia–Africa Conference in Bandung. In fact, few people remembered the first conference, even though it was the ancestor of many later initiatives from the non-aligned conferences to sundry United Nations activities. But in 1955 the conference marked a major change in the world order, the entry to international politics of a new group of countries that came to be known as the Third World.

The new order was not achieved without violence, both in terms of the transfer of power in many countries between the old empires and the newly independent governments, and in terms of international political alignments. It aroused great passions and new loyalties; it engaged many thousands, if not millions, of newly aware political activists. It changed the political dimensions even in the centres of the old empires, in London, Paris, Amsterdam, Brussels and Lisbon. A new perception of the world and of the role within it of the new states was created. Around that perception developed a body of theories, which we have called here Third Worldism. By now, of course, many of the proposals of this ideology have become absorbed into the political 'common sense' of the world, and it is difficult to identify them today.

The idea of the Third World was a radical critique of the order of world power that had governed international affairs until that time.

The world of empires, it was said, had produced two devastating world wars in the first half of the twentieth century, and also a string of savageries inflicted upon the subject majority of the world's peoples. Empire was part and parcel of an economic system, capitalism, which had been equally destructive in economic terms, in the swings of boom and slump, and particularly in the Great Depression between the wars. The emancipation of the world's majority, the Third World, offered the opportunity for a new political and economic order based on what Sukarno called the 'newly emergent forces'. In a world so recently released from the terrible war of 1939–45, and plunged into a new Cold War, the hopes embodied in the Bandung Conference could not help but be inspired.

At the heart of the new ideology was a series of propositions about the possibility of national economic development in the countries of the Third World. Why were those countries so poor when the Europeans and North Americans were so rich? How far could markets be shaped or superseded to force the pace of national economic growth? What should be the role of government in that process? The preoccupations of analysis, explanation and prescriptions for government action came to constitute a new branch of economics, 'development economics'. In fact, the theorization began much earlier than the 1950s and took up themes that emerged after the Great Depression following 1929. It seemed then as if capitalism had exhausted its potential, and new alternatives were needed for all countries. Economists from countries which exported in the main raw materials – Latin America and Eastern Europe – were particularly concerned to formulate methods by which their countries could escape slump. The earlier and later concerns merged, as we see in the evolution of one strand of thought in Latin America.

The Origins of Development Economics

The new states recognized early that maintaining political independence required economic power; rewarding those who had thrown off foreign domination required rising incomes. Many different routes led to the problem of 'economic development'. What did it mean? In Europe and North America, countries had gone through a process, lasting in some cases more than a century, in which most workers had left agriculture (and rural areas) and become industrial (or at least urban) employees. In economese, a declining share of national output was being created in sectors with a low productivity of labour (traditional agriculture) and a rising share generated in high-productivity sectors (particularly industry, and within industry, manufacturing). This structural change was seen as the key element in rising incomes and national power.

The structure of an economy was changed by disproportionate investment in the high-productivity sectors. If manufacturing were expanded more swiftly than the rest over a period of years, then the change could be accomplished. There was a set of problems that flowed from this diagnosis – how to mobilize the resources for a programme of sustained investment, how to acquire the imported equipment for the growth of manufacturing, the infrastructure and power supplies, and the technically skilled workforce. In the late 1940s, it seemed that all these tasks should be undertaken by the state. The new governments undertook the deliberate transformation of their societies.

In so far as economists had concerned themselves with these questions earlier, it had been assumed most often that growth in the world trading system would in time overcome the problems of poverty and backwardness. In a world market, if there were no restrictions and competition determined prices, then each country would become specialized in those forms of production which it was most efficient for it to undertake. And this would allow the 'comparative advantage' of each country ultimately to produce an equalization of incomes (a case formally demonstrated under special assumptions by a leading contemporary economist, Paul Samuelson, in the late 1940s).[1]

For those confronting what seemed to be the endemic poverty of the majority of countries, this theory appeared to be no more than an excuse for complacency and a rationalization of the wealth of the richest people and countries. Poverty was not inevitable, nor could the problem of poverty safely be left to the normal working of the world market. All around was the evidence that the governments of the rich countries had not merely relied on the market; armies, prison camps, legal systems, investment and tax policies – not to mention straight robbery – had all played a role in their capture of a disproportionate share of the world's wealth. The group of poor countries, identified as 'underdeveloped' in the late forties, could not afford to await the possible long-term effects of free trade.

The dispute was not simply about different means to the same end. There were two different conceptions of economic development. On the one hand, the orthodox economists, known as 'neoclassical', envisaged a world economy in which different countries played specialized roles, and were therefore economically interdependent. To them, economic development could only mean working towards a given level of income, since each national economy would be different, depending upon its specialization. The radicals, on the other hand, saw national economic development as a structural change in the *national* economy rather than a relationship to a world economy, and a change such that each country produced most of what it needed at home; thus, each country would be, to a greater or lesser extent, a microcosm of the world, not a specialized contributor (indeed, the specialized economy, the 'monocultural' agricultural exporter, for example, was seen as peculiarly subject to endemic poverty). With a fully diversified home economy, it was thought, self-generating growth was possible on the basis of an expanding home market, regardless of what happened in the world at large.

The starting-point for these preoccupations was the attempt to explain why the orthodox theory of world trade did not work for the poor countries – why for them, it apparently produced impoverishment. In Latin America, one of the most famous founders of development economics, Raúl Prebisch, began his work at this point; his conclusions became the inspiration of the United Nations Economic Commission for Latin America (ECLA, or CEPAL in Spanish).[2] He argued that, although the theory was not working in the twentieth century, it had worked in the nineteenth. Then, Britain and other European powers had depended on imported raw materials in order to expand domestic manufacturing. Imports from Latin America (made possible by European investment there) had in turn expanded the economies of Latin America, making it possible for them to service their borrowings from Europe and to import manufactured goods as well. The division of labour, an exchange of agricultural for industrial goods, had been mutually beneficial.

However, in the twentieth century, a changed structure of relationships turned the beneficial relationship into a malign one – 'reality is undermining the outdated scheme of the international division of labour', as Prebisch expressed it.[3] The United States, a much larger and much more self-sufficient economy, replaced Britain. Its need for imports from Latin America was low; Latin America could no longer earn the means to purchase vital manufactured imports, and must therefore cover its purchases with its limited gold reserves. The hoard at Fort Knox grew while Latin America became increasingly unable to expand; its failure to be able to import then contracted the world market, to the disadvantage of the exporters of manufactured goods. By 1944, Prebisch was warning of a long-term disequilibrium in the world economy as the result of the 'inner-directed development' of the United States, a problem revealed in the growing shortage of US dollars available to Latin America for the purchase of vital imports (a case subsequently applied to Europe as the 'dollar problem').[4]

Parallel to this argument, Prebisch developed another and more far-reaching one. In the Great Depression, he noted, the prices of agricultural exports declined much more than those of manufactured goods. Countries specializing in one or the other therefore faced very different effects of slump. With further work, Prebisch concluded that the phenomenon was not simply the result of slump but reflected a long-term trend, a growing inequality of exchange. Why might this arise? Because, Prebisch suggested, the exporters of manufactured goods (what he now called the 'centre' or 'centres' of the world system) had a monopoly of the supply of such goods and could therefore control their prices. Exporters of agricultural goods (the 'periphery') were many, and thus competition drove down prices.

This argument explained slump, short-term movements. Prebisch then went on to propose that the explanation of long-term deterioration lay in the faster pace of technical development in manufacturing: monopoly controls of the prices of manufactured exports ensured that declining costs of production (as the result of technical innovations) benefited only the sellers of manufactured goods, not the buyers, whereas the reverse was true for the growers of agricultural goods – 'while the centres kept the whole benefit of the technical development of their industries, the peripheral countries transferred to them a share of the fruits of their own technical progress'. A later revision shifted the emphasis from a monopoly of the supply of manufactured goods to a monopoly of the supply of labour; trade-union controls in Europe and

North America prevented wages falling in a slump and ensured their steady long-term growth, forcing the prices of manufactured goods to remain high; for the cultivators of the soil, the reverse was true, producing a growing inequality: 'the less that income can contract at the centre, the more it must do so at the periphery'.[5] Later, empirical work on long-term price movements in international trade seemed to confirm the Prebisch thesis of continuing deterioration,[6] and other writers gave new explanations; Hans Singer related the issue to a declining demand for raw-material inputs in manufacturing output as the result of technical advances making economies possible.[7]

By the late forties, the United States had acquired an unprecedented domination of the world economy. It had become the 'cyclical centre' of the system, according to Prebisch, able to determine the world business cycle and ensure domestic full employment, and oblige the periphery to conform to the interests of Washington.

However, there was a way out. The centre's domination arose from its monopoly of manufacturing. Industrialization of the periphery could begin to restore the equilibrium – it would reduce the dependence of Latin America on imports and so reduce its need to export; it would increase domestic employment and incomes, so expanding the domestic market, and thus the demand for a further round of industrialization. The benefits of technical progress in manufacturing would now be retained in the country concerned. However, it would be impossible to industrialize if manufactured goods could be freely imported from the centre; competition from more advanced and larger-scale industries at the centre would stifle the new industries of the periphery. This was the basis of the strategy of controlling imports in order to force the pace of growth of domestic manufacturing industry in a poor country – what became known as 'import-substitution industrialization'.

Such a strategy paid no heed to the theory of comparative advantage and the concept of an international division of labour with national specializations. Industrialization would proceed according to the selection of industries to be protected from imports; general protection would stimulate general industrialization, regardless of the costs of local production. The state had the power, it seemed, to determine the shape of the domestic economy.

Prebisch and his immediate followers were not revolutionaries. They were not opposed to foreign capital nor to international trade. Theirs was not a recipe for autarky, but for what Prebisch called 'healthy protectionism'. Nor did they feel any industry should be pursued at any price – the 'measurable well-being of the masses' was more important than national self-sufficiency.[8] Others who came afterwards spoke of the exploitation and robbery of the periphery, of the need for a violent break in international trade and domestic organization.

Prebisch's case was also not as novel as it seemed at the time. Indeed, it could have been identified as no more than a rationalization of what had already happened. In the late forties, protectionism was the norm for all countries. In the case of Latin America, the world slump of 1929–33 cut the purchasing power of the continent's exports by 60 per cent, and ended the possibility of much borrowing abroad. Most countries were obliged to suspend the convertibility of their currencies, cut imports radically and take measures to stimulate the production of domestic substitutes. The results were impressive – whereas the annual rate of growth of manufacturing output in the United States in the ten years after 1929 was negative (-0.6), Colombia's was 8.8, Brazil's 6.4, Mexico's 4.3 and Chile's 3.3 per cent.

The results were, however, the accidental byproduct of government efforts to save foreign exchange, not the product of a deliberate policy of industrialization. After 1945, efforts became more deliberate, particularly since they were now supported by industrial beneficiaries – as Macario puts it, 'Originally dictated by external factors, industrialization became, especially under the pressure of vested interests, a fundamental objective of the economic policy of the governments concerned.'[9] Furthermore, the process was doubly protected, for the demand for Latin America's raw-material exports now revived; there was therefore no shortage of foreign exchange to purchase the imports which were still needed, and, indeed, exports could be taxed by maintaining a value for the local currency which was artificially high – and therefore made imports cheaper.

Rationalization or not, the prescriptions of CEPAL and Prebisch exercised a powerful influence among Latin American intellectuals and a rising generation of social scientists. The effect on governments was more limited, except in the sense that policy agreed on other grounds acquired a CEPAL vindication. But there was no causal 'model' at work.

Even without the CEPAL philosophy, in the 1950s a multitude of other poor countries outside Latin America adopted programmes of industrialization which depended on limiting imports. For the newly independent powers, it became the norm, as much an emotional and moral principle of new nationalism as an economic tactic. The intervention of the state to determine which industries or sectors should grow and which should not, became direct participation in these countries too. It seemed as if state capitalism, in part or whole, was the norm for the 'peripheries', even when described as one or other form of socialism – the royal Buddhist socialism of Cambodia, the Arab, African, Indian, Burmese, Indonesian forms of socialism, and many more. The frequency with which new governments defined a nationally specific socialism suggested some elements in common other than past subjection – similarities of culture, social structure and aspiration, factors greeted with acclaim at Bandung in 1955.

It took more time to find the right term. Alfred Sauvy claimed he invented the term, the 'Third World', modelled on the Third Estate of the 1789 French Revolution. That was in 1952. In 1956, a Paris journal, *Tiers Monde*, adopted the term. But this was advanced intellectual opinion. It took another ten years for the phrase to become used more generally, but then only by radicals. It identified not just a group of new states (joined later by the older states of Latin America), nor the majority of the world's poor, but a political alternative other than that presented by Washington and Moscow (the first and second worlds).

The Schools of Thought

By the late 1960s, the analysis of the nature and causes of economic backwardness, and the formulation of proposals to overcome it, had become very substantial. It is as if the world's attention had suddenly become focused on the question, producing a veritable flood of books, journals, reports and documents, whole libraries of scholarship. From the first identification of the crude economic equations, study had spread into subtle appraisals of history, culture and psyche. Most of the work was, however, critical of the inherited wisdom of the West, and to a greater or lesser degree radical; it was a new perspective on what seemed a newly discovered world.

Nonetheless, the economic formulations remained fundamental. International trade, it was assumed, could not develop the backward countries; on the contrary, trade made the problems of backwardness worse. Countries, it was said, were the basic units of the system (not sectors, industries or companies), and each national economy needed to go through a series of clearcut historical phases as the process of cumulative investment continued, in order to arrive at a 'developed' destination (a theory famously formulated in Rostow's *The Stages of Economic Growth: a Non-Communist Manifesto*, 1960). However, raising levels of investment was difficult, since each backward national economy was characterized by a set of rigidities; the structure of the economy inhibited change, and made it virtually impossible for domestic capitalism to support continued and healthy growth ('healthy' usually implied the production of a desirable set of goods). It followed that orthodox economics, founded upon the analysis of the market and private capitalism, was of little help in moving a backward economy forward. Only governments could mobilize the resources, only governments possessed the political power to break through the bottlenecks, bend the inflexibilities and force the pace of growth.

However, within these broad assumptions, there were many variations in the theory of development economics that spanned the political spectrum. Four variations are identified here, with inevitable arbitrariness. Two others, the first and the last, which fall outside the terms of reference of 'development studies', are included to highlight their contrast with the four.

1. Classical and Marxist

In so far as economists in the past concerned themselves with 'economic development', it was as a movement 'towards opulence and improvement', as Adam Smith expressed it,[10] rather than structural change in a national economy. It was assumed that the operation of a free market would ultimately lead to general prosperity for all countries participating (a position taken over by the neoclassical economists of the 1970s). The market evoked the resources required for development; structural relationships were created, sustained and dissolved by changing market prices; there were no long-term inhibiting factors that prevented development.

Marx was the economist who added history to this picture, with a major emphasis upon the historical process of the growth of capital and its successive self-transformations. But he also assumed that as capital spread its influence geographically, the more backward areas would increasingly be transformed in the same way as the more advanced – the market forced all into development. Bukharin and Lenin qualified this, since in their time it seemed the European empires invariably allied with the pre-capitalist ruling orders (as, for example, the Indian princes) and the process of creating capitalism was inhibited. However, in his most famous work on the subject of the 'backward countries' [11], Lenin envisaged their industrialization; [12] the imperial 'centres' were increasingly restricted to financing the rest of the world, to 'rentier' and 'bond-holding' states, while the future proletariat was being created in the colonies. There was one element, none the less, which recurred later: the population of advanced countries was becoming parasitic on the labour of the workers in the colonies, a proposition half echoed in the argument that the trade unions of the 'centres' forced the impoverishment of the 'peripheries'.

2. The conservative reformers

The conservative reformers were the main leadership in the field of development economics. Directly influential with a number of governments – particularly in Latin America and India in the fifties, in Africa in the sixties – they provided much of the intellectual inspiration for the activity of many international agencies (particularly the United Nations Conference on Trade and Development and the International Labour Organization, as well as the idea of a new international economic order, the 'basic needs' programme, and the content of the Brandt Commission Report). [13]

At its simplest, the problem of development was identified as raising resources on a scale sufficient to achieve a level of investment that would change the structure of the economy. In very poor societies, incomes seemed to be too low to support a level of national savings which would be adequate to the task. On the other hand, it was assumed that resources would not be available from abroad – from borrowing, aid or through trade – on a sufficient scale. Indeed, external support of this kind was thought to jeopardize fatally a government's attempt to develop – international trade was subject to long-term deterioration in the exchange between raw materials and industrial goods; it was highly unstable; it diverted the economy away from feeding the domestic poor to supplying rich foreigners; it weakened the national government's autonomy, its capacity to pursue long-term plans; and sooner or later, the advanced countries would close their markets to imports as they had done in the early thirties.

The central problem, then, was the mobilization of resources from the domestic economy. The formulation – between investment and growth – received proper theoretical expression in what was known as the Harrod–Domar model, and became the inspiration of fledgling planning commissions. There was dispute about whether investment should be 'balanced', moving all sectors together at once (so preserving complementarities and proportionalities), or should concentrate on the 'big push' (Rosenstein–Rodan), on unbalanced growth (Hirschmann). But the central idea, a gathering together of efforts which would achieve what W. W. Rostow named, with singular but misleading vividness, 'economic take-off' remained dominant.

It was thought that increased savings, directed by the government to industry, with protection against industrial imports, was the recipe for development; major changes were not required either in the domestic social structure (although these might also be desirable) or in international economic relations.

3. The radicals

The radicals challenged this position. There had been sustained investment, they said, but society had not been transformed. Not only did the poor remain exactly as before, but the structure of the economy had scarcely changed and, above all, in Latin America imports remained decisive despite many years of import substitution and the economy was still highly vulnerable to external changes. The Chilean economist, Osvaldo Sunkel, writing in the late sixties, concluded:

The import of capital and intermediate goods necessary to produce consumer goods has been substituted for the import of consumer goods themselves. The structure of manufacturing production is now organized basically to produce for the consumer and the traditional export sector has been left to 'produce' the investment goods. This seems to me the fundamental reason why our economies have become more dependent, more vulnerable and more unstable.[14]

The failure, it was argued, arose because the existing social structure inhibited the effect of investment. A severely unequal distribution of income cut the size of the domestic market and also skewed it towards upper-income consumption goods. Unequal land distribution severely reduced the capacity of the rural majority to sustain market demand and also reduced the incentives to cultivate more. Import barriers forced foreign companies to make the minimum manufacture legally required in the country (to escape the restrictions on imports), but, because the market was so small, their costs were very high, the product inferior, and increased profits were drained out of the country instead of going to domestic investment. For most countries, the domestic market was too small to support the development of efficient heavy and intermediate industries; for these economic federations were needed – the Latin American Free Trade Area (as also the Andean Pact, the Central American Common Market, etc.).

This line of argument merged with that of the next group. Paul Singer criticized the CEPAL philosophy for ignoring the way in which the external trade and capital relationships (now identified as 'economic dependency') not only produced a particular type of economy on the periphery, but also a particular type of social structure, which was no less inhibiting for growth. The exploitation of the periphery by the centre was part and parcel of the exploitation of the Latin American working class in each country.

4. The revolutionary nationalists

Revolutionary nationalists started here. Not only was it impossible to break the external links of the economy, but it was also impossible to promote domestic development of the right kind (that would help the mass of the population), because the existing class structure blocked all change. The 'structural rigidities' now included precisely those people and classes CEPAL relied upon to transform the domestic economy. The old ruling class rendered domestic reform and development and economic independence impossible. The world system was dominated by imperialism, a group of great powers with the largest share of the world's capital, companies, banks and armed forces, and they operated through a close alliance with the classes that ruled Latin America. There was no way that this pattern could be changed through the exist-ing ruling classes, for their very power depended on retaining and strengthening subordination to imperialism. All the talk of import-substitution industrialization, with or without national planning and large public sectors, was thus irrelevant to the central task of breaking the domestic social order. That was impossible without revolution and the use of popular armed power to destroy the old order by force.

It was a case explored in detail by Paul Baran, Samir Amin, Andre Gunder Frank[15] and a host of others. In conjunction with a political tradition derived from the experience of revolution in Cuba, Fidelismo, and to a lesser extent, in China, it became the inspiration in the 1960s for a host of guerrilla groups in Latin America, which became known as national liberation movements. And so it was in much of the rest of the developing countries also. Each continent produced its models of the total domestic transformation – China and Vietnam in Asia; Algeria, Mozambique, Angola and Guinea-Bissau in Africa; Cuba and Nica-ragua in Latin America.

5. Revolutionary internationalists

There was a further development, which was neither widely known nor influential, but which nevertheless completed the spectrum of estimates of the difficulties in pursuing economic development. For now it was argued that the structure of world capitalism made national economic development impossible, even if there were domestic revolution in a backward country. Removing the old ruling class, nationalizing the means of production (and expropriating foreign capital), redistributing income and land, forced accumulation, would not suffice to overcome the paralysis imposed by the changed structure of world capitalism.[16]

In Michael Kidron's *Western Capitalism since the War*,[17] advanced states and their associated national capitals had become so powerful that it was impossible for the backward nations to begin to compete. The minimum size for the economies of scale of modern industry ruled out development for a majority of countries (one estimate suggested a population of ten to fifteen millions was the bare minimum, but that most advantage accrued to countries with fifty million or more in-habitants):[18]

They [the weaker powers] are compelled to make huge single-shot expenditures in facilities for which the minimum sizes are set by the immense capitals of the north [the developed countries] in terms of their own huge absolute sizes, gained after decades of concentrating the world's surpluses in their hands. The minima have now become so large that no country in the south can hope to attain them on its own. None can hope to bring together what it takes to exchange equal values with the advanced capitals or to exchange equal clout.[19]

Once this became apparent, there could be no geographical spread of the system from its more to its less advanced areas – 'The extension of the system in the strict sense of capital replication, or in a looser sense, of proletarianizing a growing proportion of the world's population, ended.'[20]

Development economists examined the symptoms of this growing problem – increasingly uncompetitive exports from the developing countries, saleable only with heavy subsidies which constituted yet again a net transfer from poor sellers to rich buyers. Political instability flowed from the collapse of hopes of development, which in turn produced military instability, a further drain of resources out of development investment. Only a revolutionary change in the centres of the system, the more developed countries, could change the context for the economic development of the periphery.

6. The neoclassical school

There had been critics of the received theses of development economics from the beginning,[21] but it had been very much a minority view, a pre-Keynesian trend of thought. From the late sixties, however, this school expanded with astonishing speed, to become in the seventies a new dominant orthodoxy in the industrialized countries. The neoclassical critics argued that there was great doubt about any long-term deterioration in the terms of trade between agricultural and industrial goods; that there was no peculiar merit in industrialization; that the 'rigidities' and bottlenecks which supposedly vindicated the intervention of the state were in fact the result of earlier public interventions or distorted prices. There were, they affirmed, no long-term problems which could not be overcome through the free operation of unrestricted markets. Governments were needed both to provide the framework for production, and to move towards efficient prices, but not to seek to direct the national economy towards predetermined ends; if they did that, perverse results would either defeat the public purpose or have negative effects elsewhere in the economy. The most important task of government was systematic reform in all sectors – labour, financial, business, capital markets, and government itself – in order to ensure that prices accurately reflected real scarcities in the world. We shall return to the practical effects of these arguments later.

In sum then, the development economists – those whose views have been listed above (2–5) tended to agree that capitalism had become transformed to the point where it could no longer repeat the process of the dispersal of development that had occurred in the nineteenth century. 'The capitalist system,' wrote Baran in the mid fifties, 'once a mighty engine of economic development, has turned into a no less formidable hurdle to human advancement'.[22] It was an argument that echoed those who had seen in the Great Depression of the thirties the sign that capitalism had finally exhausted its potential for growth. Yet others later went further, to deny that in the earlier period capitalism had produced growth in the periphery – from the beginning, Europe had imposed and sustained what was now seen as underdevelopment on the periphery; there had always been an inexorable asymmetry.

There were different reasons why this was said to be so, but they frequently amounted to some idea of 'unequal exchange' – whether this was seen as virtual robbery,[23] as an accident of the structure, or as a systematic phenomenon whereby the exports of the periphery were undervalued while their imports were overvalued.[24] Free trade always favoured the more developed power, so where such conditions prevailed, they always increased inequality between the trading countries. Different reasons were proposed for this (as we saw in discussing the thesis of the long-term deterioration in the terms of trade between agricultural and industrial exports). For example, it was said that the low income level of the backward made it impossible to establish industries of the most efficient size; imports would always be cheaper. Paul Baran, like Prebisch, identified monopoly as the source of unequal exchange; the industrial countries had a monopoly of the supply of industrial goods and could hold up their prices when producers of agricultural goods could not. Amin linked the high prices of industrial exports not to a monopoly by the industrialized countries, but to a monopoly of the supply of labour by the trade unions of the industrialized countries – 'It was monopoly that made possible the rise of wages' (in the more developed countries), producing 'an unequal specialization which always expressed a mechanism of primitive accumulation to the advantage of the centre ... the "development of underdevelopment" '.[25] Furtado argued that the class struggle in the centre pushed wages up and obliged the state to maintain full employment, which in turn sustained an expanding domestic market; on the periphery, weak trade unions had the reverse effect.

Whatever the reasons, conservatives and radicals agreed that 'the outside world was public enemy number one'.[26] But almost as important at various times were the internal obstacles to development. In the early fifties, Baran identified these as the old ruling orders – 'a political and social coalition of wealthy *compradors*, powerful monopolists, and large landowners, dedicated to the defence of the existing feudal, mercantile order ... this coalition has nothing to hope for from the rise of industrial capitalism, which would dislodge it from its position of privilege and power'.[27] It was a case which emerged in different forms in many arguments, particularly those concerning what came to be known as 'dependency' (the dependence of the backward on the advanced).[28] Indeed, in the period of disillusion with import substitutionism in Latin America in the early sixties, it was to the social obstacles to growth that Prebisch reverted in seeking to explain why the process had failed – the upper income groups remained preoccupied with luxury consumption,[29] which was one of the factors distorting the pattern of investment and limiting the general growth of the market. Later, his gloom intensified – the small surplus generated on the periphery seemed always to be expropriated by the centres, by the rich and by the state (especially where the military were powerful); trade-union action might check the rich and the state, but only at the cost of high rates of inflation; 'in the advanced course of peripheral development', he concluded pessimistically, 'the process of democratization tends to become incompatible with the regular functioning of the system'.[30]

Such gloom was far from the high hopes of the early fifties. Then the world market might be an obstacle, but at home, if power could be won, there was nothing to stop growth. What had hitherto been squandered or hoarded by the rich would become available to fuel growth; at the time of the second Indian Five Year Plan (1955), Baran boldly asserted that 'there can hardly be any doubt' that 15 per cent of India's national income could be invested without cutting mass consumption, since 25 per cent was already absorbed by the 'unproductive strata'. But it required bold political action; without it, 'The injection of planning into a society living in the twilight between feudalism and capitalism cannot but result in additional corruption, larger and more artful evasion of the law, and more brazen abuses of authority.'[31]

Others saw potential in the vast mass of very poorly paid workers. Low incomes narrowed the market, but it meant also that there could be an immense growth in the labour force at relatively low cost. One of the leaders of the new movement offered a simple model to prove the efficacy of this paradox.[32] From the opposite corner came those who saw as the only hope the limitation of population growth, a case that became increasingly popular as the difficulties of development became more apparent.

The experience of the Soviet Union played a particularly important role in shaping the perceptions of some of the new governments. For there, it was said, industrialization had been autarkic and particularly swift; the process had telescoped the historical stages of development – from light to heavy industrial development – by beginning with the stimulation of heavy industry. Planners in many backward countries were fascinated by heavy industry; it was always the key, it was thought, to economic independence, to full development. Elements of the first Russian Five Year Plan were emulated in the first Chinese plan, with its emphasis on the growth of steel output, and in the model which was the inspiration for the second Indian Five Year Plan.[33]

The heavy industrial emphasis of the Stalinist model of planning conflicted with the views of those who believed that economic development should be directed at increasing employment. The development of heavy industry was notoriously profligate in the use of scarce capital, and produced very few jobs. One of the first economic rejections of the Stalinist model led to a whole school of thought, crystallized in a long-term research programme by the International Labour Organization, concerned with increasing employment, particularly through more labour-intensive forms of production. This in turn led on to the United Nations' 'basic needs' programme to identify and meet a minimum level of consumption among the poor of the less developed countries.

In practice, heavy industrial programmes proved very burdensome. Understanding why giant public-sector enterprises were so often a drain on, rather than a contribution to, the savings for future development was one contributory thread in the radical change of opinion in the seventies. If the Third Worldists were right and their views were re-volutionary, the seventies saw an astonishing victory for counter-revolutionary thought. The neoclassical economists (at least some of whom had formerly been ardent Third Worldists) attacked the entire system of thought – the idea of the economy as a rigid structure; of the government as a benevolent, strong and rational agent; of industry in general, and heavy industry in particular, having some peculiar merit; of the domestic market being superior to exports, domestic capital to foreign, of self-sufficiency to interdependence. The very idea of con-scious long-term direction of the economy by the government was questioned.

Import substitution came to be identified as the very source of the problems of backwardness – high-cost, low-quality industrial output, neglect of agriculture and popular consumption, worsening income distribution, an entrenched position of foreign capital inside the econ-omy, a bias to capital-intensive manufacture: in all respects, it was said, industrialization through import controls robbed the masses, inflated the profits of a minority and increased the power of the state. The remedies had come to be seen as the cause of the illness.

By the end of the 1970s the 'less developed countries', as they were now known, were exporting more manufactured goods than raw materials, a change producing 'a spiritual revolution as great as that experienced by economists over the age of thirty who were converted to Keynesianism in 1936'.[34] By 1980, the more developed countries exported 36 per cent more primary commodities than did the less de-veloped. From the perception of the 1950s, the world had been turned topsy-turvy.

Ideologies, and their substructures of economic theory, are no better than the prejudices of the age and the classes from which they derive, but it is rare for such a complete transformation to take place in such a short time. It is a mark of how unconscious most participants are that the change received little systematic attention – it seems that, pragmatically, one thing led to another, even though the 'another' contradicted the 'one'. The truth was less simple, and much of the rest of this account is spent in seeking to identify some of the complexities of a reality that fitted neither side in the dispute.

2 = Asia: The Gang of Four

Given the Third Worldist arguments about the new character of the world economy, how did the developing countries fare in the post-war period? We start by looking at some of the more successful cases of economic growth, in particular, South Korea, Taiwan, Hong Kong and Singapore – the 'Gang of Four' (named, for reasons quite obscure, after the four leading followers of Chairman Mao in China after 1971). Despite being relatively small, they came to dominate the external trade of developing countries.

So swift was the rise in the exports of the Gang of Four that they seemed to pose uncontrollable threats to established producers of particular goods. Sheffield complained that the price of South Korean cutlery imports to Britain were below the Sheffield price of steel for making cutlery. Modern shoe-making factories faltered before what was described in military terminology as an 'invasion'. European ship-makers accused Korea of the 'predatory pricing' of its ships, covering only the cost of materials. Lionel Olmer, in 1984 an undersecretary in the United States government, was reduced to the indignity of appealing to the world's steel-makers not to sell technology to the Koreans, for their 1983 exports of 5.7 million tonnes threatened America's output of 75 million tonnes.

If there were elements of hysteria in some circles, for neoclassical economists the Gang of Four seemed to vindicate the promise of free-market economics. Before the four existed, it had been necessary to invent them in order to justify the theory; and after they expanded, not a little invention went into rendering the facts of their performance consistent with the postulates of the free market. Yet others, identifying the performances more realistically, compared three of the Gang of Four to East European economies in terms of state participation.[1]

The neoclassical economists stressed that it was public policy which achieved the swift growth of the four countries. Emulation was therefore within the grasp of all governments – 'The almost irresistible conclusion,' one analyst decided, 'from Korean development experience is that with proper economic policies and a continuation of reasonable international aid levels, most developing countries could sustain growth rates as high as 10 per cent.'[2] Whether or not aid per head of the population on the Korean level could be extended to all developing countries, it seemed most unlikely the world could absorb a comparable volume of exports. If China had exported in 1981 at the Korean level of exports per head, Chinese exports would have had to increase 2,512 times (or 42 per cent more than all the exports of all developing countries). China and India together would have produced exports equal to half the value of world trade.[3]

The experience of the Gang of Four seemed to offer support for the theses and prejudices of everybody. What in fact occurred?

The Republic of Korea (South Korea)

Structure and change

In 1953, agriculture produced some 47 per cent and manufacturing under 9 per cent of the Korean gross national product; in 1981, the comparable figures were 16 and 30 per cent. By at least one measure of 'economic development', South Korea had developed. Furthermore, its manufacturing sector had been transformed – the contribution of heavy and chemical industries to total industrial output, 23 per cent between 1953 and 1955, was 29 per cent from 1960 to 1962, and 42 per cent from 1974 to 1976.

Figure 1 shows three series of rates of annual growth – for gross national product, manufacturing output and exports – from the mid fifties to the mid eighties. It shows clearly the quite remarkable process of expansion. In gross product, only one year shows contraction (1980) and after 1962 growth never fell below 5 per cent except in 1980 (in six years, growth was above 10 per cent). In manufacturing the rates are even higher – in twenty-nine years, the growth rate was above 10 per cent in twenty-one, and above 20 per cent in ten. And the overseas appetite for Korean goods grew even more swiftly – in real terms, by 18 per cent per year after 1970. In most years, the rate of growth was above 20 per cent, and in five, above 50 per cent (in 1973, the rate was

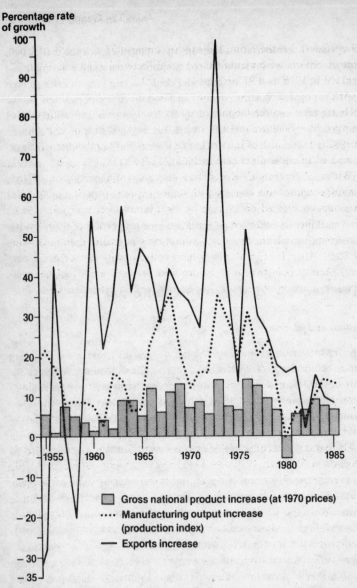

Figure 1. *South Korea: increases in gross national product, manufacturing output and exports, 1955–85*

Sources: *Principal Economic Indicator 1984*, no. 3, Bank of Korea, 1984, and *Economic Bulletin*, EPB, Seoul, various issues

99 per cent). Furthermore, the export composition changed – 17 per cent of exports were manufactured goods between 1960 and 1962; 82 per cent in 1975, and 91 per cent in 1981–2.

As the population grew – from 25 million in 1960 to 40 million in the early eighties – so the labour force was transformed. Two thirds were engaged in agriculture in 1960, two thirds engaged outside agriculture in 1982 (about a fifth of the workforce was employed in manufacturing, compared to under 6 per cent in 1960).

Within a generation, Korea had changed from being one of the poorest countries to a country with some measure of social wealth. Life expectancy increased on average by eight months per year after 1960. Universal literacy had been achieved, and the proportion of the relevant age groups completing secondary education was greater than in Britain or Italy. After 1971, real wages increased annually by some 7.5 per cent. More people than ever before were at work and at higher real incomes; a nation of peasants had become one of urban workers.

Origins and phases

The Japanese colony

From before the First World War until 1945, Korea was an integral part of the Japanese Empire. Tokyo imposed a peculiarly cruel regime upon the Koreans, but also introduced a modern administration, monetary system, railway network and education (by 1945, about a quarter of the population had acquired some formal education).

There was also a considerable expansion in agricultural and industrial production. Between 1910 and 1940, manufacturing output increased on average by 10 per cent per year (the manufacturing share of Korean gross product rose from 1 to 15 per cent, while agriculture declined from 62 to 40 per cent). The composition of manufacturing output also changed – light industry (mainly food processing and textiles) declined as a proportion of the total, from 72 to 45 per cent (1926 to 1939); chemicals expanded from 6 to 26 per cent, and metal products from 4 to 10 per cent. Much of this growth was export led – for some two thirds of manufacturing output went overseas, to the rest of the empire.

The economy was dominated by the Japanese. Most of the capital employed in manufacturing was Japanese-owned, and most of the technicians came from Japan. By 1940, there were 700,000 Japanese living in Korea – running the administration, most management, and some of the larger agricultural estates. Seventeen per cent of the labour force was Japanese. None the less, there were about a quarter of a million Koreans employed in factories in 1940, with another couple of million Koreans living in Japan, and possibly another million in mainly industrial occupations in Manchuria. It was, in principle, an experienced workforce, and this probably softened the impact of the Japanese evacuation in 1945.

The end of the Second World War saw the removal of the ruling order of Korea, its business and technical class. The problems were exacerbated by some wartime destruction (although this was not as extensive as elsewhere), the loss of Korea's external markets and raw-material imports through the collapse of the imperial trading system, and the partition of the country between its heavy industrial and mining north (occupied by the Russians), and the light industrial and rice-growing south (controlled by the Americans). The number of industrial establishments was halved; employment fell by 40 per cent. The southern administration inherited two thirds of the population, nearly half the arable land (70 per cent of the rice-growing areas), and much of the light industrial capacity.

1945 to 1960

Up to 1948, the US military administration established some modicum of order before handing over to a South Korean regime. However, before much rehabilitation could take place, the country was overwhelmed by a new and far more destructive war. The fifties were dominated by the desperate struggle to recover from this catastrophe.

One important accomplishment, however, marks the period before the Korean war: the reform of the land system. The Americans expropriated Japanese holdings, and pressed the new Korean administration to purchase all large Korean landed estates on specially favourable terms. By this means, the landowner class was eliminated. No free market in land was permitted to develop thereafter, and the maximum size of holding was limited to three hectares. These draconian measures, however, did not stifle growth – after 1952, agricultural output increased annually 3.5 per cent on average.

The new Korean administration also introduced a system of compulsory procurement of rice and barley not unlike that operated in

Eastern Europe. In 1950, the state assumed a monopoly of grain marketing. This was diluted later, but even in the mid seventies, half the marketed rice and most of the barley was purchased by the government. Prices paid to the farmers were below those of imports, and sometimes below the average costs of production – 'Government grain was in effect requisitioned from the farmers ... [who] suffered much loss because of forced sales to the government.'[4]

The Korean War, the first open conflict in the long contest for world supremacy between the United States and the Soviet Union, involved new levels of destruction. Some 1.3 million people were killed, and millions more maimed or rendered homeless. The economic costs have been estimated as equivalent to nearly two years' gross product; the 1953 value of industrial output was possibly one third of the level of 1940.[5]

The war led to the two Koreas maintaining very large military establishments. Officially, defence took a third of government spending in the seventies. The Japanese aphorism – 'Rich country, strong army' – seemed to be reversed in the Korean case, where business appeared to ride on the back of the war-making machine. However, the economic impact may have been less significant than the political – the two Koreas maintained regimes of great insecurity that demanded continual sacrifices. The military sustained dictatorship, and dictatorship, an accelerating rate of investment and output.

The crippled South Korean economy was supported only by massive American military and civil aid, as well as tight economic controls (including protection against imports). As Figure 1 shows, industrial production grew annually by nearly a fifth from a very low base point in the mid fifties before slowing to a still respectable 8–9 per cent. Incentives to businessmen to export were steadily increased; by 1959, exporters paid no tariffs on imported raw materials and had access to favourably priced export credit (perhaps producing the sudden increase in exports in the late fifties shown in Figure 1). A period of intense political instability interrupted this growing concentration on exports – President Synghman Rhee was overthrown in 1960, and the military seized power the following year.

*

1961 to 1979

The eighteen years which followed were the years of the widely acclaimed Korean economic miracle and the stable long-term dictatorship of General Park.

The period began with a continuation of the faltering steps to expand exports (but without 'liberalization' – the relaxation of import controls), growing increasingly urgent as the date approached for the progressive decrease in aid from the United States. The economy had become overwhelmingly dependent upon dollar injections and it did not seem possible that a major slump could be avoided simply by cutting imports down to the declining size of foreign aid. Nor was there much optimism that the target of an annual growth rate of 7 per cent per year (presented in the 1962 five-year Economic Development Plan) could be achieved. The Korean currency, the won, was halved in value (to encourage exports), interest rates were allowed to rise (to encourage domestic savings), restrictions on external trade were eased (so that exporters acquired virtual freedom to import provided they exported), and tax incentives to export were increased.

To the general astonishment, the recipe seemed to work and, as it worked, fuelled an increasing obsession with exports as the key to growth. This was not an alternative to import substitution – the government continued to protect the domestic economy, although on a changing basis (the ban on the importation of cement, metals, chemicals and fertilizers later gave way to a ban on transport equipment and machinery).

With success, the government's ambitions grew. Even as the neo-classical economists were discovering a Korea which seemed to vindicate a free-market economy, the Korean state introduced the 1973 Heavy Industry and Chemicals Plan, to force the disproportionate growth of capital-intensive industries (shipbuilding, steel, machinery, petrochemicals) regardless either of relative prices or of notions of comparative advantage. While the increase in world oil prices (1973–4) and world slump forced a reduction in these aspirations, the government persisted (and increased its overseas borrowing to ease the domestic shortage of resources). Investment as a share of gross product increased between 1976 and 1979 from 25 to 35 per cent, and four fifths of the investment went to the heavy and chemical sectors.

The investment boom along with general world factors produced a powerful increase in inflation (exaggerated by a major increase in Korean participation in Middle Eastern construction projects that produced shortages of skilled labour and vital materials at home). To ease the shortages, the government allowed an increase in imports, at the same time as rising domestic prices were making it increasingly difficult to export (and the won was not devalued fast enough lest this increase the prices of imports and so fuel inflation). The increase in the volume of exports declined from 14 per cent in 1978 to 1 per cent in 1979. There was a balance-of-payments crisis just as rising interest rates abroad swiftly increased the burden and cost of Korea's overseas borrowings, oil prices increased and the onset of world slump cut the overseas demand for Korea's exports.

In October 1979, President Park was murdered and, for a time, the military lost control. For nearly twelve months, the Korean people were able to express some of their feelings about the breakneck speed of growth, the disciplines of work and low pay for very long hours, the extraordinary levels of repression, all additional constituents of the Korean miracle.

After 1979

The crisis of 1979–80 produced in time a much more wide-ranging reassessment of the economic and political direction of the country. The Fifth Plan (1982–6) attributed the problems of growth to the government itself – 'Excessive government intervention in the private sector ... discouraged private initiative and efficiency of investment, which are vital to growth in a market economy.' The Minister of Planning subsequently elaborated a more detailed account:

Labour became increasingly more expensive in Korea, and the nation's business sector was neither small nor passive enough to require extensive government intervention and guidance. Furthermore, the relatively favourable international economic environment that contributed so much to Korea's economic growth over the previous two decades no longer existed.[6]

In Seoul, other versions from within the government alleged that heavy industry (shipbuilding, vehicles, heavy machinery) were so inefficient that only indiscriminate public subsidies kept them in operation. Holding down interest rates (to cheapen capital and so increase investment) had, it was said, reduced the willingness of people to save and created semi-legal markets outside public control. The resulting shortage of domestic savings forced an increased dependence on borrowing abroad (by the end of 1985, the cumulative debt was about $47 billion, a higher level per head of the Korean population and as a proportion of the gross product than any other developing country, including Brazil).

The government had begun to recognize the problems in early 1979; even in 1978, there had been talk of the need to liberalize imports in order to increase domestic competition and efficiency. There was much resistance,[7] and not until 1981 did the government have sufficient authority to outline a programme of reforms (urged on by the International Monetary Fund and supported by a World Bank 'Structural Adjustment Loan'). In that year, the process of denationalizing the state's banks was begun; interest rates were allowed to rise. In 1984, special regulations governing foreign banks were ended, and some reductions in import tariffs introduced. There was still a long way to go – it was said that the government continued to finance favoured borrowers with special rates and to supervise the banks, and tariffs remained very high on many imports.

The crisis of 1979 to 1980 is of particular interest. The government was drawn back from its strategy of creating a heavy industrial base (to support, among other things, its military capacity) and obliged to begin measures of liberalization. Liberalization was not impelled simply by domestic needs – it was also an attempt to open Korea to American imports as a *quid pro quo* for retaining access to the United States market. But the domestic reasons were also important. The heavy-industry orientation had starved of funds the exporting light industries and jeopardized the whole economy. It had produced a set of uneconomic industries. Pruning was now aimed at concentrating resources on a few key heavy industries (which were not chosen, however, by simple deductions of comparative advantage). The economy had become very much more complex,[8] it was no longer susceptible to the crude imperatives of public policy and it had created a substantial business class that was unwilling to accept the government's unilateral definition of the national interest. The building of an independent national economy – albeit, of a special export-oriented kind – now had to give way to an increase in the integration of the Korean and the world economies.

Industries

In the first phases of accelerated export production in the 1960s, the theory of comparative advantage appeared a plausible explanation of the process. Up to the present, this might also be applicable to a major part of Korea's exports. Thus, textiles and garments were the foundation of the high growth, and remained equal to about a third of the total export value in the early eighties. It was here that the heavy-industry expansion of the seventies was said to have had the most deleterious effects in starving the industry of investment. Electronic equipment, so dependent, in the areas in which South Korean specialized, on low-paid literate young women workers, might similarly be accommodated in the theory. In the mid eighties, it was expected that exports in this field would rapidly overtake exports of garments.

At the other extreme, South Korea proved unable to develop large-scale machinery exports. The spearhead of the government's efforts in this field, the publicly owned Korea Heavy Industries and Construction Company, was a symbol of this failure. Many of its divisions were separated and distributed to private groups or shut down in the early eighties.

However, it is most difficult to see Korea's comparative advantage in one of its most spectacular successes, *shipbuilding*. In the sixties, the industry produced small coastal craft and trawlers, an annual output of about 20,000 gross tonnes. In the sixties, the government drew up a plan to exploit the boom in the oil trades by moving into tanker construction. Despite the radical revision of ambitions following the world slump of 1974–5, expansion continued – to create an annual capacity of 700,000 tonnes in 1976, and 4 million tonnes by 1983. By then Korea had overtaken all established rivals with the exception of Japan (with, at that time, 13 million tonnes capacity). Between 1973 and 1983, gross world output of ships declined by about a half (and Japan's output by more than a half); South Korea had increased its output by 15,000 per cent, to take, in the first half of 1983, 23 per cent of the world market. To put it in another way – in 1973, Sweden's output was 230 times South Korea's; in 1983, Korea's output was five times larger than Sweden's.

It is true that Korea had advantages in its relatively low wages (estimated to be a third of Japanese and European levels), the available length of working time, productivity (its equipment was of the largest scale and most advanced technology as it had been built so recently) and reliable and swift construction times, a result of high organization and discipline. But shipbuilding was a capital-intensive industry, supposedly characteristic of a capital-abundant economy. It was government that made the difference, financing company expansion in the face of declining demand and low-capacity use, forcing mergers and a cartel to reduce domestic competition, and obliging companies to adopt a particular pattern of specialization. In sum, it appeared that government, not the operation of a free world market, had created a 'comparative advantage'.

The same might also be said of *steel*. Output from the state company, Posco, started at one million tonnes in 1973, and was about 12 million tonnes by 1984. Exports of 5.7 million tonnes in 1983 led to the protests from Washington and produced price declines in the highly cartelized market of Japan. Korea had no domestic supply of coking coal, oil or iron ore (it had purchased mines abroad – in Pennsylvania, Canada, Australia); labour costs per unit of output are not a very significant element. Modern technology and highly disciplined organization must have made an important difference, but not without the full panoply of the privileges the government made available to the industry.

The government's attempts to invent comparative advantages are now being tested in the *vehicle-manufacturing industry*. Components have been made since the Korean War (the 1983 value of vehicle-component exports was $300 million), but the assembly of vehicles only developed after a 1962 ban on imports; at the same time, production was restricted to companies with a majority Korean ownership, and the proportion of a vehicle which had to be manufactured in Korea was steadily raised (it is now 90 per cent). The government maintained powerful financial pressures to prevent the domestic market expanding in order to force an export orientation (before the eighties, the peak domestic purchase of cars was 89,000, in 1979). In 1974 (when 9,100 cars were produced), targets were set for an output of half a million by 1980 and one million by 1985. However, after 1979 (when output was 114,000 cars), the industry went into severe crisis, and output did not exceed this figure until 1983 (121,000 cars). The industry recovered, and targets were proposed of half a million by 1986, 2 million by 1991 (with exports of 900,000) – and 4.5 million for all vehicles. A private forecast by Hyundai proposed that the total vehicle output by 1991 would be between 5 and 6 million (of which 3 million would be exported).

These were heroic ambitions, and it seemed that they were just as unlikely to be achieved as were the targets for shipbuilding in the early seventies. They were impossible without a privileged framework of operations provided by the government and a safety net in slump. In 1979, the Ministry of Commerce estimated that Hyundai's Pony cost $3,972 to make, compared to its more sophisticated rival, Toyota's Corolla, costing $2,300. Yet while the companies made spectacular losses, they expanded capacity (capacity increased some 55 per cent between 1979 and 1981 – when it was said to be only 24 per cent utilized). The magic of this exercise was achieved courtesy of the national treasury.

In sum then, while the backbone of the export performance of South Korea might be attributable to a genuine comparative advantage, the second generation of growth industries seemed more likely to be the products of government gambles. There were problems in both respects. Lower-cost producers affected the basic exports; in under a decade, China expanded its garment exports so swiftly that it became the fourth largest exporter among the less developed countries. (Korean officials estimated Chinese wages were 30 to 40 per cent below the Korean level.) Also, the new industries directly affected old-established sectors of production in the industrialized countries, evoking protectionism in the richest markets.

The state

In the sixties and seventies, the state dominated the entire process of rapid economic growth. Between a fifth and a quarter of the gross national product was government spending; public investment was about 40 per cent of the national total, and public savings were between a fifth and a third of the whole. The government had appropriated the five leading commercial banks in the early sixties and, with the Bank of Korea and direct public-sector activities, the state controlled two thirds of national investment – 'the single most important economic factor explaining the distinctly subordinate position of the private sector'.[9] On top of this, by means of political patronage, discriminatory tax, credit and pricing policies, medals and awards, orders, bribery, bullying, and monthly conferences between Ministers and businessmen, the wishes of the state shaped the whole development process. Those that refused or evaded the detailed direction faced the possible confiscation of their assets and prosecution (to set the tone, General Park prosecuted most major businessmen at the beginning of his regime for possessing 'illicit wealth').

Even in the early eighties, the government was still busy intervening to force mergers, specialization and monopolies. Hyundai was nominated as sole maker of marine engines; Kia was ordered to cease car making, and Daewoo marine-engine manufacture; fifty-three of the sixty-eight shipping companies were collapsed into sixteen. But it took much greater effort than earlier, and more frequently failed. When the government ordered companies to release land hoards to reduce their indebtedness, they refused. The *chaebol*, the fifty giant private companies, were coming of age, although the Chairman of Daewoo could still complain that 'The government tells you it's your duty and you have to do it, even if there's no profit. Maybe after the year 2,000, Korean businessmen will be able to put their company's interests ahead of those of society or government.'[10]

The government also provided a safety net for floundering companies. It used public expenditure as a means of stimulating growth in the classic Keynesian fashion. Yet, although the heart of Korean development was as state capitalist as any East European economy and as Keynesian as any West European social democracy, it was distinguished from both by the flexibility of approach and speed of change. Exports required an opportunism normally excluded from state planning. One commentator described the government style as 'not so much a deliberate one of careful planning and debate, but more one of diving in, getting started, observing results, adjusting policy, and repeating the process until the appropriate mix is found'.[11] Although it was swimming in the fast-flowing tides of world trade, South Korea was none the less, as regards the role of the state, as 'socialist' as most of the countries that applied that term to themselves.

Explanations

The analysis of South Korea's economic performance has been dominated by the search for explanations. Roughly, these divide into factors concerning the peculiarities of Korea or of the external forces acting upon it. At its most superficial, the analysis becomes either an extended compliment to Korean abilities or a denunciation of the fickle priorities of the United States and multinational capital.

The crudest version of the 'internal' case explains Korean development as the product of low wages. Since low wages are general in developing countries, South Korea's advantage is limited. Korean wages were not the lowest in the world at the beginning of fast growth, and, as earlier noted, have increased faster than in most developing countries (in real terms, by over 7 per cent per year since the sixties). However, productivity gains more than offset the increase in wages, so that the labour cost of output fell; explaining the productivity gains, however, takes us far from the original proposition.

The more sophisticated case attributes the success of Korean development to the interaction of government policy with social factors: a high propensity to work and save (a condition sometimes rather vaguely attributed to a Confucian tradition, without its being clear what this is and why it does not seem to work elsewhere). The government created, it is said, a 'free-trade' regime for exports – that is, Korean exporters were granted the right to purchase inputs to exports at the lowest price in the world market (so neutralizing the advantage of rival exporters). Other factors were incentives, labour policy, and an exchange rate which for much of the time reduced the price of exports and made imports relatively expensive. As a result, Korea's comparative advantage could be clearly expressed.[12]

How would we demonstrate that this analysis is correct? For, on the face of it, it would seem that Korea *subsidized* exports, or redistributed income domestically in order to cheapen exports 'artificially'. According to this view, external markets gained from the sacrifices imposed upon the mass of Koreans. Furthermore, it would seem implausible that two sets of prices, domestic and export, could be maintained for long without one coming increasingly to influence the other – either exports would increasingly influence domestic prices (in which case, 'free trade' would become 'laissez-faire', and the government would be obliged to relinquish ambitions to determine the shape of the economy), or the reverse would occur (and exports would decline). Nor does the timing fit, for export expansion began in 1959, whereas the policy changes to which export growth is attributed by the neoclassical account occurred later – 'There is no clear correlation between the liberalization of 1964–

5 and the start of rapid growth.'[13] Nor is it clear that Korea did, in its recent phases, pursue any evident 'comparative advantage', and certainly not imperatives determined by markets; it certainly began by 'exporting the output of labour-intensive processing stages, or, to put it in a less savoury fashion, in the packaging of labour for export'[14] (and even this is true only if Korean labour costs reflected the real scarcity value of Korean labour) but thereafter, the speculative gambles of the state, backed by its capacity to mobilize resources and force the population at large to support the process, were dominant. Korea did not pursue simple export promotion; to this day, it substitutes for imports as a tactic of forcing industrial growth.

The process was blind – success bred, with sufficient pragmatism, more success. Without such pragmatism, combined with gambles and the capacity to centralize resources, it is difficult to see how the state capitalism of South Korea, operating in a particular world context, could have achieved optimal market conditions. The neoclassical account of Korean growth, however, turns analysis into moral justification, vindicating the profitable regardless of either judgements of real scarcity pricing or of the morally repugnant.

However, the second line of argument, more common among defenders of Third Worldism, encounters equal difficulties. Is Korean development the byproduct of the military and civil aid of the United States? Between 1953 and 1960, this equalled 9 per cent of the Korean gross national product, 75 per cent of gross investment, 70 per cent of the value of imports and nearly half public expenditure. US civil aid was very important in the financing of infrastructure and education. However, accelerated growth came later and was the result of attempts to cope with declining US aid; perhaps aid was a necessary condition of development, but it could not be a sufficient one. Military aid continued at a relatively high level, but its effect was to relieve some of the burden of Korean military spending rather than to promote civil production. However, this was not true of Korean involvement in overseas military operations – Korean sales to US forces in Vietnam, with supplies to troops in both Korea and Vietnam, accounted for nearly half Korean overseas earnings in the second half of the sixties (the proportion was down to 9 per cent by 1972).[15]

Was Korean development the result of the changing priorities of investment by multinational (or trans-national) companies? At worst, this could mean South Korea is a kind of ventriloquist's dummy, rendered inert when the ventriloquist lays aside the doll (or multinational priorities change). In fact, South Korea is not a notable recipient of foreign investment; if we consider foreign investment in a selection of less developed countries, with Mexico as 100, then South Korea is 17.6; Brazil is 235.3; Thailand 19.1 (all between 1972 and 1976). Foreign investment as a ratio of gross national product in South Korea was 5.5, in Brazil 9.6, Colombia 10.6, Taiwan 6.2 and Turkey 10.5.[16] In any case, the volume of foreign investment does not correlate with the scale of exports – in 1980, Brazil, with the largest foreign investment, had exports of $9.2 billion, compared to South Korea's $19.2 billion. Furthermore, foreign investment *followed* accelerated growth rather than leading it. The largest foreign investor by nationality were Japanese companies (with 61 per cent of the total in 1978, 48 per cent in 1984), and their entry came after the normalization of Korean–Japanese relations in 1965. They were generally small and medium-sized companies for whom the one Korean plant was the sole overseas investment, and usually operated jointly with a Korean partner. The great transnationals were rather remote in such a context. Finally, the share of foreign investment appeared to be declining in many newly industrializing countries in the seventies and eighties.[17] Korean companies certainly seemed to be replacing some of the largest Japanese operations in the field of electronic goods.

The foreigners came after growth began and were heavily concentrated in particular fields. The pioneers in the first half of the sixties were Koreans. In other sectors of key export production at different times – ships, footwear, iron and steel, metal manufacturing, nonmetallic minerals (especially cement), rubber goods (especially tyres), precision instruments, wigs, plywood – there were no foreign companies.

The factors cited as explanations obviously played some role, but not as effective causes. For that we need to understand the interaction between a peculiar (and temporary) set of conditions in Korea and new phases in the external environment. Korea was not manipulated from outside, but did exploit changing opportunities. The characteristics of boat, captain and crew were important, but without a wind there could have been no movement. However, we must await the examination of other cases before we seek to identify the wind.

Taiwan

The economic development of the 'province of Taiwan' (the name preferred both by the government of mainland China, the People's Republic, and by the administration of Taiwan, the Republic of China) is as remarkable as that of South Korea; indeed, some see it as more remarkable – 'the most successful of the developing countries', in the words of I. M. D. Little.[18]

Agriculture provided 35 per cent of the net domestic product in the early fifties, 9 per cent in the early eighties. The share of manufacturing increased from 12 to 33 per cent. The employed population increased two and a half times, while primary-sector employment fell from 55 to 19 per cent of the whole (an absolute decrease of 300,000). Manufac-

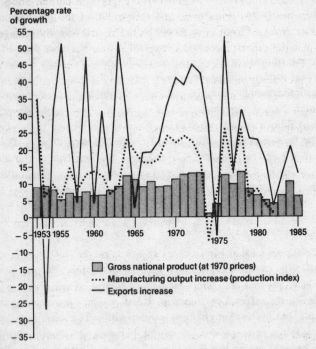

Figure 2. *Taiwan: increases in gross national product, manufacturing output and exports, 1953–85*

Sources: *Taiwan Statistical Data Book*, 1983, and *Far Eastern Economic Review*, various issues

turing employment grew from just under 14 per cent (or 400,000 in all) to 32 per cent (or 2.2 million).

Figure 2 shows the annual economic performance between 1953 and 1985. The gross national product includes no negative rates in the thirty-three years; in three years only did the increase fall below 5 per cent (1974, 1975 and 1982); in nine years, it was above 10 per cent. In manufacturing, only 1974, the year of the first slump of the current period, shows a negative rate (− 6 per cent), with three years below 5 per cent (1974, and 1981 and 1982, the years of the second slump); in nineteen years, the rate was over 10 per cent, and in nine, over 20 per cent.

Exports showed much wider swings, with two years of negative growth (1954 and 1975); six of a rate below 10 per cent, but nineteen with increases above 20 per cent, and seven above 40 per cent (1956, 1959, 1963, 1970, 1972, 1973 and 1976). Exports, at current prices, increased nearly 200 times over, and their share of the gross national product increased from 11 to 50 per cent. The structure also changed – raw-material exports increased sixteen times over but, as a share of the total, fell from 95 to 8 per cent. Textiles, clothing, leather, wood and paper products, insignificant in 1952, had expanded to over 55 per cent of the whole by the mid seventies. Other goods expanded swiftly in the seventies – non-metallic manufactured goods, metal products and transport equipment among them. Electronic products, barely 1 per cent of exports in 1960, were 18 per cent by the early eighties (a share for the first time larger than that of textiles and garments). In 1982, Taiwan became the largest exporter of electronic products among the less developed countries (with Mexico second and South Korea fourth).

The comparison with South Korea

Taiwan is much smaller than South Korea, both in terms of population (under half that of Korea) and land surface (Taiwan is about 15 per cent of South Korea's surface area). Furthermore, Taiwan was colonized for a longer period by the Japanese and deliberately cultivated as an exporter of agricultural goods to the rest of the empire. As a result, the rural infrastructure (roads, railways, electricity supply, irrigation systems) was more highly developed – on 15 per cent of the land surface of Korea, Taiwan had in the early seventies 353 sq km of railway and 1,036 km of highway per 1,000 population, compared to 156 and 1,000 in Korea.

Both Korea and Taiwan had radical land reforms. But the Koreans did not use agriculture, as the Taiwanese did, as the basis for export production; given Japanese policy during the period of colonization, the Taiwanese strategy would seem more sensible for the province. As a result, industrialization came after agricultural development in Taiwan, but before it in Korea. Agricultural wages continued a more rapid growth as a result – between 1965 and 1975, Taiwanese agricultural wages increased by 7.5 per cent annually (industrial wages by 5.4 per cent) – compared to the Korean rate of increase of 4.8 per cent (and 7.8 per cent in manufacturing). The rural market accordingly expanded swiftly, producing, according to some commentators, a dispersed territorial pattern of development instead of high concentration in the large cities. Of course, greater rural prosperity did not rule out a net transfer to the urban industrial sector, achieved through land taxes, a rice–fertilizer barter arrangement, and the use of revenue from agricultural exports to purchase the import of industrial equipment for a protected domestic market. More generally, the domestic market has been allowed to expand more swiftly than in Korea; in car manufacture, for example, whereas the Koreans curbed the domestic market to force exports, the Taiwanese for a long time produced only for home consumption (as a result, in the early eighties, there were fifty cars per thousand people in Taiwan, seven per thousand in Korea).

Taiwan's manufacturing industry is more dominated by light industry, by small family-based and labour-intensive operations (90 per cent of provincial output comes from small and medium companies). Nearly 70 per cent of jobs are in units employing ten or fewer workers. A third of the value added in Korean manufacturing came from units employing 300 workers or fewer, but 57 per cent of Taiwanese. Ten general trading companies provide half Korea's exports, and the largest three (Hyundai, Daewoo, Samsung) a quarter; 38,000 companies produce three quarters of Taiwan's exports. Daewoo's 1981 export target was said to be twelve times larger than the 1980 exports of Taiwan's five largest companies.

However, this picture of small company activity is much modified if the public sector is included. Throughout Taiwan's development, the state has played a decisive role just as it did in South Korea. The new regime of 1949 was committed to state capitalism in the industrial field,[19] and this fitted the emergency priorities of the fifties. Two thirds of the civil aid received from the United States was used to fund public-

sector spending (particularly in infrastructural and educational investment), with another 27 per cent employed in public–private joint
ventures. In 1951, 80 per cent of industrial output derived from public
corporations, a share which declined sharply in the sixties, but expanded
again in the seventies as the government built up a major heavy industrial programme (as happened in South Korea). Between 1973 and 1979,
the public sector undertook over half the fixed-capital formation. In the
late seventies, public corporations built up major deficits (again as in
South Korea) which obliged a programme of reforms – mergers,
rationalization or closures.

While the state does not seem to have intervened in such detail as in
Korea, it has none the less exercised the decisive controls. Most of the
banking system was in government hands, and was used in the seventies
to fund the public-sector heavy-industry programme. Selective credit
controls were used to favour priority projects, and interest rates
favoured exports (as did a changing import-substitution programme).

The military burden on the Taiwanese economy was substantial (as it
was in South Korea). Over half a million men served in the armed
forces in the fifties (or some 14 per cent of the 1950 male population),
and official defence spending equalled 12 per cent of the gross national
product (80–90 per cent of public spending).[20] The military share of the
national budget was still over 40 per cent in the eighties (and the official
military budget excluded many items of 'military spending'). In the
fifties, United States aid made the burden tolerable. Between 1949 and
1967, US aid reached the cumulative total of $4 bn, or $425 per head
of the population (Taiwan's income per head in 1960 was $110). It was
large, but less than the military aid received at different times by South
Vietnam, South Korea, Zaire, Turkey, Yugoslavia and Egypt. It particularly helped the maintenance of imports – in the fifties, imports
exceeded exports in value by some 60 per cent.

From the early sixties, aid declined (and what was left was converted
to loans). It was this factor which drove the government to expand
exports and encourage foreign investment. Foreign capital became significant in the late sixties – some 6.5 per cent of average fixed-capital
formation in manufacturing was foreign-owned between 1967 and 1975
(nearly half went to the electrical-machinery, electronics and chemicals
industries).

In the crisis of the seventies, Taiwan was hit more heavily than South

Korea in the first slump (1974–5), but less in the second (1980–82). Korea borrowed heavily and, as we have seen, with rising interest rates and a strengthening dollar, the cumulative debt proved a severe burden in the early eighties. Taiwan did not increase its borrowing so swiftly, so the second slump was less severe; by the early eighties, the cumulative debt was some $6m, more than matched by Taiwan's assets abroad of $9 bn.

Phases of growth

The Japanese period
The Japanese colonial administration of Taiwan developed the island as a source of agricultural exports for the empire. Railways, roads, a rural credit system, health and educational facilities (by 1945, three quarters of the primary-school age group was at school), were all devoted to this end. The irrigated area of agriculture similarly expanded from one third to two thirds of the whole between 1906 and 1942. The value of exports doubled between the twenties and forties.

Factory production – mainly agricultural processing – also expanded. Sugar refining was particularly important here, and Taiwan came to supply 75 per cent of Japan's sugar consumption (as well as 30 per cent of its rice imports). Most of the factories were very small, but by the early forties, about 130,000 workers were employed in them. There was some diversification – into chemicals (mainly fertilizers for agriculture), ceramics and, during the Second World War, metal manufacture and aluminium production.

The postwar years (1945–54)
In 1945, Taiwan – like Korea – lost its ruling order, its administration and an important part of its skilled labour force. It also lost a clearly defined role in the imperial trading system through losing its markets. Unlike South Korea, it had suffered extensive damage from Allied bombing. However, it remained one of the most advanced areas in the new short-lived republic of China, which included Taiwan in the mainland (1945–9).

The forces of the Republic of China, the Kuomintang, were driven from the mainland in 1948 and 1949. Over a million refugees arrived in Taiwan to constitute a new ruling order, an administration, business class and army. As a matter of extreme urgency, the new government bent all efforts to restore agricultural production in order to make secure the domestic food supply (part of the process included the radical land-reform programme). Furthermore, the regime needed agricultural exports in order to purchase the industrial imports upon which the province was overwhelmingly dependent. The old landlords were diverted into industrial activities (as happened in the People's Republic).[21]

These were emergency measures for survival. In the same way, the regime controlled all imports, and maintained an overvalued currency in order to cheapen the purchase of those imports needed. As Figure 2 shows, the economy expanded swiftly, although unevenly. Despite the overvalued currency, exports increased on average by 22 per cent per year up to 1960.

The transition to an export economy (1954–64)

The economy recovered, but was still extremely vulnerable. The markets for agricultural exports seemed limited, and United States aid was likely to be only temporary. Policy makers in Taipeh in the last half of the fifties debated the strategies for the future, influenced perhaps by the liberal views of American aid officials and the surprising success of Hong Kong in industrializing and expanding exports. Piecemeal reforms were introduced – the new Taiwan dollar was devalued by between 50 and 80 per cent at the end of the fifties; foreign-exchange allocations to buy imports were eased, and import quotas ended (but tariffs remained high). Import controls and general regulations, however, remained elaborate.

In the early sixties, it became increasingly apparent that the United States would reduce its aid, converting what was left to loans. This provided the spur to seek to expand exports (imports being already tightly controlled) and induce an inflow of foreign capital. The second aim required changes both in incentives, foreign-exchange regulations and import restrictions – as well as a political settlement with Japan.

The export economy, Mark 1 (1964–72)

From the early sixties, the growth of manufacturing output and manufactured exports became exceptionally rapid. With success, confidence grew. The manufacturing structure was reshaped by overseas demand, and overseas markets were diversified. In the late sixties, the government began increasingly to seek to take command of the process of reshaping in order to move the economy away from labour-intensive to more capital-intensive activities, to 'deepen' the structure of production. The public sector was to be the key instrument in this endeavour. These ambitions were outlined in the Fifth Four Year Plan (1969–72).

The export economy, Mark II (1972–80)

The increase in world oil prices and the world slump checked these aims, but the basic task (now embodied in the 'Ten Great Projects' and the Sixth Plan) was only temporarily diverted. The programme – in steel, aluminium, petroleum, basic petrochemicals and synthetic fibres – placed a heavy burden on the supply of capital to build industries with long maturation periods and a high vulnerability in a world marked by overcapacity in these fields. The government persisted, however, since it saw the public-sector heavy-industry programme as a means of stimulating the economy (in Keynesian terms) in the face of world contraction.

However, as noted above, public-corporation debts afflicted the drive and forced severe cutbacks (which in turn affected private operations dependent on public purchases). The new plan (to 1985) deliberately reduced public investment and the proposals for heavy industry expansion.

Liberalization (1981–)

The economy did not decline as it had done in the first slump (1974–5), and it was pulled back into high growth by the revival of demand in the United States. None the less the ten-year attempt to create an 'upstream' base to the economy was checked. The world economic order in slump imposed strict restraints on the shape of the domestic economy, but, as a reward for self-discipline, external markets expanded in 1983 and the following two years, producing a resumption of general growth.

The heart of the exports expansion was trade with the United States, generating unprecedented surpluses for Taiwan. Washington made increasingly loud protests and threats, and the Taiwanese government made concessions on imports – duties were cut in 1983 and 1984, and plans to reach an average import tariff of 6 per cent within three to five years were publicized.

Furthermore, if ambitions in heavy industry were frustrated, the government none the less promoted a restructuring plan to increase the skill content of manufacturing. It was expected that the People's Republic – which had already caught up with Taiwan in the export of toys, canned food, footwear, sporting and paper goods – would sooner or later replace Taiwan in garments and textiles, dyes, plastic goods and some consumer appliances. Electronic products – new prototypes of microcomputers, computer peripherals, cordless telephones, video and telecommunication equipment – were seen as some of the items which would replace the declining sectors.

Explanations

Many of the explanations applied to South Korea's development were used also with Taiwan. The Chinese growth pattern, it was said, was no more than a byproduct of United States aid or military priorities, or of foreign capital; the export basis made Taiwan peculiarly vulnerable, etc. As we have seen, few of these points can be sustained in a serious examination of the Taiwanese experience. Some of the neoclassical economists examining the Taiwanese performance attributed the success to policy, as with Korea. After a phase of import-substitution, where domestic growth exhausted the potential, policies produced free trade for exports where Taiwanese cheap labour could exercise its comparative advantage by utilizing the cheapest world inputs to exports. Cheap Taiwanese labour certainly was, but less through the operation of a market priced to show real scarcities than through state efforts to hold down wages, ban strikes, keep trade unions weak and avoid welfare legislation protecting workers (and thereby raising labour costs). The invisible hand was more of an armed fist. In such circumstances, it involved only faith (or class prejudice) to affirm that the price of labour reflected its world scarcity rather than that the people of Taiwan were obliged, through cheap exports, to subsidize the rest of the world. What might be irrational for the Taiwanese people – subsidizing the rest of the world – might be rational for the Taiwanese government, with its great hunger for imported armaments.

Some observers have also suggested that Taiwan's success was no more than a byproduct of Japan's dramatic growth – Taiwanese labour employed Japanese machinery to produce goods for export to the United States. This might have had some plausibility in the sixties, but

Taiwan diversified – Taiwan–Japan trade grew at half the rate of Taiwan–world trade – and its dependence upon Japan grew steadily less.

Taiwan and South Korea exhibited important common features, not least in the drive for heavy industry in the seventies. Both exhibited great instability in growth up to the early sixties, and then a sustained high level of growth for a decade before the greater fluctuations of the seventies. Both tended to move into the same pattern of fluctuations in the sixties as the domestic economy of each became increasingly directed by the same external markets. However, South Korea's performance was far more unstable than Taiwan's, with greater swings in output, and especially exports. These different patterns relate both to differences in the commodity composition of exports and to differences in scale in domestic production.

In the mid eighties, despite the extraordinary long-term performance, it still remained to be seen how far both countries could make the transition to a modern, technically advanced industrial economy. In the short term, the boom of 1983–4 produced great dependence upon the United States market, which, with its decline in 1985, created severe difficulties for both countries. As always, there was excessive gloom. Some neoclassical economists had attempted to explain the long-term growth of the two economies as the result of a Confucian culture, and it was only appropriate that the failure of Taiwanese business to grasp the investment opportunities of high technology, to move the economy from the short-term difficulties of 1985 to long-term sophistication should be attributed to the same source; the Chairman of the Council of Economic Planning and Development of the government (Y. T. Chao) pronounced that weak investment in high-technology sectors in Taiwan was the result of 'a Chinese culture and historical burden it will take years – maybe even generations – to change the mentality'. Culture was always sufficiently ambiguous to offer explanations for everything from all points of view.

Hong Kong

Hong Kong is a striking contrast compared to South Korea and Taiwan, and also to Singapore, the next case to be examined. The city is the nearest approximation to the neoclassical model. It is, however, very small and has been, for most of its history, the protected colony of a dominant world power, Britain. It is now increasingly dominated by the People's Republic of China, operating as a kind of very large export processing zone and offshore banking centre. Both relationships, to Britain and to China, make Hong Kong a very special political case rather than a neoclassical prototype.

The state

Hong Kong lacks a state in the development sense, an agency which endeavours to change the economy to achieve a target pattern of future output. There is no economic strategy nor long-term plan, no great state investments wielded as instruments of public ambitions. Indeed, the Hong Kong government strives to avoid the creation of the information which would make possible the formulation of such ambitions. There are thus no subsidies nor incentives to nudge business in given directions. There are no controls on the movement of currency in and out of the colony, no central bank, no monetary policy. There are no controls on external trade, and no balance of payments figures are collected.[22]

However, the government does more than it acknowledges, more than what officials call 'sitting on our hands'. It promotes exports and services, and defends the interests of its companies abroad. It now builds and rents factories, in addition to providing infrastructure, including industrial estates and new towns, schemes of urban renewal, land reclamation and road and major transport projects. There are export credits, technical assistance, and regulations governing some working conditions. It has sponsored major housing programmes since the early fifties, with many economic ramifications. It has also vigorously promoted education – education to the age of fifteen is now compulsory (and at the primary level, free); by 1981, 61 per cent of those aged sixteen and seventeen were undergoing full-time education, and 23 per cent of those aged eighteen to twenty (the comparable figures for Britain were 46 and 16 per cent).

Particularly in the seventies (as in South Korea and Taiwan), public expenditure increased rapidly – by 16.7 per cent annually between 1971 and 1980. By 1982, public spending was equal to nearly a quarter of the gross domestic product, having risen from 7 per cent in 1960 and 13 per cent in 1970. However, unlike South Korea and Taiwan, this expansion was not related to the publicly forced growth of heavy industry, but rather to construction and building (nearly half the investment here in 1983 was from the public sector). Under budgetary strain in 1974–5 and 1981–2, the government sharply reduced spending rather than increase its borrowing.

Growth and structure

The importance of the Hong Kong case is that, within certain qualifications, it most sensitively reflects changes in external markets. There is little to mediate the relationship. Hong Kong was accordingly the first to begin the process of rapid growth, led by the expansion of manufactured exports, and has been continually restructured by the changing demand of overseas markets (and the appearance of new low-cost producers emulating Hong Kong's performance). Hong Kong's exports thus show us the nature of world demand, uncomplicated by state intervention.

The considerable fluctuations in growth are shown in Figure 3. However, the expansion of manufacturing was checked only in 1974, and of exports, in 1974 and 1982. In the two decades between 1961 and 1981, the labour force more than doubled, and employment in manufacturing peaked at 48 per cent of the workforce in 1971 (in 1981, it was 41.2 per cent). In the interim, the composition of exports has changed considerably, upgrading the skill inputs and the value. Between 1973 and 1981, the exports with the highest rates of growth were machinery and transport (+ 324 per cent), electrical machinery (+ 302 per cent), 'other manufacturing' (+ 280 per cent) and industrial materials and fuels (+ 220 per cent).

Heavy industry played virtually no role in this growth. Apart from some cement and steel production (for the construction industry), shipbuilding and power, there is little traditional 'base' to the economy, or, to reverse the image, there are no 'commanding heights'. Furthermore, light industry is highly concentrated on particular commodities. Two thirds of exports in the late seventies were in three sectors – textiles and garments, electrical machinery and apparatus, and plastic goods. In the case of electrical machinery and apparatus, this was

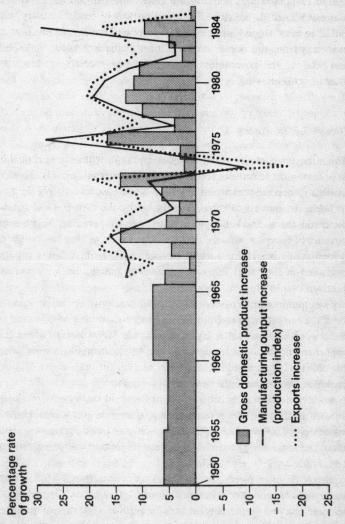

Figure 3. *Hong Kong: increases in gross domestic product, manufacturing output and exports, 1950–84*

Sources: 1950–70: *World Bank Tables*, p. 101; 1977–80: Census and Statistics Dept, Hong Kong Government, 1981; 1981–4: *Far Eastern Economic Review*, various issues

overwhelmingly dominated by one item, transistorized radios (International Standard Industrial Classification 383).

The basis of Hong Kong's early growth in manufactured exports lay in a happy conjuncture of circumstances in the late 1940s. Shanghai had been the textile manufacturing centre of pre-war China. The mill-owners, however, with skilled labour, fled before the march of the Red Army to the sanctuary of the British colony. The new orders for machinery to make up wartime losses and depreciation were on the high seas, and were diverted to the island. The supply was created. And in war-torn south-east Asia the initial demand was overwhelming. Later British buyers came in search of new supplies for cheap garments, and were followed by American purchasers. The overseas markets seemed limitless and rapidly expanded Hong Kong's supply – 3.5 per cent of the island's exports in 1950 were garments, 35 per cent in 1960 and 44 per cent in the mid seventies (when nearly half the manufacturing labour force was engaged in this sector).

Increasing import controls in Europe and North America (finally embodied in the Multi Fibre Arrangement) and the rise of new producers reshaped Hong Kong's output. Limits on quantities forced the city's output into higher-priced exports (while importing cheaper textiles for the domestic market from China) and encouraged mill-owners to move production to lower-cost sites outside Hong Kong (where the import quotas into European or North American markets were often not filled). Hong Kong accordingly became, of the less developed countries, one of the largest overseas investors.

A widening variety of other industries grew in the wake of garment exports. From 1960, the manufacture of electronic goods grew swiftly, employing 89,000 workers by 1980. Watch- and clock-making began at about the same time, expanding by some 56 per cent per year from the mid sixties; by 1980 Hong Kong had become easily the world's largest exporter of time-pieces (well ahead of Switzerland). In miscellaneous plastic goods, the value of exports increased on average by 37 per cent per year in the two decades to 1980, though the composition changed radically, varying from flowers to toys and household goods.

As in Taiwan, the companies are predominantly small or tiny operations, labour intensive and family run. This structure favoured swift responses to changeable overseas fashions. In electronic manufacture, four fifths of companies (employing a third of the workforce) employed under nine workers; only twelve employed one hundred or more workers.

Foreign investment was more important than in South Korea or Taiwan, but much less than in Singapore. It was heavily concentrated in particular sectors – 38 per cent of the assets in the electrical and electronic industry, 12 per cent in textiles, 7 in chemicals and just under 6 in watches and clocks. China had the largest stake (along with a holding of 40 per cent of Hong Kong's financial operations), followed by US registered companies. About 10 per cent of the city's exports were said to be under foreign control (compared to 20 per cent of Taiwan's, 15 per cent of South Korea's and 70 per cent of Singapore's).[23]

Services and labour

However, manufacturing is a declining share of the city's economy now. Hong Kong is returning to its original servicing role, but now with services of much greater value – shipping, air transport, tourism, banking and insurance. Hong Kong's port is the fifteenth largest in the world, and its container port, the fourth. Its airport is the eleventh largest in terms of passenger movement. In the early eighties, the island received nearly 3 million tourists, contributing spending equal to 8 per cent of the value of exports. The city's finance sector attracted nearly twice as many banks as Singapore, with half the total funds engaged in offshore operations; Hong Kong was the third largest gold market in the world.

Hong Kong is thus tending to move towards a much more highly specialized servicing role in Asian and world trade. It is a pattern a number of more developed countries are approaching, although at a much higher level of income than Hong Kong's. Not that Hong Kong has been slow to expand incomes – wages increased annually by 5.4 per cent between 1964 and 1973, and by 3 per cent in the two decades to 1982. But in 1981, nearly two thirds of the workforce still earned less than the equivalent of $340 (US) per month. Furthermore there were considerable fluctuations in income – thus, in the slump of 1974–5, unemployment rose to 15 per cent and about a quarter of all workers were on short time with the result that take-home pay declined by about 15 per cent). Man-hours worked in 1981 were said to have fallen by a fifth. The proportion of people working is high (including children) and the hours long – the average working week in the early seventies was some fifty-six hours; 175,000 workers (or 30 per cent of the industrial labour force) worked seventy-five hours or more weekly.

The uncontrolled character of the Hong Kong economy, protected politically first by Britain and now increasingly by China, made possible expansion in response to overseas demand during the long boom in the world economy. By the time that boom came to an end in the early seventies, Hong Kong's businessmen had learned the art of shifting production swiftly to new markets, expanding while global demand stagnated or even declined. The neoclassical argument appeared to be more valid than in any other case. However if it were valid, it was difficult to see why Hong Kong had not developed just as swiftly in the nineteenth century or in the 1930s, for all the same domestic factors in terms of policy obtained in the earlier periods. The resulting structure of production had the peculiarities of its origin – the lack of heavy industry, the high concentration on particular exports, the lower level of technical development and innovation than the other three in the Gang of Four. However, Hong Kong was a vital case since the differences and similarities, when compared with the other three, illuminated both the strengths and the weaknesses of the doctrine of comparative advantage.

Singapore

With the city-state of Singapore, we move back to the world of state-directed economies. If Hong Kong could be seen as a working model of the neoclassical thesis, Singapore is an example of the social democratic one, with the predominant state capitalism of mixed economies, replete with consistent Keynesian policies. If the criterion of success is the speed of expansion of exports, then Singapore and social democracy are the winners, for there has rarely been a process of growth so swift. By the eighties, Singapore – with an income per head approaching European levels at $6–7,000 per year – was being obliged to retire from the class of less developed countries.

The state intervenes in almost everything – from the long-term and the strategic, the regulation of currency and the shaping of a future industrial structure, to the reproductive habits of Singaporeans and the quality of the goods that tourists can buy, and even the dropping of litter and the length of hair permitted to tourists. The Prime Minister, Lee Kuan Yew, in 1982 summed up the spirit of paternalism: 'Every time anybody starts anything which will unwind or unravel this orderly, organized, sensible, rational society, and make it irrational and emotional, I put a stop to it and without hesitation.'[24]

The government is active in all the same activities as other governments, as well as owning strategic sectors of all the main industries – trading, airlines, shipping, shipbuilding, radio and television, electronics and engineering, munitions and aircraft, steel and petrochemicals. Through its holdings it has guided the economy through successive transformations. However, one of its most powerful controls is that exercised over labour.

Labour and trade unions

Control of the labour market takes the form of an explicit annual wages policy, implemented in three ways. First, through the decisions of the tripartite National Wages Council and those of the Central Provident Fund which, together, determine the net income to be received by the mass of workers. Second, through the close supervision of the trade unions exercised by the National Trade Union Congress (NTUC), a body controlled by the appointed officials of the dominant political party, the People's Action Party (PAP), and through the periodic removal of issues from the purview of the trade unions – thus, general working conditions are either regulated by statute or reserved exclusively to management. Finally, immigration is tightly controlled, immigrants closely supervised, and the reproduction of the labour force influenced through incentives discouraging the low skilled and encouraging the professionally qualified. The contrast with Hong Kong could hardly be greater.

Establishing this structure of controls was a long-drawn-out process in which PAP defeated its left-wing rivals, the Barisan Socialis. The legislative framework was then gradually created, in the first instance to end strikes (man days lost in dispute, running at 388,000 in 1963, fell steadily to 2,500 in 1970, and thereafter, up to 1986, were negligible); a 1968 ordinance defined managerial prerogatives, and an Employment

Act laid down minimum conditions of employment (covering hours of work, maximum overtime, maximum holidays and pay increases).

The Central Provident Fund, set up in 1955, operated as an insurance operation into which employees and employers were legally obliged to pay set proportions of income to secure retirement pensions and other public welfare benefits (of which the purchase of public housing became one of the most important). By 1984, the compulsory contributions had been increased thirteen times; starting at a level of 10 per cent of labour costs (5 per cent each to be paid by employer and employee), they had become 50 per cent by the eighties (23 and 27 per cent respectively by employee and employer). This extraordinary level of forced savings means the CPF is no longer primarily an insurance fund, but rather an instrument of public finance – to raise savings, to invest, to counter inflationary pressures, to finance the government (the CPF at the end of 1982 held 78 per cent of government stock on issue). By 1982, total CPF funds had come to equal two thirds of all individual deposits in Singapore's banks. The steady rise in real wages and living standards masked the change.

Wage controls have been important in preventing wages reflecting real scarcities (something the neoclassical case depended upon). With a small labour force, strong encouragement to birth control and tightly controlled immigration, an expanding economy constantly tended to reach the limits of labour supply. To relieve this, the government periodically relaxed immigration controls, but then became alarmed at the possible loss of control as the labour force grew. In the late seventies, it was decided to try to transform the industrial structure so that it became decreasingly dependent upon the supply of labour; it became much more capital intensive. In 1979, the government issued a three-year programme to increase labour costs by 20 per cent per year (but not wages – most of the increase went to the CPF). Low-productivity industries were to be encouraged either to upgrade production or leave Singapore (with privileged re-entry rights for imports). In the poetic formulation of the Trade and Industry Minister, the aim was to 'compel employers to disgorge unnecessary labour and invest in labour-saving equipment and machinery to economize further in the use of manpower'.

The confidence was misplaced. The second slump in the early eighties cut the overseas demand for Singapore's exports and a slackening in the domestic demand for labour. The check was temporary, and in 1982 the government decided to phase out the use of immigrant workers, retaining them up to 1991 only in construction, shipbuilding and repair and domestic services. ('Immigrants' always meant manual workers, not European, American and Japanese professional or business expatriates.) This time, however, the government did not seek to increase labour costs, but to increase the length of shifts, from eight to twelve hours. Fewer workers were to be worked longer.

The year 1985 saw Singapore's growth fall disastrously – to −1.7 per cent – as the United States economy slowed, cutting Singapore's exports. Exports elsewhere did badly because Singapore's dollar, tied to the United States currency, appreciated in value through 1985. Ship-building and oil refining were especially badly hit, and the four-year property boom in the city collapsed; 90,000 workers were laid off. However, since two thirds of them were immigrants and were expelled from the city, the increase in unemployment did not exercise any down-ward pressure on wages.

In December 1985, the opposition parties won a third of the vote in the assembly elections, to the shock of the government. And in January of the following year, the first strike in eight years occurred.

The Prime Minister's son, as one of his father's ministers, was en-trusted with the task of drawing up the diagnosis (through the report of a wide-ranging economic committee). On the one hand, the growth of the city's economy was clearly much more dependent on outside forces than on its own genius. On the other, high wages (exacerbated by the rising Singapore dollar) had made Singapore's output uncompetitive. Labour costs were high because of a labour scarcity, made worse by controls on immigration in a boom and because of the high rate of forced savings through the CPF scheme. Furthermore, with such a high rate of savings (equal to 42 per cent of gross domestic product, the highest rate in the world), much of it going through public hands to major state projects, local companies were squeezed out and the econ-omy's growth depended more and more on foreign capital. In practice, two thirds of local savings had gone to fuel the property boom.

It was a radical indictment of the social-democratic recipe for Singa-pore's development; the recommendations made included wage re-ductions, ending the central settlement of wages (in favour of local productivity-related deals), a relaxation of the ban on immigration, a cut in the employer contribution to the CPF, and a general decline in government intervention (with privatization) and dependence upon large foreign companies. The long record of success did not protect Singapore from enforced liberalization.

Origins

The domestic order of Singapore was created through the tight control of the labour movement. In Hong Kong, labour was always over-shadowed by the People's Republic, where 'class struggle' was defined as purges initiated officially by the Party. Singapore's domestic politics were, however, intimately related to external issues – the federation with Malaya. The PAP right-wing leadership, indeed, saw the merger as a way of smothering the left, and as a means of securing a clear role for Singapore – as the industrial supplier to an import-substituting federation (Malaya supplying Singapore with raw materials, primarily rubber). The Malay leadership of Kuala Lumpur, alarmed at the Chinese majority of Singapore being added to the Chinese of Malaya, brought in the Malays of Sabah and Sarawak as counterbalance.

As Figure 4 illustrates, the economic strategy was not without success in the first half of the sixties. Growth took place despite the campaign of intimidation launched by Indonesia's President Sukarno (which did, however, affect Singapore's re-export of goods from Indonesia). But the relationship with Kuala Lumpur proved the main problem – the Malays did not concede Singapore a monopoly of manufacture, and PAP could not resist championing the Chinese of Malaysia. In 1965 the merger came apart.

At once the import–substitution–industrialization strategy lost much sense. There was now no rich hinterland to which Singapore could play manufacturing centre. Yet a city-state is inevitably dependent upon imports, particularly of foodstuffs, so there was no alternative but to seek to expand exports and encourage the inflow of foreign capital. The problem was exacerbated by the withdrawal of British military forces, which obliged the Singapore government to assume responsibility for its own military defence – the import of armaments was now a priority.

Strategies

The government initially identified selected sectors of labour-intensive manufacture (textiles and garments, footwear, electrical and electronic

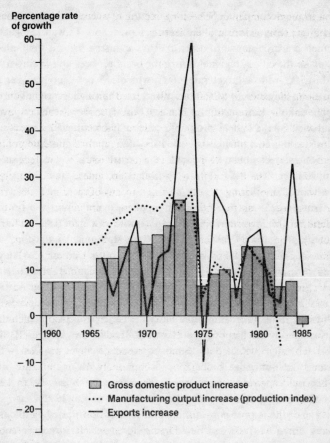

Figure 4. *Singapore: increases in gross domestic product, manufacturing output and exports, 1960–85*
Sources: 1960–77: *Yearbook of Statistics 1977/78*, Singapore; 1977–85: *Far Eastern Economic Review*, various issues

goods) as the instruments for export promotion. Figure 4 illustrates how successful this approach was. Indeed, it was more successful for Singapore than any of the other three in the Gang of Four. The city absorbed the impact of the final British military evacuation in 1968 (at its peak the British forces had employed some 50,000 people), and had gained from the boom produced as a result of United States military intervention in Vietnam. It also gained much from the expansion in oil exploration in the South China Sea, becoming the key centre for this activity.

In the early seventies, like South Korea and Taiwan, Singapore launched a programme to develop heavy industry. With it went efforts to make the city a 'regional centre for brain services and brain-service industries', with a target rate of growth of 15 per cent per year. In industry, Singapore was to concentrate on the development of oil refining and the manufacture of plastics, synthetic fibres, turbines, industrial machinery, optical products, office equipment, aerospace parts, construction equipment and scientific and medical instruments. In services, the city was to become the centre of a world-class communications network (sea, air, telecommunications, etc.), of finance, medicine and tourism.

Between 1965 and 1980, the economy grew in real terms by 9 per cent annually. The government boasted it would reach the 1980 Japanese income per head by 1990. Even the two slumps did not deflect the trajectory disastrously – real manufacturing output declined by 16 per cent in 1975 and 6 per cent in 1982. Otherwise, the growth was substantially greater than that of the other three of the Gang of Four. At 1967 prices, Hong Kong's gross domestic product grew 153 per cent between 1965 and 1977, when Singapore's increased 235 per cent (for manufacturing output the figures were 215 and 385, and for exports, 193 and 234). The structure of output and of exports changed no less swiftly towards skill-intensive goods.

Services expanded even faster. Financial and business services were, in value of output, only just below manufacturing in 1982. Singapore has the eighth largest port in the world (excluding the Eastern Bloc) in terms of non-oil trade, and the fourth including oil. Its airport is among the world's most modern, and had the most rapidly expanding passenger throughput in the seventies. Singapore is the regional headquarters for the oil industry, including over a hundred US oil companies (in 1977, the oil sector took nearly 40 per cent of foreign investment). Government plans aimed to strengthen this position in services by capturing two thirds of the Asia dollar market and developing a gold futures market. By the early eighties, two thirds of the gross domestic product was generated in services – banking, shipping and ship repair, transport, telecommunications, consultancy services, medical and health care, tourism and trade.

The manufacturing economy, like Hong Kong's, was quite narrowly based. Five industries in the mid seventies employed 66 per cent of the manufacturing labour force to produce 73 per cent of the manufacturing output: oil refining (30 per cent of output and 1.5 per cent of the labour force); electrical machinery and electronic products (15 and 23 per cent); food and beverages (11 and 7 per cent); transport equipment (shipbuilding, oil exploration equipment, aircraft components – 10 and 14 per cent); and textiles, garments and footwear (7 and nearly 20 per cent). The government aimed to reduce the last group in particular, and expand in the fields of computers and peripherals, video equipment, office, communications and process control and military equipment.

Foreign investment was of decisive importance in Singapore's growth, and is the feature of the country most in contrast to what has been called a social democratic model. The boom in oil exploration, from the Vietnam war, and in banking, brought in a multitude of foreign companies. By 1980, it has been estimated that 13 per cent of manufacturing establishments were foreign owned, contributing 87 per cent of the combined value added.

Singapore's growth is quite different, as is Hong Kong's, from the other two. There is no common or standard model. In many ways, Singapore has been more tightly controlled by the state than any of the others, and has had a higher rate of export growth. Of course, it would be invalid to say one was the cause of the other, since so many other factors go into making up a high rate of growth, including the accident of geography and the historical moment. But that is to qualify the neoclassical case in a profound respect.

The Gang of Four

From the late fifties, Hong Kong, from about 1961, Taiwan, from 1962–3, South Korea and, from 1965, Singapore – all expanded their gross products relatively swiftly, and by means of the growth of manufactured exports. They began with garments and textiles, and progressed through a variety of miscellaneous products to electronic components; in the seventies the degree of sophistication in the commodities exported increased steadily. With or without stagnation in the global economy, the process now seems sufficiently well rooted to continue.

The initial impulses were different. Hong Kong was passive, a small vessel caught by an external wind. South Korea and Taiwan, having lost their role in a Japanese imperial trading network, were temporarily sustained by United States aid. The ending of that aid drove them to try to find alternative means of gaining foreign exchange, without which they could not import the means necessary for survival. For Singapore, the ending of the British connection and the Malaysian federation precipitated a similar search. Three of the cases had also an important military drive, especially true for insecure South Korea and Taiwan. In an important sense, for three of the four there was little option other than to pursue exports; given the relative self-sufficiency of local markets and the protectionism of the industrialized countries in agricultural goods, there was also little option in terms of what sort of goods should be exported. However, while it is possible to identify the necessity for this type of aspiration, this is far from explaining the successes in pursuing the aim. (We shall return to this in the next chapter in connection with the Latin American case.)

If the impulses were the same, the performances were not. South Korea seems to have experienced the greatest fluctuations and Singapore the most sustained and exceptionally high growth. The heavy-industrial crisis at the end of the seventies was most severe for South Korea. All experienced the highest and most sustained growth between 1965 and 1973. Thereafter, much greater fluctuations set in (although the average rates are still high), and the fluctuations of all four tend to become much more synchronized.

The policies pursued were frequently different, as were the attitudes, endowments, histories and sizes. If a neutral state is required to explain Hong Kong's growth (as the neoclassicists would have it), it does not explain the performances of the other three, where there was consistent state intervention. South Korea, Taiwan and Singapore are triumphs of state capitalism, but Hong Kong and Singapore are also triumphs of free trade. Hong Kong and Taiwan are characterized by a mass of small companies, the nineteenth-century picture of unbridled competitive capitalism; Korea and Singapore by giant companies (foreign owned in Singapore's case). Taiwan and South Korea supported what appear as almost intolerable military burdens that were lacking in the case of Hong Kong. Singapore was also, although to a lesser extent, impelled by a context of military insecurity. Despite all the differences, external demand shaped a similarity of response.

By most historical criteria, the four did develop economically, and they did so, contrary to the postulates of development economics, through the promotion of exports; and, contrary to the pessimistic outlook of development economics, through the export of manufactured goods. The process did not lead to greater instability than would otherwise have been the case, nor did it – in the case of South Korea, Taiwan and Singapore – frustrate attempts to create some measure of heavy industry. Efforts were curbed, as we have seen, but not entirely nullified – by the eighties, South Korea was an important exporter of some elements of heavy-industrial output.

On the other hand, for three of the four cases there was no simple reflection of 'market forces' either. Not only did the state direct the process, participating closely, it also – in the case of South Korea and Taiwan – imposed what might be seen as a predatory agrarian policy not unlike those in the Eastern Bloc. The experience does not vindicate export-promotion policies any more than it repudiates import-substitution industrialization. In practice, an opportunistic combination of both approaches was employed.

In Latin America, a number of countries also experienced sustained growth over a long period, but of a different type. It is appropriate to examine two cases of this type – Mexico and Brazil – before advancing some judgements of the issues at stake.

3 = The Latin Americans: Brazil and Mexico

Brazil and Mexico are very much larger economies than the four Asian countries we considered in the previous chapter. In 1982 (a bad year for both of them), Brazil's gross domestic product was 55 per cent and Mexico's 7 per cent larger than the four Asian countries combined. Indeed, Brazil would be the eighth largest non-Communist economy in the world if rated with the industrialized countries, its GDP being 86 per cent of the seventh largest, Canada. Among developing countries, only China was larger (in product terms, by 5 per cent). Mexico, if rated among the industrialized countries, would be the tenth largest, its GDP just larger than Australia's and 94 per cent of that of the ninth largest, Spain.

They were also much richer than the Asian countries in the fifties. Even in 1982, South Korea's product per head was still only 82 per cent of Brazil's and 84 per cent of Mexico's. The manufacturing sector of the two Latin American states was also much larger; the four Asian countries together were equal in 1980 to 76 per cent of Brazil and 83 per cent of Mexico. Both the Latin Americans were rich in natural resources, unlike the four Asians.

They were also very different in terms of government development strategy. The efforts of the four Asians were directed at playing a specialized role in a world economy; the Latin Americans sought the expansion of the domestic market and of a non-specialized economy to supply it. Given their much greater size, the emphasis made more sense than it could ever have done for the four Asians.

Brazil was the more consistent in pursuing this 'import-substitution-industrialization strategy', apart from a brief phase in the seventies and after 1982. But even in the years when Brazil opted for export promotion, it was a policy grafted on top of the old orientation of protection. Mexico, with its long border with the United States, found it difficult to pursue the substitution of imports with the same dedication, although the government tried to do so, particularly in the main industrial region, the Central Valley. But whatever the differences between the two, they were much less marked than the differences between them and the Asian countries – the four tried to use the world market to force growth; the two tried to exclude the world from their markets.

However, in the seventies, both the Latin Americans found their foreign-exchange earnings too low to purchase the imports they needed and, to a limited extent, embraced export promotion. But even at its peak, exports were small. Exports as a proportion of gross domestic product for Brazil and Mexico in 1980 were 9.6 and 8.2 respectively – compared to 34, 47, 72 and 162 per cent for South Korea, Taiwan, Hong Kong and Singapore. The Latin Americans exported about 14 per cent of their manufactured supply, when the four Asians were all above 100 per cent (respectively 109, 110, 336 and 386, showing, in the last two cases, the important role of re-exports). Indeed, Brazil's manufactured exports equalled only 41 per cent of South Korea's, and Mexico's 40 per cent. The same contrast exists with the industrialized countries – countries with a value of exports roughly the same as Brazil's (for example, Norway), have a much smaller gross domestic product (22 per cent in Norway's case). On the other hand, economies with a gross domestic product as large as Brazil's, export vastly more; Italy with a 1982 product just under 40 per cent larger than Brazil's, exported four times as much.

However, whatever the differences, the long-term growth of the two Latin Americans has been spectacular. Brazil increased its gross national product on average by 6.3 per cent annually from 1932 to 1979 – roughly 7 per cent between 1948 and 1961, and from 1974 to the eighties, with an 11 per cent rate from 1968 to 1974. Value added in manufacturing increased five times over in twenty years (1960 to 1980), and exports (in current prices) rose from just over one billion dollars' worth to 23 billion. Between 1964 and 1980, 3 million tonnes of steel output grew to 12.9 million; 5.5 million tonnes of cement to 27 million; the capacity to produce 200,000 vehicles grew to 1.2 million. The average life of millions of urban dwellers in the cities of the south and the centre was no less transformed than that of the average Korean (and the absolute numbers in Brazil were much larger than in Korea).

Mexico experienced two decades of annual growth of 6–7 per cent –

6 per cent in the fifties, nearly 8 in the sixties, 6–7 in the first half of the seventies, and 8 per cent from 1977 to 1981. When much of the world stagnated in the seventies, Mexico doubled the volume of its industrial output. The capacity to generate electricity grew from 6 to 16 million kw; the length of paved highway from 68,000 to 208,000 km; the number of registered vehicles, from 1.8 to 4.5 million. These were remarkable and substantial achievements in the long struggle to achieve material abundance.

The Structure of the Economy

In the thirty years after 1950, Brazil and Mexico made the transition to an industrial economy. In 1955, the contribution of agriculture to national product was 21 and 18 per cent respectively; in 1981, 13 and 8 per cent. Industry, which contributed 31 and 30 per cent at the beginning, thirty years later provided 33 and 37 per cent. However, it should be noted that in the late seventies, the share of agriculture increased in

Table 1. *Brazil: Distribution of the Value of Manufacturing Output by Industry (percentage shares), 1962, 1973 and 1980*[1]

	1962	1973	1980
Traditional industries*	49.2	41.9	34.5
Non-traditional industries (total)	50.8	58.1	65.5
Metallurgy	10.7	12.2	16.7
Machinery	2.9	7.2	6.4
Chemical products	9.8	12.1	17.1
Non-metallic minerals	4.3	3.4	4.0
Electrical and communications equipment	4.8	4.9	5.4
Transport equipment	9.6	8.9	7.6
Paper and paper products	2.7	2.8	2.8
Rubber and rubber products	1.9	1.5	1.5
Pharmaceuticals	2.0	2.0	1.2
Perfumery	1.0	1.2	0.9
Plastic products	1.2	1.9	1.9

Note: discrepancies in totals are due to rounding.

* Food processing, beverages, tobacco, textiles, garments, footwear, furniture, printing and publishing.

Brazil, as did the share of primary industry in Mexico: both took a small step back to the old structure.

Within manufacturing, heavy industry expanded disproportionately; see Table 1.

In Mexico, manufacturing output expanded on average by over 7 per cent per year in the seventies, with higher rates of growth in the heavy and chemical sectors – 9.4 per cent in chemical products; 9 per cent in metal products, machinery and equipment, and in basic metals. These four have increased their share of the value of manufacturing since 1950 from 25 to 49 per cent, while 'traditional industries' decreased from 73 to 49 per cent; see Table 2.

Table 2. *Mexico: Distribution of the Value of Manufacturing Output by Industry (percentage shares), 1950, 1960, 1970 and 1978*[2]

	1950	1960	1970	1978
Food, drink, tobacco	36.4	36.8	29.0	25.8
Textiles, garments, leather	26.1	18.8	16.8	16.3
Wood, paper, publishing	10.8	8.1	7.6	7.2
Chemical products, etc.	7.8	11.2	13.5	13.7
Non-metallic minerals	3.5	4.1	4.4	5.4
Basic metals	4.1	6.2	6.8	8.2
Metal products	9.3	12.6	19.6	21.3
Other	2.0	2.2	2.3	2.1

The heart of the modern engineering industry – metal products and machinery and equipment (division VII in the Mexican Industrial Census) – increased physical output by 86 per cent between 1970 and 1978. The high growth subsectors in this division were: domestic electrical apparatus (+178 per cent), electronic equipment (+126 per cent), cars (+124 per cent), car components (+87 per cent) and electrical equipment (+83 per cent).[3]

The changes in the structure of employment were less dramatic, and much less than in the Asian four. In 1960, 55 per cent of Mexican workers were recorded as employed in agriculture, 20 per cent in industry; in 1980, the figures were 36 and 26 per cent. For Brazil, the same comparison was, in 1960, 52 and 15 per cent, and in 1980, 30 and 24 per cent. Between 1960 and 1976, Brazil officially increased non-agricultural jobs from just under 12 million to 19 million. In Mexico, the government claimed that 7 million new jobs were created in the seventies, 3.2 million of them in the burst of growth at the end of the decade. However, despite the declining proportion employed in agriculture (forestry and fishing included), the absolute number continued to increase (by 16 per cent in the seventies). On the other hand, the size of the manufacturing (as opposed to industrial) labour force increased by 44 per cent, but its share declined slightly, from 13.4 to 12.4 per cent.[4]

For such large economies, despite reservations, these were impressive changes. They affected in absolute terms far more people than the changes in the four Asian countries. How did they relate to the intentions and activities of government?

Strategies and History

Brazil has persistently shown a tendency to high growth, based upon successive waves of displacing imports. Thus, employment in the textile industry increased from 2,000 in 1895 to 26,400 in 1905 and 53,000 in 1907 as local products reached the point of replacing foreign goods. In terms of the total supply of manufactured goods, imports supplied 36 per cent of demand by the twenties (and under 10 per cent in clothing, footwear, furniture and wood products). Import substitution without public intervention was already well established.

The 1929 world financial crisis began the slump. The price of Brazil's main export, coffee, fell by 60 per cent in the following two years, and this halved Brazil's capacity to import. The government responded with tight controls over imports and over the external exchanges, and from 1932, industrial growth suddenly became swift – over 10 per cent annually up to 1939 (compared to 1.5 per cent per year in the twenties).[5] Shortages of imported raw materials slowed growth during the Second World War (to 5·5 per cent per year), but after 1945 the pace was resumed. There had also been a relaxation of import controls, and imports increased rapidly, producing a sizeable deficit on external trade in 1947. When tighter controls were reintroduced, it was with the more conscious intention of providing an impetus to domestic growth of manufacturing. It seemed to work – industrial output grew by 8 per cent per annum to 1962. Nor was industrial growth inhibited by a lack of imports, since Brazil's coffee exports fetched relatively high prices in these years (and Brazil supplied three quarters of the world's traded coffee in the fifties, but only 40 per cent by 1970). But growth was heavily concentrated on the domestic market – exports grew to the early sixties by no more than 1.3 per cent annually.

The package of policies pushed down imports as national output rose. By 1964, imported consumer goods provided 1.6 per cent of domestic supply compared to 64.5 per cent in 1949 (when the value of domestic supply increased nearly sixty times over); imported intermediate goods had moved from 25.9 to 6.6 per cent of domestic supply (which increased five times over); capital goods from 63.7 to 9.8 per cent (and domestic supply increased eight times over). The success in substituting for imports showed the limits of any further impulse from this source – and it was to the supposed exhaustion of import substitutionism that the slowdown in Brazil's growth in 1962, 1963 and 1964 (to 1.5 and 2.4 per cent in the last two years) was attributed, while inflation exceeded 100 per cent.

This was part of the economic background to the seizure of power by the Brazilian armed forces in 1964. The new regime instituted a wide-ranging purge of all opposition throughout Brazilian society and a most repressive domination. They also attempted to create a new economic order by emulating the effects of slump – cuts in public expenditure, increased taxes and increased prices of public-sector goods, reduced real wages and subsidies – both an increase in 'flexibilities' and a net shift of resources from mass consumption to government and profits. Through tax concessions and subsidies, much-enhanced encouragement to export was offered, as well as an easing of import restrictions.

The effects appeared startling; the Brazilian economy expanded as never before – in real terms and on average by nearly 10 per cent per year. Exports increased by nearly a quarter on average annually up to 1973. The domestic market boomed – helped by new provisions of consumer credit for the purchase of houses and consumer durables. Imports also soared – as a share of the domestic supply of industrial goods, from 6.9 per cent in 1965 to 17 per cent in 1974.[6]

In 1974, the world economy went into reverse. It was the most severe slump since the Second World War. Brazil's export markets were directly affected, and the price of imported oil increased rapidly; the terms of trade deteriorated by 18 per cent. However, the government did not transmit this external downturn into the domestic economy. On the contrary, it endeavoured to keep up public spending to sustain high growth, while reintroducing import restrictions. If we continue the projection of the rate of increase in imports after 1974, by 1979 the country's imports were 22 per cent below the trend line. Export incentives were also strengthened so that renewed import substitution was accompanied by export promotion; however, it seems that the import defences were considerably stronger than the incentives to export.[7] The government also sought to ease the external constraints on growth by greater borrowing – Brazil's cumulative debt increased from $12.6 bn in 1973 to $41 bn in 1978.

Like three of the four Asian governments examined in the last chapter, the Brazilian planners also introduced a programme for the development of heavy industry. The second National Development Plan aimed to secure Brazilian self-sufficiency in pulp and paper, petrochemicals, fertilizers, steel, and non-ferrous metals by 1979. Part of this programme included intensified efforts to substitute for imported capital goods.

The hopes that the slump would prove temporary began to fade in the late seventies, as governments everywhere were obliged to begin to grapple with the possibility of long-term stagnation in world trade. In the case of Brazil, by 1979 continued domestic growth was attracting excessive imports, and two thirds of export revenue was being absorbed in servicing the external debt. A new effort to right the external balance was required. For the first time in thirty years, the government directed efforts to expanding agricultural exports (thereby, after a long period of relative neglect, seeking to exploit one of Brazil's less equivocal 'comparative advantages'). A brief attempt to liberalize imports foundered on the fragile external balance, despite a major devaluation of the currency.

The increase in incentives for exports cheapened them in relation to domestic prices. The gap between the two was some 40 per cent for transport equipment; 33 per cent for rubber products; 32 per cent for non-metallic mineral products; 31 per cent for paper, and 24 per cent for wood products. The effort to shift resources from domestic consumption to the consumption of the rest of the world had attained substantial proportions, but it was constantly threatened by the fact that the difference in prices tended to be wiped out by the effect of domestic inflation (the periodic mini-devaluations of the cruzeiro were not large nor frequent enough to keep exports cheap). This, along with a sudden escalation in the size of the external debt, contributed to the crisis of 1982–3, which we will examine later.

Mexican strategies were afflicted in a similar manner to those of Brazil. While import-substitution policies could only have limited effects in the areas closest to the United States frontier, in the Central Valley they were of greater power. However, domestic inflation constantly tended to produce a cheapening of imports (and more expensive exports) forcing tighter controls on imports and stagnation in exports. In the unstable external circumstances of the seventies and eighties, this combination was exaggerated by the effects of cumulative debt and produced two crises, that of 1975–6 and the much larger one six years later. The external problems were exacerbated by the attempt to force domestic growth through an expansion in public spending to offset world slump in 1974 (public spending as a proportion of gross domestic product increased from 8 to 10 per cent between 1971 and 1975). The peso was devalued and public expenditure cut. The brief recovery of stability was, however, ended when the vast oil reserves of Mexico became apparent; this seemed to offer a guaranteed external income which would obviate the need to curb growth in the interests of controlling imports.

Oil exports seemed to make possible not only an import level which was close to Mexico's capacity to absorb imports, but also, in the short term, expanded overseas borrowing. The borrowing fuelled the expansion of the domestic market and a public heavy-industry programme in oil, power, steel and capital goods. For four years up to 1981, the economy expanded very swiftly. But the increase in imports and the weight of debt grew even faster, to produce crisis.

A number of key issues need closer examination here. How far did Brazil and Mexico share in the process of internationalization of trade seen in the case of the four Asian powers? How far did foreign borrowing jeopardize their performance? And what was the role of foreign investment?

The trade balance

As we noted earlier, Brazil and Mexico, despite the relative neglect of primary production, depended upon the export of primary products to earn foreign exchange (in 1980, over 60 per cent of their exports were 'non-manufactured'). Unlike the four Asians, the export of manufactured goods could not be a primary force in generating domestic growth. None the less, non-traditional exports tended to grow – from 15 to 29 per cent of the whole in the case of Mexico (1960 to 1977), and from 3 to 26 per cent for Brazil. In both cases, however, in the late seventies and early eighties, this process was reversed – Mexico became more dependent upon the export of one primary product, oil, and Brazil on agricultural exports.

Brazil's non-traditional exports were diversified, particularly in engineering goods – from simple machine tools to heavy armaments, capital ships and light aircraft. It also made special efforts to export manufactured goods to other developing countries, particularly to the large prosperous oil producers (Nigeria, Iran, Indonesia and Iraq). In the seventies, at least some of Brazil's manufactured exports were approximating to those of the four Asian powers – that is, part of an international pattern of specialization rather than simply the surplus after domestic consumption has been satisfied.

The same tendency was apparent in the Mexican case. But in the second half of the seventies expanded oil production severely inhibited the development of manufactured exports by driving up the value of the peso (a change not unwelcome to the Mexican government since it cheapened imports and borrowing abroad). Oil revenue expanded the domestic market, so that potential exports were drawn into local consumption. The trend to expand manufactured exports peaked in 1975 (at 22 per cent of total external revenue) and then declined to 11 per cent by 1980 (oil sales increased from 6 to 59 per cent in 1982). The strongest growth was experienced in chemical products and machinery. Electrical, electronic and transport equipment increased as a share of manufactured exports from nothing in 1960 to 16 per cent in 1970 and 38 per cent in 1977.

Both Brazil and Mexico could conceptually be divided into three economies – a traditional raw-material-exporting economy supplying the bulk of exports; a heavily protected industrial economy supplying the domestic market; and a new international economy, a fragment of a specialized global system of manufacturing. The relationships between the three were unstable, and the third grew almost by default, with main government attention being given to the second. In Mexico's case, the international economy could be divided in two: the border region and 'other international production'.

The border region

The border region was delimited in 1966 as a twenty-kilometre strip the length of the frontier with the United States, where free trade prevailed. Companies were granted the right to create 'in-bond' plants (they came to be known as *maquiladores*) that is, the right to import capital equipment and raw materials provided the output of the plant was entirely exported. In essence, in-bond plants were a variation on the concept elsewhere embodied in 'export-processing zones'. By this means, the Mexican government sought to exploit the advantage of cheap local labour, and to establish a zone that protected an import-substituting regime further south.

From seventy-three plants (employing 16,000 workers) in 1967, the number grew to around 500 (with 76,000 workers) in the mid seventies, when the value of the exports of the *maquiladores* was close to that of Mexico's manufactured exports from the rest of the economy. In 1972, the privileges of in-bond-plant status were accorded to factories anywhere in the country. By 1984, the numbers employed had grown to 230,000.

The wage factor proved, depending upon the peso–dollar exchange rate, a powerful lure to foreign companies supplying the United States market. In the late seventies, plants of the same company on different sides of the border paid roughly $1.23 per hour in Mexico, $3.10 in the United States. However, the increasing value of the peso, spurred by domestic inflation and a failure to devalue fast enough, eroded this differential, and heightened the desirability of other locations further south, in Central America and the Caribbean. Many of the Caribbean islands in the late seventies had wage rates of $1 per hour or less (and in Haiti, 0.25 cents). Furthermore, the Mexican government added other payments to the wage – contributions to welfare funds, special taxes, etc. – increasing labour costs by between 27 and 40 per cent. Much of the Caribbean added only between 8 and 10 per cent of the wage to labour costs. Mexico's strength lay in its combination of relatively low wages, with the skills and literacy of the labour force, geographical proximity to the United States and good communications. Where only labour costs were important, alternative locations could prove attractive, forcing a division of labour in geographical location between more and less skill-intensive operations.

International production

The success of the in-bond plants, despite fluctuations in the exchange rate, showed the potential for Mexico to become incorporated in international systems of production, to parallel the experience of the four Asian countries. It was also seen outside the in-bond sector, in general production for export. In the seventies, an increasing number of international companies favoured Mexico as a location for production for the United States and other overseas markets (even where they produced for the Mexican market as well, unlike the in-bond plants). The attractions were similar – in vehicle production, labour costs in the mid eighties were said to be a fifth of those payable in the United States. Unlike the Asian four, Mexico could be competitive in the production of goods expensive to move because of weight and size (for example, vehicles), and could therefore play a role similar to that of Spain in Europe. In the early eighties, there was talk of General Motors and Ford raising Mexican vehicle output from the 350,000 then current (by all companies) to 1.8 million per year. In 1982 Ford completed a half-billion-dollar plant in Chihuahua to manufacture 400,000 engines, 90 per cent for export, and another car plant for small cars in Hermosilla. General Motors and Phillips constructed electronic-component plants; the General Motors operation was designed to manufacture all the company's electronic parts for the vehicles assembled in the States. Car-component manufacturers followed the car assemblers – Spicers, Perkins, Eatons, Kelseys, Hayes.

Much of this occurred almost by default. State governments and city authorities were keen to encourage it, but often the Mexican government regarded foreign capital as an infringement or an affront to Mexican nationalism. It was a marginal addition to the main priority, the development of an independent national economy. Being marginal, the international segment of the economy was not protected from the byproducts of an import-substituting economy – the vagaries of the exchange rate, for example – nor was there any encouragement for Mexican capital to be involved in these ventures. There were thus no Mexican Hyundais. In the boom at the end of the seventies, domestic inflation, bottlenecks in the supply of raw materials and intermediate goods, as well as the exchange rate, must have jeopardized the viability of export production considerably. Without that domestic boom, Mexico might have moved much further along the road of the Asian four. As it was, the external constraints pushed Mexico in exactly the opposite direction – away from manufactured exports to the export of a single raw material, oil. The oil boom temporarily postponed the internationalization of Mexican manufacturing.

The boom had other effects that worried planners in both Mexico and Brazil. Each surge of output seemed to require an increasing volume of imports. In the early seventies, Mexican imports grew in real terms by 25 per cent annually; they shrank by 9 per cent between 1975 and 1977, and then grew up to 1981 by a heroic 35 per cent per year (as a ratio of gross domestic product, imports grew from under 7 per cent in the early seventies to 15 per cent in 1980). For an import-substituting economy, this was a poor performance. Some saw it as intrinsic to the imperfect structure of the economy, its 'dependency', but a simpler explanation related it to the value of the peso; dollar-denominated imports were generally cheaper than domestically produced goods. Thus, the advantage of protection was nullified by the exchange rate.

Debt

In the seventies, as we have noted, governments of both Brazil and Mexico tried to sustain continued growth by keeping up public spending and investment at home, and by increased borrowing abroad (which allowed imports to remain high even though exports might stagnate). It was fairly cheap to increase external debts when the Brazilian cruzeiro and the Mexican peso were relatively overvalued. Like many others, both governments calculated that stagnation in the world economy would not continue indefinitely; when the demand for the exports of the two countries revived, export revenue would increase faster than the burden of repaying the debts. It was a not unreasonable gamble at the time. But in the peculiar conditions of the early eighties, the gamble became disaster – the value of the dollar rose sharply, increasing the weight of dollar-denominated debts; interest rates remained very high, so annual payments for loans with variable interest rates rose much higher than expected; slump affected export revenues; and, for Mexico, oil prices sagged.

This conjuncture of forces coincided for both countries with the first bunching of repayments, which could therefore be covered only by further borrowing. The debt increased alarmingly – for Brazil, from $32 bn in 1977 to \$50 bn in 1979, and then, each year to \$57, \$64, \$78 and, in 1984, \$96 bn.

The race between increasing exports and increasing debt could not be won in such circumstances. The markets became increasingly nervous; Poland virtually defaulted, and a scatter of other sovereign borrowers came very close to default. Brazil's relationships with Iran, Iraq and Nigeria were threatened by war and by declining oil revenues with which to buy Brazilian goods. Slump contracted the demand for Brazilian exports (and primary commodity prices fell swiftly) as the industrialized countries flirted with increasingly dirty restrictions on imports. The ultimate folly of the British counter-invasion of an obscure group of islands in the south Atlantic threatened to carry off into default not only Argentina, but all large borrowers in the same area.

For Brazil, coping with debt was a war of attrition. But it was left to Mexico to make the high drama of 1982. The same sequence of events drove the external debt from nearly \$50 bn dollars in 1980 (double that of 1976) to \$84 bn in 1982. Servicing and repayment charges were then taking \$25 bn per year (a figure not far off Poland's cumulative debt).

Debt was the cutting edge of the crisis. It made the gambles of both regimes unsustainable, and imposed upon them priorities created in outside markets. The protected economy collided with the powerful centralizing forces of world finance. The outcome was a partial integration in the world system.

Foreign investment

In Brazil and Mexico, unlike three of the four countries of Asia (not Singapore), foreign capital played an important role, and the more backward the economy, the more important that role was. Corresponding to the three types of economy identified earlier – raw-material-exporting, import-substituting and manufactured-goods-exporting – were three types of foreign capital. In raw materials, foreign capital declined, being replaced by local or public companies. Foreign capital operating in order to escape the high barriers to imports (and gain the monopoly profits of a protected domestic market) was important from the thirties to the sixties. The third type of foreign operation became more important as manufactured exports were encouraged in the seventies.

By the end of 1956, the investment of US-registered companies in Brazil was the fourth largest American holding abroad. The absolute level continued to increase, but in the sixties it began to decline relatively. That trend continued in the seventies, so that the foreign share of the equity of companies operating in Brazil declined from 34.4 to 22.5 per cent (1971 to 1979); by 1979, the holding of the state was the same size as that of foreign capital.[8] The decline was marked in the more expansive sectors of modern manufacturing where foreign capital had been consistently powerful. Thus, in machinery, 72 per cent of the equity was said to be foreign-owned in the early sixties, 68.4 per cent in 1971, and 36.5 per cent in 1979. In electrical and communication equipment, the comparable figures were 61.6, 64.9 and 37.5 per cent; in plastic products, the 48.7 per cent of 1971 fell to 25.9 in 1979. There were also declines in other sectors favoured by foreign companies – tobacco, pharmaceuticals and transport equipment.

In Mexico, foreign capital remained important, although again overshadowed by the holdings of the Mexican government. The official figure for direct foreign investment in 1980 was $27 bn; of this, two thirds was in manufacturing and over two thirds belonged to US-registered companies (representing some 2–3 per cent of the investment overseas of American companies). Foreign companies were said to control over half the output of private mining (but private mining was overshadowed by the nationalized sector), 84 per cent of the rubber industry, 80 per cent of tobacco, 67 per cent of chemicals, 62 per cent of machinery and 79 per cent of electrical equipment. Traditional industry, consumer goods and heavy industry remained overwhelmingly Mexican. However, again there was some suggestion that shares were falling, particularly later in the period when there was some withdrawal of the activities of United States companies abroad.

In contrast to three of the four Asian powers, direct foreign investment played an important role in the early phases of development in Mexico and Brazil. It was state capital that early on counterbalanced this foreign investment. But as growth accelerated, private domestic capital grew with increasing speed, a process the reverse of that in the Asian countries (where private domestic capital began the process).

The State

As in the case of the Asian countries examined (this time excepting Hong Kong), in Brazil and Mexico the process of growth and structural change was initiated, directed and supervised by the state. Both were far from the classic model of market-directed capitalism,[9] and might well be construed as triumphs of state capitalism. Nor was it a matter of left-wing politics – the seizure of power in Brazil by a right-wing military force led to an increased emphasis on the directing and participating role of the state.

As in South Korea and Taiwan, the control of credit gave great power to the Brazilian government. At its peak, two thirds of all loans were made by state-controlled banks (and 40 per cent by the giant Banco do Brasil, the assets of which were equal to the combined assets of the top twenty private banks). The expansion of public spending and activities was also the key factor in sustaining high domestic demand, just as the pattern of subsidies to commercial activities maintained the export performance – public spending, equal to 17 per cent of gross national product in 1947, was nearly a third of GNP in the early seventies. Government purchases were a decisive force in the expansion of key sectors, particularly in capital goods. The public sector at one stage handled about half the gross domestic product, undertook half the gross capital formation in the capital goods industry and accounted for nearly a quarter of the equity in manufacturing. In heavy industry – mining, iron and steel, petrochemicals, energy, oil refining and distribution – public corporations were either monopolies or dominated the industries. Of the twenty largest Brazilian companies, nineteen were in the public sector (and forty-five of the hundred largest), led by the largest of all, the oil company, Petrobras (with, in 1983, 28 per cent of the aggregate capital investment in the top twenty), and followed by three government operations: Electrobras, Telebras, Companhia Vale do Rio Doce.

In Mexico, the public sector contributed a quarter of the value added in the gross domestic product, employed a fifth of the workforce and paid two fifths of the national wage bill. It dominated the basic industries: in steel (with four companies), power, mining (with fourteen companies), fertilizers, fisheries, transport (all the railways, two airlines, Mexico City's underground railway, and many municipal bus operations), oil, petrochemicals and many others. As we have noted, oil production (in the hands of the state) provided the fuel for growth in the second half of the seventies. Public investment increased by 20 per cent per year between 1977 and 1981 (and fell by 20 per cent in 1982 and 40 per cent in 1983). Low-priced inputs to the private sector came from public companies in oil, gas, electricity, steel, cement, fertilizers and paper. The government operated a range of agricultural-processing industries (in sugar refining, food packaging, milk skimming, baking, sisal manufacture, maize-oil processing, etc.). Finally, in 1982, in order to guarantee private-sector foreign debts, the government nationalized fifty-three domestic banks (which brought equity holdings in over three hundred other companies).

Public-sector spending provided a key factor in propelling growth. As a proportion of gross domestic product, it increased from 12·5 per cent in the sixties to nearly 20 per cent in 1972 and 28 per cent by the mid seventies. The deficit of the public sector (also as a proportion of gross domestic product) rose from 1.8 per cent in 1970 to 8.7 per cent in 1975 and 11.3 per cent in 1981 (with a fall in 1976 and 1977).

Thus, in both countries, the state and the multiplicity of activities in the public sector were decisive forces, both directly, through direct participation in production, finance and transport, and indirectly, through the control of credit, taxation and incentives. With this great role went a strategic shaping of the economy, the initiation of the main phases of development and detailed intervention – as when the Mexican government instructed private companies to cut the range of car models manufactured (unless the company exported at least half of its output), banned foreign participation in the production of heavy diesel trucks after 1986, and ended the proprietary branding of pharmaceuticals. At every stage, this pattern of development relied on very large private companies, and ensured that private business activity included a large share of political lobbying.[10] In Brazil and Mexico, the state appeared to be the force that activated the growth of capitalism.

Agriculture

Neoclassical economists criticized import-substitution strategies for producing a neglect of agriculture. It was not the result of restricting imports in general, but rather of a package of policies designed to force industrial growth. Restricting industrial imports produced a kind of local monopoly, 'overpricing' industrial goods. Preferential interest rates for industrial investment discriminated against agricultural investment. An industrial boom increased the demand for industrial labour and led, it was said, to 'excessive' wage levels in industry compared to agriculture (a differential exaggerated where minimum-wage legislation covered only factory labour). Subsidies to food prices to stabilize industrial wages and controlled prices paid to cultivators both expanded the urban demand for food and reduced the incentives to farmers to meet that demand. In time, it was said, agriculture was relatively impoverished and tended to stagnation.

In countries where agriculture was an important source of the exports needed to earn the revenue with which to purchase equipment and raw materials for industrialization, stagnation in agriculture had direct effects on the progress of industry. In part this could be overcome by subsidizing agricultural exports, but then farming became divided between the well-remunerated exports and the neglected home-consumption sector, between commercial crops and basic foodstuffs.

The inferences were not inaccurate in the case of Brazil. The obsession with industry for three decades did lead to a relative neglect of agriculture, exaggerated by price controls on basic foodstuffs (milk, bread, vegetables, oil, beef and beans) to curb inflation. Export incentives accrued to the minority of farmers with the acreage and capital for large-scale production (about a fifth of all farmers, mainly concentrated in the south). Indeed, favouring exports tended to increase the conversion of land to commercial crops. Take, for example, one of the most important agricultural states of the south, Rio Grande do Sul. In the two decades after 1960, one of the most important commercial crops, soya beans, increased in annual output from a quarter of a million tonnes to 5.7 million, while two key items of the basic diet, beans and manioc, declined by 28 and 14 per cent respectively. Meanwhile, 39,000 farms were sold and 700,000 members of farm families left the state. Large farms and agro-businesses replaced them. For the country as a whole, in the seventies, soya-bean output increased from 1.5 to 15.2 million tonnes, while rice production increased from 7.6 to 9.7 million tonnes, and beans declined from 2.2 to 2 million tonnes.

In Mexico something similar happened, while the overall pace of agricultural growth tended to decline – from a 6 per cent annual increase (1945–55) to 4.2 per cent (1955–65) and then 2.1 per cent (1965–75). The large commercial farmers operating on newly irrigated land in the north-west sustained high rates of expansion and exports, while the mass of cultivators, working small communal holdings in rain-fed or semi-arid areas, could not keep pace with the growth of domestic demand. From 1969 to 1981, the output of the two staples, maize and beans, grew by a total of 32 and 13 per cent, when soya-bean production increased 181 per cent.[11] Production of maize, beans and rice per head of the population grew between 1966 and 1981 by 0.5, −2.8 and −0.2 per cent.

The poor farmers had their revenge. To feed the population now required an increasing volume of imported food, which in turn ate into the resources available to purchase the inputs to industry. Import-substitution industrialization had increased dependence upon imported foodstuffs.

The Conjuncture

The main factors leading to the financial crisis in Mexico and Brazil in 1982 and 1983 have already been enumerated. It was a much more extreme version of events noted in the last chapter in the four Asian countries – the results of world slump on economies where growth was being sustained, in many cases, through an ambitious heavy-industry programme. In the case of the two Latin American countries, the depth of the crisis was much more severe (although the events of 1980 in South Korea should not be underestimated). For Mexico, the gross domestic product declined in 1982 and 1983 (by −0.5 and −4.7 per cent); manufacturing output went down even further (−7.6 and −14.0 per cent); and gross investment more still (−16.4 and −25.3 per cent). Real wages officially fell by about a third over two years, and some 1.2 million jobs were said to have been lost. The retiring regime of President Lopez Portillo, demoralized in its closing year, descended into a scale of corruption unusual even for Mexico.

However, Mexico made – in the short term – a surprising recovery. Imports were drastically cut (−58.5 and −58.3 per cent in 1982 and

1983) and exports boosted, helped by a massive devaluation of the peso (73 per cent in 1982 and 33 per cent in 1983). The budget deficit was reduced by cutting subsidies, increasing taxes, increasing public-sector prices and cutting public expenditure and investment. With this 'good behaviour', the Mexican government won two extraordinary re-schedulings of a major part of its debt.

Furthermore, in the medium term, there seemed to be favourable circumstances. The decline in the peso boosted export industries and tourism. Despite the cruel fall in the dollar value of wages in the border region – from $2.09 per hour in early 1982 to about 90 cents in the spring of 1983 – employment expanded. However, a boom in the United States not only lifted Mexico's exports, it also lifted the value of the dollar and sustained high interest rates, to Mexico's loss in terms of the burden of debt. The ending of the boom in late 1984 lowered interest rates and the value of the dollar, but sharply contracted the demand for Mexico's exports, particularly oil. The United States growth produced unexpectedly swift growth in Mexico in 1984 (growth was 3.5 per cent, compared to a target of 1 per cent), and a big increase in imports. Thus, the economy was once again quite swiftly threatened with severe pressures, symbolized in a rapidly increasing deficit on external trade when debt servicing still remained high. Earthquakes added disaster to the growing difficulties of 1986 (when the spot price of oil touched $10 a barrel – against a budget figure of $22).

The crisis had had another important effect. It forced the Mexican government to commit itself to ending what was called an 'indiscriminate import-substitution model'. On a wide number of issues, the government relaxed the regulations. The requirement on domestic ownership of companies was quietly eased. A programme of de-nationalizing was begun (with over three hundred companies returned to private ownership in 1984). The government moved to make another – covert – devaluation of the peso and to permit virtual convertibility. There were sharp cuts in public spending – including the symbolic sacking of fifteen deputy Ministers and fifty director-generals; the President imposed a 10 per cent salary cut upon himself, and a pay freeze on the administration at large. In trade, a series of measures was taken to encourage exports: import licences were replaced by tariffs; exporters were permitted to import goods up to the value of 40 per cent of their exports without paying tariffs or value added tax;

maquiladores were permitted to sell a fifth of their output in the Mexican market; imports were to be automatically admitted where domestic products were priced at 50 per cent or more above imports; and special incentives were offered to foreign trading companies to take Mexican exports. A basic transition was being impelled by means of the international financial market so that Mexico's growth should be rather more a function of external demand than of domestic desires.

Brazil's short-term crisis was more long drawn out. Gross domestic product, increasing by 4 per cent in 1981, showed no change in 1982 and then fell by nearly 4 per cent in 1983 (product per head fell 11 per cent in the same three years). Real industrial production fell 11 per cent, and hit particularly hard former key sectors of growth – consumer durables (-27 per cent), capital goods (-20 per cent) and vehicles (-33.3 per cent). The government responded, like that of Mexico, with a devaluation of the currency, deflation of the economy and radical cuts in imports. Exports responded to the new measures with remarkable speed, turning the external trade balance from a deficit to a surplus of over \$12 bn in 1984. The cost of the changes in domestic terms were no less horrifying than in Mexico – over 40 per cent of São Paulo's workforce lost their jobs over a two-year period; there was a general strike; the hungry raided Rio's supermarkets; and violent crime and corruption seemed to attain new heights.

However, as we noted with the four Asian powers, the attempt to expand exports to the United States obliged the exporting governments to make concessions on imports from the United States. The Brazilian instincts lay in the opposite direction, as was shown in 1984 when the government refused a World Bank loan because it stipulated import liberalization. However, the new civilian regime promised a new combination of policies. The former military order had combined opposition to a welfare state with a large public sector and government; the new civilian order promised a commitment to the alleviation of poverty with, as the draft National Development Plan put it, 'a reduction of the presence of the state in the productive sector'. Indeed, the state capitalism of the past was seen as one of the sources of income inequality.

Thus, the borrowings that were made to sustain an import-substituting economy in the seventies returned in the eighties to force, not merely an increase in export promotion, but the beginnings of the domestic changes required to support exports. There were still many obstacles – not least, a domestic business class most nervous of confronting imports – but it seemed that even in these two more extreme cases, the days of economic nationalism were numbered.

Despite all the reservations advanced by the neoclassical economists, Brazil and Mexico demonstrated that high rates of sustained economic growth were possible for long periods on the basis of import controls. The two countries achieved a radical transformation of the domestic economy, affecting many more people than in the four Asian countries. As in the Asian countries, it was a state-initiated and state-directed process, not one determined by a private market, and that state role was enhanced when the right-wing military were in power.

The two groups were very different. The Latin Americans were much larger and richer, endowed much more substantially with raw materials. That made possible continued raw-material exports while the main attention was devoted to the expansion of the domestic market. Thus, differences in government strategy, the precise mix of import substitution and export promotion, could be related to different material endowments rather than different governmental persuasions. The Latin Americans took for granted a growing world demand for their exports through much of the post-war period; the world of the seventies, however, exposed their dependence, a dependence grown archaic in the new world of manufacturing exports. Paradoxically, the exports of the two Latin American countries remained much closer to the nineteenth-century pattern than did those of the Asians.

The state-dominated process of industrialization did seem to encourage the concentration of capital in giant companies, public or private, a sort of premature monopoly or oligopoly. The heavy industrial programmes also seemed to encourage over-investment that made the economy particularly vulnerable to external slump. These features seemed to be common to the Latin Americans and South Korea, as well as to Eastern Europe, the most complete forms of state capitalism. The Latin Americans also shared with the East Europeans the relatively poor performance of agriculture in the production of basic foodstuffs.

Dependence upon the growth of the domestic market also seemed to produce a pattern of production which matched the existing unequal pattern of the distribution of income. Indeed, Brazil seemed positively to encourage income inequality in order to have a large enough relatively high-income market for its output of consumer durables and vehicles. Income differentials in both Mexico and Brazil were thought to have increased, whereas in the four Asian powers, they had remained narrower. If the data is correct, it suggests that export-promotion industrialization produced less income inequality. On the other hand, Hong Kong was able to supply the mass of people with cheap goods because it supplied the world market on a scale that reaped the full advantages of both optimal size and the cheapest inputs available in the world.

The crisis of the early eighties put in question all the features of the pattern of development of Mexico and Brazil which appeared least consistent with the emerging pattern of the world economy. A national ruling order was beaten into a shape which was more appropriate to a world of comparative advantages – and in the short term, that entailed a slight return to the earlier specialization in primary production. We have seen how the aspirations of General Park in South Korea were frustrated after his death: the country was forced into a narrower specialization (although still quite remote from the 'comparative advantage' an independent judge might have defined). Brazil and Mexico were much more diversified and with a much more thoroughgoing orientation towards a self-sufficient national economy. It is understandable, therefore, that the process of reorienting them should be more violent. The financial crisis was the lever of the world economy which prized open the Latin American economies and forced liberalization and so integration.

The Latin Americans had delayed the readjustment long past the time when it would have been easier. There were too many interests vested in import substitution and the rate of growth was too high to risk changes of direction. The Asian countries changed much earlier, when sustained world growth seemed the norm for all eternity and business forecasts were all brave. Furthermore, the state in South Korea, Taiwan and Singapore seemed much more powerful relative to business than in Brazil and Mexico; the removal of the Japanese and British ruling orders left a vacuum the state could fill, a sociological factor with no parallel in the Latin American cases. By the late seventies, export promotion could only be grafted on top of import substitutionism in conditions of world stagnation, heightened competition and general pessimism. It required the stark threat of financial catastrophe to bludgeon business into line (and, even then, there was strong evidence of continued business resistance to liberalization).

Yet neither Brazil nor Mexico retreated into autarky as they had done in the slump of the early thirties. The two governments recognized that the world was a different place and realized that interdependence had become the condition of survival. Others did not see the change – the left in both countries continued to call for economic isolation, 'self-generating growth', 'self-reliance', and an end to 'dependency'. The old conditioned reflexes were skew of the new world order. Celso Furtado, distinguished Brazilian economist and economic adviser of the op-position to the military, called in 1983 for a return to reliance on the domestic market, a radical redistribution of income to reshape the market and an end to foreign borrowing and the export drive. And on the right, there remained sections of business that depended upon state protection to survive. They did not know the stern warning of Engels on the relationship between local power and the international market:

> The industrial bourgeoisie can govern in a country only whose manufacturing industry commands for its produce the universal market; the limits of the home market are too narrow for its development.[12]

4 = A Global Manufacturing System

There is simply no precedent in history for the dynamic rate of change in the geographical spread of global output in our era.[1]

Was the high growth performance of the four countries of east and south-east Asia and the two of Latin America peculiar to those six, or was it part of a more generalized phenomenon? Did everyone become enamoured with the magical properties of exports? This chapter examines the export performance of the less developed countries and the changes in some sectors of world production.

Exports and the Less Developed Countries

Twenty-seven less developed countries are listed in Table 3, the twenty-seven that exported goods worth one billion dollars or more in 1980. The list excludes countries which were mainly oil producers, although there are some arbitrary selections here – Indonesia and Nigeria are omitted, Mexico included. The countries are listed according to how big their exports were relative to gross national product. Of course, this is misleading – it favours the small countries. They have to export in order to import the goods they cannot afford to make at home because the domestic market is too small; if all countries were the same in terms of their pattern of output, the ratio of exports to gross domestic product would fall as the size of a country increased – to the point where the world was the same as the country, and both exports and imports became zero.

The twenty-seven countries – of the ninety-six recorded by the World Bank as low- and middle-income (less developed countries) – include 53.6 per cent of the population of the world. They are divided into five groups, according to the proportionate size of exports. Of the twelve leading countries, as we can see in Table 3, half had populations below 10 million, and only three were as large as 20–30 million. South Korea stands out as a special case – with a population of nearly 40 million, and an export ratio of 27 per cent. However, if we compare these twenty-seven to the six more developed countries of Figure 6, we can see that they are well behind – Belgium's performance ranks it higher than Taiwan, and Holland would be among the top five in the list. Most remarkably, the major economy of West Germany would be sixth, a ratio which conceals the enormous absolute size of West German exports (worth ten and a half times those of South Korea).

The top six countries in Table 3 are not the same as the six we have examined. They include Israel and South Africa, with Brazil and Mexico (with large gross domestic products in absolute terms) well down in the fourth group. Figure 5 also shows the value of manufacturing exports, and it might be thought that this would favour countries with an abso- lutely large manufacturing sector (that is, large countries). In fact, the leaders are still small – Taiwan, Hong Kong, South Korea, South Africa and Singapore (each with manufactured exports valued at over $10 bn). However, a number of large countries now become more prominent in the ranking – China, Mexico and Brazil (with the much smaller Yugoslavia) come into the first ten, although India does not. The gap between the more and less developed now becomes larger. None the less the twenty-seven were important in world trade – their combined exports were 10 per cent larger than those of Japan, and about 91 per cent of those of the United States.

Table 3. *Less Developed Countries: population and size of exports as a proportion of gross domestic product, 1980 (ranked)*[2]

Country	Population, 1980 (millions)	Exports as a percentage of gross domestic product
I. 50–100%		
Singapore	2.4	99.8
Hong Kong	5.0	90.6
Taiwan	17.8	51.5
II. 15–49%		
Israel	3.8	28.1
South Korea	37.8	27.1

South Africa	28.5	18.9
Portugal	9.8	15.1
III. 5–14%		
Malaysia	13.1	11.1
Tunisia	6.2	10.9
Yugoslavia	22.1	9.8
Sri Lanka	14.5	9.3
Greece	9.3	6.8
Philippines	46.7	6.2
Pakistan	79.7	6.0
Thailand	45.5	5.6
IV. 3–4.9%		
Uruguay	2.9	4.8
Guatemala	6.8	4.7
Mexico	65.6	3.6
Kenya	15.3	3.5
Chile	10.9	3.4
China	965.5	3.4
Brazil	116.5	3.3
V. 1.4–2.9%		
Peru	17.4	2.8
India	659.2	2.8
Colombia	26.1	2.7
Turkey	44.2	1.5
Argentina	27.3	1.4
Total	2299.5	
Percentage of world total	53.6	18.6

What sort of exports were these manufactured goods? Figures 5 and 6 separate out two types of exports – machinery and transport equipment and 'other manufacturing' (excluding textiles and garments). Again, for machinery and transport equipment, one might expect those countries with the largest manufacturing sectors (and the largest capital goods and heavy-industry sectors) to predominate. None the less, as we can see from Figure 5, Singapore and Taiwan are the largest exporters in the list. Singapore exported machinery and transport equipment equal

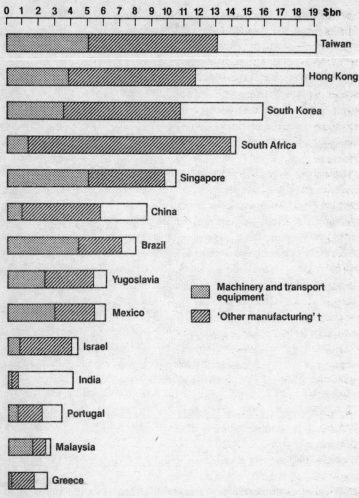

Figure 5. *Less developed countries:* value and structure of manufactured exports, twenty-seven leading countries, 1980*

Source: *World Development Report*, World Bank, various issues

* Excluding 'non-market industrial economies' (Poland, Bulgaria, Hungary, USSR, Czecho-slovakia, German Democratic Republic) for lack of comparable data.

† Other manufacturing: the residual from the total value of manufactured exports, SITC sections 5 to 9, less section 7 and division 68.

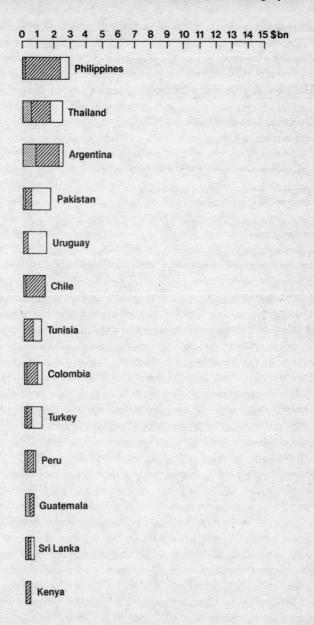

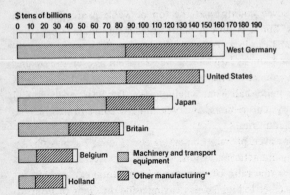

$ tens of billions

0 10 20 30 40 50 60 70 80 90 100 110 120 130 140 150 160 170 180 190

West Germany

United States

Japan

Britain

Belgium   Machinery and transport equipment

Holland   'Other manufacturing'*

Figure 6. *More developed countries: value and structure of manufactured exports, six countries, 1980*
Source: as for Figure 5.
* See note to Figure 5. NB: scale in tens of billions of dollars (unlike Fig. 5).

to \$2,083 per head compared to Belgium's \$1,438, West Germany's \$1,426, the Netherlands' \$890, and Taiwan's \$280. The degree of specialization in Singapore is thus remarkably high. However, size is also important, and some of the larger countries now become more important in the list – Brazil is fifth, Mexico sixth and Yugoslavia seventh. But the gap between the more and less developed now becomes extreme – the combined exports of the twenty-seven in this class of goods was worth only 38 per cent of those of the USA and West Germany, 47 per cent of Japan's and 82 per cent of Britain's. None of the twenty-seven remotely approaches Belgium; the leader, Singapore, has a little over one third of Belgium's score.

'Other manufacturing' is a mixed bag, and not a very satisfactory measure of diversification or flexibility. In the ranking, however, larger countries become more prominent – China (fifth), Brazil (seventh) – although India at nineteenth illustrates that mere size is not the only important factor. The less developed countries are more prominent here than the more developed, showing perhaps a lower degree of specialization; the combined exports of the twenty-seven are 18 per cent larger than the United States', 30 per cent above Japan's, and 42 per cent above Britain's; West Germany's output is slightly larger than that of all twenty-seven together.

In sum, the seven countries at the top of Table 3 are peculiar in certain respects, but it is only a matter of degree. South Korea and South Africa stand out in a group of relatively small countries. Yet still none of the seven loom as large in the world system as even the smaller more developed countries. The largest exporter of manufactured goods, Taiwan, exports under half what Belgium does. The heart of the global manufacturing system remains overwhelmingly concentrated in the more developed countries.

The trends, however, promise something else. Figure 7 shows this by comparing the manufacturing exports of the twenty-seven in 1960 and 1980. In all cases, the ratio of manufacturing to total exports has increased, in some cases to high levels (leaving aside the Gang of Four, to 82 per cent for Israel; 73 per cent for Yugoslavia; and 72 per cent for Portugal). Some large economies have also approached high levels – 59 per cent for India, 50 per cent for Pakistan, and 47 per cent for China.

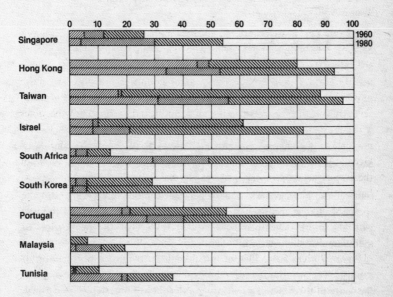

Figure 7. *Less developed countries: change in the structure of manufactured exports, twenty-seven leading countries, 1960 and 1980*
Source: as for Figure 5.

Continued overleaf

Figure 7 – continued

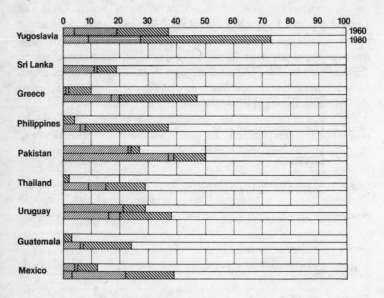

But again, the proportions still tend to be below those for the more developed countries – 68 per cent for the United States; 86 per cent for West Germany; 96 per cent for Japan; 74 per cent for Britain; 51 per cent for the Netherlands; and 74 per cent for Belgium (1980). But the speed of change means that the twenty-seven are fast closing the gap with the more developed countries in respect of the proportion of manufactured exports to all exports.

Figure 7 gives some idea of the changing technical sophistication of exports. The more advanced the exporter, the more the tendency for the share of textiles and garments to fall (but not invariably – see South Korea, Taiwan and Yugoslavia). New exporters expand most swiftly, on the other hand, in textiles and garments, whether small (as Sri Lanka) or large (as China). The new exporters displace their more advanced rivals, just as the Gang of Four displaced Japan (the share of Japanese

Figure 7 – continued

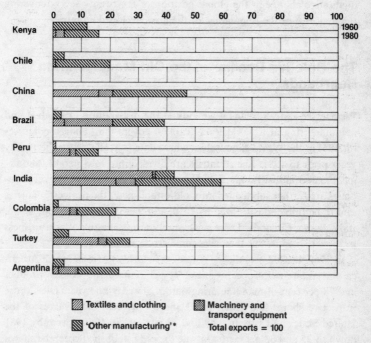

Textiles and clothing

'Other manufacturing'*

Machinery and
transport equipment

Total exports = 100

* See note to Figure 5.

exports in textiles and garments fell from 28 to 4 per cent in the two decades). In no country was there a decline in the share of machinery and transport equipment; the average for all twenty-seven increased from around 2 to just under 10 per cent (from 4 to 23 per cent for the first group of countries).

The manufacturing exports of the less developed countries are heavily concentrated in a few countries. Thus, 85 per cent of the manufactured exports of 'low-income countries'[3] derive from three countries – China, India and Pakistan; half the manufactured exports of the twenty-seven come from the top four (Taiwan, Hong Kong, South Korea and South Africa), 81 per cent from the top ten. None the less, while the high exporters are peculiar, the trends affect all the twenty-seven – all increased exports, all experienced a disproportionate increase in manufactured exports, and within that category, an increase in the exports of machinery and transport equipment. There seems to have been a qualitative change in the global position of the twenty-seven, covering the majority of the population of the less developed countries.

The Relative Decline of the Old Manufacturing Heartlands

We can see similar trends if we look at the distribution of product and manufacturing at a world level. Table 4 covers the hundred countries (of 125) in the World Bank tables where data is available for the twenty years prior to 1981. The countries are divided into low-income, middle-income and industrial-market economies.[4] The industrial-market economies are further subdivided into 'old-established', the thirteen countries said to be fully industrialized by 1950, and 'newcomers' (Ireland, Spain, Italy, Japan, Finland). There is inevitably some measure of arbitrariness in these divisions, but they give some crude sense of change.

In 1960, the old-established core of the world system in North America and Western Europe produced 71 per cent of the world's product and 78 per cent of manufacturing output. Twenty-one years later, those respective shares had fallen to 60 and 59 per cent. The shares of the United States and Britain – 49 and 53 per cent in 1960 – were by 1981 down to 35 and 33 per cent. Outside the old-established core, the shares moved from 29 and 22 per cent to 40 and 42 per cent. In 1960, the old-established core held a greater share of world manufacturing than product, but by 1981 the position was reversed.

The heart of the shift in shares was from the old-established to the newcomers and the middle-income group. Combined, their shares changed from 21 and 19 to 35 and 37 per cent. The low-income group's share of world product was reduced, but in the case of manufacturing it was slightly increased. On a different set of figures, the World Bank estimates that the trend will reduce the share of Western Europe and North America in manufacturing to under a half by 1990. Furthermore, it affects all sectors of industry (except paper, printing and publishing).

The issue is not about flows of goods, exports and imports, but about the location of the capacity to produce. Indeed, trade flows often go in the reverse direction – expanding industrial capacity in the less de-

Table 4. *Shares in Gross World Product (current prices) and Value Added in Manufacturing (1975 prices), 1960 and 1981, by groups of countries* [5]

	Share in gross world product		Value added in manufacturing		Share of manufacturing increase
	1960	1981	1960	1981	1960–81
1. Industrial-market economies					
(a) Old-established	71.1	59.9	78.1	59.1	56.0
United States	43.2	30.0	46.0	28.8	26.0
Britain	6.1	5.2	7.2	4.3	
(b) Newcomers	8.5	18.0	9.5	22.0	24.0
Japan	4.7	14.7	n.a.	n.a.	n.a.
2. Middle-income economies	12.7	16.7	9.3	15.3	16.2
3. Low-income countries	7.8	5.5	3.1	3.7	3.7
China	3.7	2.7	n.a.	n.a.	n.a.
India	2.5	1.5	1.3	1.0	n.a.
	100.0	100.0	100.0	100.0	100.0

Note: discrepancies in totals are due to rounding.
World totals exclude the Eastern Bloc (the centrally planned economies of COMECON) due to lack of comparable data.

veloped countries requires increased imports of industrial equipment from the more developed. In the seventies, as the newly industrializing countries increased their industrialization efforts, the current value of exports of engineering goods from the more developed countries tripled, as did the export surplus on engineering goods for the industrialized countries (1973–9).

Let us look at some of the industries most affected by this movement of world capacity.

Selected Industries

Textiles and garments

The textile and garment industry is usually identified in the more developed countries as the industry most affected by imports from less developed countries. It is here that the governments of Western Europe and North America have exercised the greatest ingenuity, hypocrisy and brutality to evade the logic of free trade. Apart from agriculture, trade in textile goods has been the most strictly controlled of all sectors, yet it has not saved jobs in the developed countries. Employment in these sectors has fallen in every year since 1973. In Europe, the production of textiles and garments now employs only 1.6 per cent of the workforce, in the United States 1.1 per cent.

The restrictions have not stopped the relocation of capacity in the industry, nor has it stopped the share of trade changing. Table 5 illustrates this.

Table 5. *Textiles and Clothing: Distribution of World Trade by Groups of Countries, 1963, 1973, 1983 (percentages)*[6]

	Exports			Imports		
	1963	1973	1983	1963	1973	1983
Textiles						
More developed	74	70	60	63	68	57
Less developed	18	22	30	30	25	34
Eastern bloc	8	8	10	7	7	9
Totals	100	100	100	100	100	100
Clothing						
More developed	67	51	38	66	78	75
Less developed	15	35	48	17	10	17
Eastern bloc	18	14	14	17	12	8
Totals	100	100	100	100	100	100

While the imports of the less developed group do not conform to the trend, the overall picture, particularly in garments, is of the decline of the more developed group in trade. This does not necessarily mean an absolute decline – between 1963 and 1982, the value of the textile trade increased more than seven times over, and of garments, nearly twenty times over.

In the fifties and sixties, the Gang of Four revived an industry in long-term decline and made it into a growth sector, a springboard for general industrialization. But by the seventies, many more were copying the tactic and displacing the Four. Physical quotas restricting exports helped the process by forcing the leading exporters into higher value lines, leaving the lower value products to newcomers. One of the countries that exploited this opportunity most fully was China; its garment exports increased by 18 per cent annually from 1977, and by 1981 China had become the third largest exporter among the less developed countries.

Microprocessing devices and electronic products

This was the other sector most notorious for high growth in the less developed countries but, because it was a new industry, it did not embody the same threat to employment in Europe and America. Nevertheless, it provided striking examples of the displacement of sectors of production there. For example, up to 1962, the United States market for black-and-white television sets was supplied from local factories. Within three years, Japanese companies had secured half the market; within three years of the arrival of colour television sets, Japanese companies had secured 17 per cent of the market; in a further six years, 35 per cent of the market. At that point, they were beginning to lose the black-and-white market to imports from Taiwan and South Korea. In 1977, the Federal government imposed restrictions – the euphemism was 'Orderly Marketing Agreements' – that cut the sales of Japanese companies from two and half to one and three quarter million for three years. The following year, South Korea and Taiwan were brought into the 'Agreement'. The restrictions prompted Japanese companies to build production facilities in the United States to escape import controls; and the high profits on sales in the United States (because foreign competition was temporarily restricted) helped prompt United States companies to purchase an increasing proportion of their output abroad. Nationality became increasingly blurred, and its elusive significance could not be captured in the statistical measures available.

Steel

Textile goods and electronic consumer goods were light industries and, despite their political significance, were not considered to be fundamental to Western economies. That was not the case with heavy industry and more sophisticated engineering products. The location of world steel capacity was another weathervane; it was an industry not at all dependent upon cheap labour (as the other two supposedly were), but combining high technology and great capital intensity, the natural comparative advantage of industrialized countries. Yet the industry had always been mobile, from the first displacement of the British as the largest world steel producer in the 1890s. In 1870, steel mills in Britain made 37 per cent of the world's output; in 1981, under 2 per cent. In 1950, steel mills in the United States made nearly half the world's steel, a share that was down to 15 per cent in 1981. On the other hand, Japanese mills, with some 2·5 per cent of the world output in 1950, held 16·5 per cent by 1975. When, in the fifties and sixties, United States steel production increased by 1.5 per cent annually (and the British, by 2.7 per cent), Japanese mills expanded by 30 per cent per year (West Germany's by 6.8, Italy's by 13.3 per cent). By the eighties, it seemed, Japan's expansion was over; in 1980, output for the first time exceeded that of the United States, but in 1982 Japanese output fell absolutely for the first time in a decade.

It was common knowledge that steel consumption began to fall as an economy became more sophisticated and world technology changed. Uses become more economical, services expand faster than industry and more lighter, synthetic materials become available to displace steel. These were the reasons, it was said, for the fact that, between 1967 and 1977, when United States gross national product increased by 30 per cent, steel consumption grew by only 6 per cent. Steel consumption in Japan increased faster than GNP to 1974, and then more slowly than GNP. Indeed, expanding steel consumption was a mark of a relatively unsophisticated economy in the last quarter of the twentieth century, not, as it had been earlier, a mark of progress; the largest steel producer in the world, the Soviet Union, exemplified this changeover.

Thus, it was to be expected that the less developed countries would increase steel consumption much more rapidly than the more developed ones, even when both had the same rate of growth, for the output of the one was likely to use much more steel than that of the other. World steel consumption would thus continue to grow, but with redistribution towards the less developed countries. Table 6 shows what happened in this respect in the seventies.

At a time when global steel production declined slightly (but consumption increased by 3 per cent), the industrial countries cut production by 17 per cent and consumption by 12 per cent, while the less

Table 6. *World Steel Production and Consumption, shares of groups of countries, percentage (absolute output, million tonnes, in brackets), 1974 and 1981*[7]

	Production		Consumption	
	1974	*1981*	*1974*	*1981*
OECD group (total)[8]	64.6(457.6)	55.4(391.5)	57.7(415.7)	50.2(372.0)
United States	*18.7(132.3)*	*15.4(108.8)*	*20.2(145.6)*	*17.9(132.5)*
EEC	*22.0(155.6)*	*17.8(126.0)*	*17.2(124.3)*	*14.1(104.4)*
Japan	*16.5(117.1)*	*14.4(101.7)*	*11.2(80.7)*	*10.7(79.3)*
Less developed	4.4(30.9)	8.3(58.7)	10.3(74.3)	13.9(102.8)
Others (including East Europe, China)	31.1(220.1)	36.3(256.1)	32.0(231.0)	34.7(256.6)
Totals	100.0(708.6)	100.0(706.3)	100.0(721.0)	100.0(740.6)

developed countries doubled production and increased consumption by nearly 40 per cent. It was little to be wondered that steel companies in the industrialized countries complained bitterly that, cut capacity as they might, the less developed countries persisted in expanding, resulting in overcapacity once again.

The shift was politically more marked in the United States. The gap between production and consumption – 13.4 million tonnes in 1974 (or 9.2 per cent of consumption) had doubled by 1981 to 23.7 million tonnes (17.9 per cent). In 1975, the Japanese and Europeans had filled 90.8 per cent of the gap. But as the gap grew, these two met a declining proportion of it – 56.9 per cent in 1983. Some thirty countries competed to make up the difference. In 1984, President Reagan, busy electioneering, ordered a reduction of the share of the domestic market taken by imports from 25.4 to 20.5 per cent, allocating to Japan, Europe and Canada all but 6.5 per cent of the market. It was this intervention that threatened, as we have seen, steel exports from South Korea, Mexico, Brazil and many others (these three had shared more than 6.5 per cent of the market in 1983). Like the Japanese before them, the Brazilians invested in the United States – in a steel-rolling complex to use Brazilian slabs in California.

Measures to control the steel trade produced perverse results. When the West German government limited steel imports from Japan, Swedish imports from Japan and exports to West Germany increased.

Limiting imports raised domestic steel prices, putting steel consumers at a disadvantage relative to foreign competitors; it was said some United States steel consumers moved to Canada to escape high steel prices – trade controls encouraged the movement of capital to escape the effects. In special steels, controls were less needed, for technology gave a clearcut advantage to the more developed countries. Yet even here there were threats – in 1983, for example, the Indonesian government began construction of the first seamless pipe plant in the less developed countries.

Vehicle manufacture

If steel was an unlikely candidate for relocation, vehicle manufacture seemed even more so. The forces of geographical inertia appeared formidable. Vehicle assembly, it had always been said, was located physically close to the market for vehicles since the cost of moving the product was high; 50–60 per cent of the value of a vehicle derived from component manufacture, and assembly attracted a whole array of suppliers of parts, the whole creating an interdependent geographical concentration of great size. It did not seem possible to move such a large complex where physical proximity was so important. The problem was further exaggerated by the increasing minimum scale of production thought appropriate (for assembly, two million vehicles annually). Close relationships were required between research and development work, production, management and marketing to make the launch of a new model successful. None of these powerful factors, it was said, was outweighed by the availability of cheap labour.

The optimal size and location of an industry is not, however, a function of engineering specifications, but of prices and profitability. None of the factors involved was permanently stable. It might be expensive to move a weighty car at one stage, but lighter materials constantly lowered the cost; in the ten years before 1985, the average weight of a car manufactured in the United States declined by over 30 per cent; technical innovations in transport, in carrying vehicles, also had the effect of lowering the cost of transport. Nor did automation nullify the effect of the other costs – for where the rival companies employed the same automated technology, differences in labour costs and other factors (for

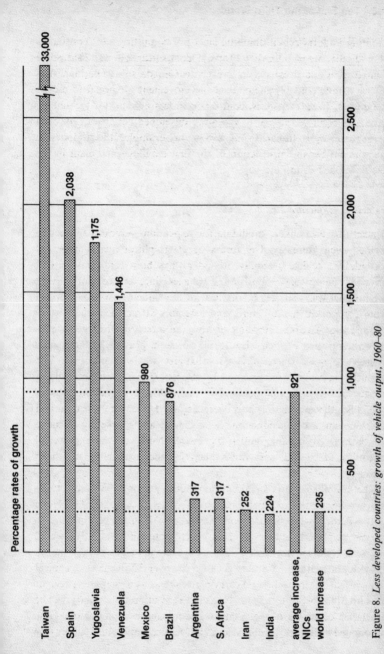

Figure 8. *Less developed countries: growth of vehicle output, 1960–80*
Sources: *UN Yearbook of International Trade*, various issues, and *Motor Vehicle Data*, London, 1982.

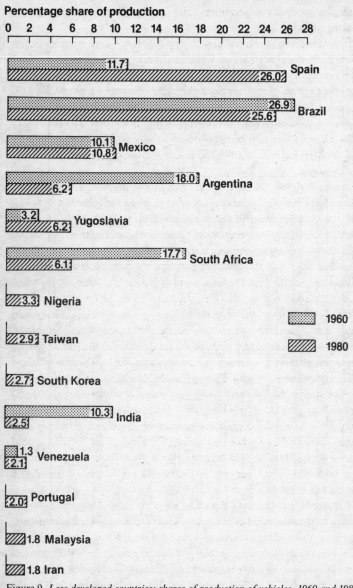

Percentage share of production

Figure 9. *Less developed countries: shares of production of vehicles, 1960 and 1980*
Source: as for Figure 8.

example, government incentives, the quality of infrastructure, etc.) became decisive.

In practice, redistribution has taken place. In 1950, companies manufacturing in the United States dominated world vehicle production (with 76 per cent of world car output); by 1979, their share had fallen to 28 per cent (and this figure included the value of components used in US-manufactured cars, but imported from overseas). In 1950, companies in Japan contributed 1 per cent of world output; in 1979, 23 per cent. In 1956, all but 3 per cent of car production was made in North America and Western Europe; in 1979, the rest of the world made 35 per cent of world output.

Figure 8 shows the rates of growth of the main vehicle producers among less developed countries (or at least, given the inclusion of Spain, new vehicle producers) in the two decades up to 1980. Figure 9 shows the different share of production taken by these countries in 1980; it also shows the high concentration of production – Spain and Brazil produced over half the total output, and the top six (these two plus Argentina, South Africa, Mexico and Yugoslavia), some 80 per cent. Figure 9 also shows the sharp relative decline in the output growth of India, South Africa and Argentina (among the leading producers in 1960). India's growth was actually below world growth (the last bar in Figure 8). Despite its large share of the total output of the less developed countries, Brazil's growth was below the average for the newly industrializing countries – with Taiwan, Spain, Yugoslavia, Venezuela and Mexico above the average. Some fast growers – for example, South Korea – are excluded from Figure 9 because they began production after 1960. In sum, the group of newcomers expanded 9.2 times over (when the world as a whole expanded 2.35 times over), to reach about four and a half million vehicles total output. As a share of world output, they increased from 3 per cent in 1960 to 6.3 per cent in 1970 and 11.8 per cent in 1980.

Unfortunately, the data does not allow us to identify what is happening to the vast number of components that enter vehicle production. However, the evidence is that geographical dispersal was more extreme here than in vehicle assembly. Nor did this cover only minor mechanical components (starter motors, alternators). Manufacturers in the United States imported 3.6 million engines in 1983, or a third to a half of the value of the engines used in the United States' output. Two thirds of the engines came from Mexico and Brazil. Furthermore, as we noted in the last chapter, investment in Mexico by Ford and General Motors suggested this flow of key components was likely to increase. Some countries pursued a deliberate policy of seeking to foster component manufacture. For example, in 1985, Proton (a joint venture of the Malaysian government's Heavy Industries Corporation and Mitsubishi) launched a new prototype car, the Mahabishi, on a domestic market of 18,000 cars per year, already supplied by six companies. The government aimed to dominate the domestic market, driving out four of the existing producers and, on this basis, develop the skills and engineering capacity to develop component manufacture for export.

It was too early to detect the new geographical pattern for the manufacture of vehicles and components, but already a number of countries close to the major markets (Mexico for the United States; Spain and Portugal for the Common Market) were being reshaped in particular ways to provide specific inputs. A world car, assembled from parts made in many different countries, provided substantial export opportunities for the collaborating countries, but only on condition that they permitted increased imports: as production and exports rose, domestic content must fall. The trend collided directly with the imperatives of import-substitution industrialization.

Capital goods

Finally, at the end of the skill spectrum in manufacture, the capital-goods industry is also subject to some relocation. The industry can be divided into five sectors: metal products, non-electrical machinery, electrical machinery, transport equipment and professional equipment. Figure 10 shows what happened between 1975 and 1985 in terms of the less developed countries' share of world production and exports in the industry as a whole, and in three subsectors. In general, changing location is limited – although the share of the more developed countries is tending to decline slowly from 50–60 per cent of world production and from over 90 per cent of world exports. In non-electrical machinery, the shares in each declined from 61 and 96 per cent to 55 and 94 per cent; in professional equipment, from 34 and 95 per cent (the centrally planned economies of Eastern Europe had 64 per cent of production

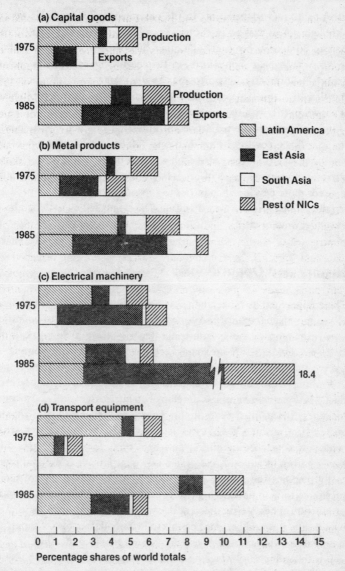

Figure 10. *Less developed countries: shares of production and exports, capital goods, by sector and region, 1975 and 1985*
Source: UNIDO, *Second World Study on Capital Goods*, Vienna, 1984 (mimeo).

here) to 32 and 91 per cent. In the other sectors, change was faster, although not as fast as in electrical machinery – from 61 and 92 per cent to 60 and 80 per cent. The other side of the coin to this decline is the swift growth shown in (c) in the chart – the role of East Asian exports is dramatically portrayed. In the same way, the powerful position of Latin America in the production of transport equipment is shown in (d), with the relatively poor export performance.

In sum then, in the main lines of industrial production, the newly industrializing countries have had some effect, albeit still a relatively small one. It should be noted that we have been dealing with *relative* shares, not absolute scales of production. It is, of course, perfectly possible for more developed countries to expand production while producing a declining share of world output. The shares tell us nothing about output or employment.

History and Opportunities

The analysis here is crude and selective, partly because we are obliged to use gross geographical categories – countries or groups of countries – and even more unwieldy industrial categories. If we could break down both, we could identify increasingly complex networks contributing to the creation of commodities, and increasing layers of geographical specialization. We could go beyond the balance of trade in 'rubber products' between more and less developed countries to identify how some localities in the United States supply aircraft and other heavy-duty tyres, and import medium-heavy tyres from localities in Europe and from some less developed countries, and light tyres for motor cycles and bicycles from localities in less developed countries. We could also more easily pinpoint those innovations which suddenly make it once more profitable to manufacture light tyres in the United States, and to start production of heavy tyres in less developed countries. At a further level of complexity, it would become possible to identify the sources of inputs to tyre-making which would once again reverse many of the flows.

It is this complexity which destroys the easy identification of patterns of production, and particularly many of the assumptions about 'centres' and 'peripheries'. In the first phases of world growth after the Second World War, industrial expansion appeared asymmetrical – there was disproportionate growth in the core regions of the more developed countries and relative decline in the less developed ones (Japan hovered somewhere in between, until the world decided it was more developed, and saved a legion of theoretical problems). The experience seemed to support a reasonable pessimism about the prospects of the less developed countries being able to expand exports indefinitely, and particularly exports of manufacturing goods. Practice showed something different, and, as we have seen, Hong Kong led the Gang of Four in the fifties towards expanded exports of manufacturing. Textiles and garments proved to be the key to the new phase – when consumption in the more developed countries increased by 3 per cent per year, exports to them from the less developed increased by 20 per cent per year. Once begun, many other goods joined the process – plastic products, footwear and so on. From 1963, the share of more sophisticated goods in the exports of the less developed countries increased – semi-manufactures declined up to 1976 (from 60 to 35 per cent) and engineering goods increased from 13 to 29 per cent.[9] In the seventies, the process went further and, in particular commodities, became significant. Between 1970 and 1976, for example, less developed countries increased their share of imports to more developed countries in telecommunications equipment from 3 to 9 per cent; in switchgear, from 1 to 6 per cent; in pistons and engines, from 1 to 3 per cent; in accounting machines, from 1 to 15 per cent; in electrical power machinery, from 2 to 7 per cent; and in sound recorders, from 0 to 7 per cent.[10] At the end, the shares were still small, but the speed of change was remarkable.

The change in performance slowly affected almost all the governments of less developed countries. In retrospect, the change appears as one of the most profound in economic theory and policy. Reorientation occurred slowly (as in India), more quickly (as in China), through violent political change (as in Chile and Turkey); some changed back and forth (as Colombia) or were changed by economic crisis (as in Mexico and Brazil); some were liberalized from full state-owned economies (as China, Yugoslavia, Hungary, Poland), some from autarkic but private economies. Even those who delayed and were most autarkic, moved ultimately (as Burma, Vietnam and North Korea); even those oil producers, where foreign exchange was less of a constraint (as Indonesia), also followed the process. Not all shifted with the same degree of success, however – catastrophe afflicted Chile, Uruguay,

Argentina and, latterly, the Philippines. But whatever the political flag flying on the vessel, whatever the vicissitudes and results, the fact of change was inescapable.

What did the change signify? A shift from the belief that only the expansion of the domestic market could force growth (foreign trade was therefore a strictly subordinate or marginal element in growth) to a faith in the capacity to expand manufactured exports indefinitely; a movement away from hostility towards foreign capital to active pursuit of it; from opposition to borrowing abroad to the reverse; the liberalization of some imports; a shift of emphasis away from public-sector activity to the private market (on welfare and health as much as in industry); a commitment to eliminating subsidies – markets must determine prices for all commodities; a shift to floating currencies; and the privatization of public-sector industry.

Such a universal process – a universal embrace of what had so recently been thought of as the outdated ethics of nineteenth-century capitalism, regardless of the claimed ideologies of different regimes, the slogans, traditions and even 'stages of development' – betokened not a change of fashion or the different ideological eccentricities of particular politicians, but some profound structural change in the world system. Of course, in each country there was a different special explanation, and it was only when one put all the countries together that it became clear that all appeared to be moving in the same direction, regardless of special explanations. Furthermore, in the background, the great swing from the theories associated with the name of Keynes to those of the neoclassical tradition offered a dramatically different theoretical underpinning to the shift in policy. An intellectual revolution had been wrought, and covertly, so that there were few convincing explanations of what had happened and why.

In sum, then, the process of dispersal of manufacturing capacity is a general phenomenon, not simply something restricted to the Gang of Four. It involved increasingly complex patterns of changing specialization, interweaving different parts of the world unknowingly in collaborative processes of production. If permitted to continue – and it was quite unclear how it could be stopped – it bid fair to end – or at least render very much more complex – the simple picture of industry in more and less developed countries.

Furthermore, the process had become part of the structure. It no longer depended upon the changing fortunes of this regime or that – of South Korea's dictator or Mexico's debt. Nor did it depend upon a high rate of growth in the world economy or among the more developed countries – as we have seen, particular sectors continued to grow in periods of general stagnation, and geographical shares in the output of particular goods can change swiftly even though total world output is increasing slowly. Indeed, slump in the more developed countries intensified the search for newer, lower-cost sources of production just as it was the debt crisis, not high rates of growth, that turned Mexico and Brazil outwards. It was slump and stagnation which forced Ford and General Motors to increase their imports of components to the United States, or even to export assembly capacity. Generalized growth was not the condition for dispersal.

However, the growth of trade, like that of world capitalism itself, does not necessarily mean an equal process of transformation of the labour force. The numbers engaged in low-productivity cultivation of the soil remained more resistant to the processes of industrialization than in the nineteenth century. The hymns of praise for a new world order of manufacturing trade are not in the first instance rejoicing for the growth of jobs and incomes so much as for profitable production. In 1980, a majority of workers worldwide were still trapped in agriculture even though its contribution to output had fallen below 20 per cent. In China, 60 per cent; in India, 62 per cent; and in the rest of low-income Asia, 66 per cent, cultivated the soil; in Africa and the Middle East, the proportion was 80 per cent. There was still a mighty way to go, once one lifted one's eyes from production to people; millions still earned only the minimum required to sustain the most basic existence.

And many countries had no share in what benefits there were. The poorest countries experienced very little change – the seventies returned them, it seemed, to the forties. They remained trapped in producing and exporting a single raw material at low levels of productivity, lacking reserves to guard against the ravages of famine. The triumphs of world capitalism were indeed more spectacular in the less developed countries than they had been in the more developed, but victories in the long march of capital accumulation should not be confused with the conquest of hunger.

5 = Policy and Economic Development

It is time to summarize the arguments. The phrases – 'import-substitution industrialization' and 'export promotion' – with which we have identified the two alternative strategies are misleading, both because they are not mutually exclusive and because they refer to long-term development strategies as well as to short-term defensive tactics. When a government is faced with a sudden imbalance between the revenue generated by exports and the cost of imports, it may well limit imports, without this being 'import-substitution industrialization'. In the interests of getting enough foreign exchange, virtually all governments promote exports, without this being a strategy of export promotion.

Both long-term strategies seek to manipulate the external balance of trade to achieve domestic transformation, but they do not aim to achieve the same domestic transformation (even though the difference is concealed in the ambiguous phrase 'economic development'). Import-substitution strategies are directed to creating a national economy independent of the rest of the world. Its growth is to be sustained by the growth of the domestic market, a 'self-sustaining' growth. For such an economy to be reasonably self-sufficient at a tolerable level of income, it would have to reproduce domestically all the main sectors of a modern economy; it would become a microcosm of the world economy (including heavy, intermediate and light industry), and would have no specialized role in world trade. The emotional and political force of the case derived from a nationalist position which often included other aims which were not essential to the main one – local companies should be owned by local people, profits should be invested at home rather than sent to other countries, innovations in technology should be developed in the country concerned rather than imported, etc. Such a strategy could only be implemented by the state; its control of external trade and financial transactions was the key to reshaping domestic activity.

Export-promotion strategies were directed not at creating a 'balanced' domestic economy, independent of the rest of the world, but at the opposite: the creation of a specialized role in a world economy. The generation of domestic incomes and employment, the size of the domestic market and, ultimately, organization and prices in the domestic economy were to become byproducts of exploiting a specialized contribution to a world market. Whereas in the import-substituting case the scale of domestic industry would be determined by demand for its output in the domestic market (and usually that would be below the efficient world size), in the export-promoting case even quite small countries could have optimal size plants (so producing goods at the lowest price). The domestic consumer would benefit by having access to goods, whether produced at home or imported, at the lowest prices in the world system. Specialization implied that only a few sectors of world production would exist in the country, which would have an 'unbalanced' industrial structure. The forms of production in which the country should be specialized would be determined by its 'comparative advantage' in the world system. But that could be determined only if domestic prices were the same as external prices – all factors were priced relative to their scarcity in the world. In such circumstances, if locally produced goods were more expensive than imports, exporters could import inputs to production from the cheapest source abroad – all competitors would then utilize the cheapest inputs available, the advantage coming only from what was locally cheaper or more efficient (the 'factors' included entrepreneurial flair). In the theoretical case, the same principle ought to operate in the labour market, otherwise the advantage of cheap labour would be lost because local circumstances – such as government minimum-wage legislation, 'monopoly' trade unions, etc. – would overprice it.

Neoclassical development economists moderated the severe demands of their case by distinguishing between 'laissez-faire' and 'free trade'. The first conformed to the criteria of the theory: there were no barriers between the external and internal markets, and the role of government was restricted to non-economic functions (the maintenance of order, etc.). The second allowed the government to intervene as it wished in the domestic economy provided the prices of the inputs purchased by exporters did not differ from those of the cheapest imports. In practice, the distinction was dubious, not only because it accepted an 'inefficient' pattern of organization in the domestic economy which would not permit the proper allocation of resources, but also because the cost of keeping separate the two entities, domestic and exporting activity, would become prohibitive.

In practice, as we have seen, import-substituting governments were required to promote exports in order to earn sufficient foreign exchange to purchase the imports which continued to be needed, and export-promotiong governments usually controlled imports. But the broad emphasis remained distinct. Let us look at the development of the two cases in more detail.

Import Substitution

It took time for the distinctions to emerge, and for the idea of a long-term government strategy to change the structure of the economy to develop. As we have seen, the *ad hoc* defensive reactions of Latin American governments in the thirties (as with those of the more developed countries at the same time) created a system of controls which, in the Latin American case, did indeed promote rapid industrialization. The system also created a class of beneficiaries, businessmen whose profits were made possible or enhanced by eliminating the competition of imports. When the original balance-of-payments problems that had led to the introduction of import controls eased, it became impossible to reduce the import controls because of the political power of the benefici-aries. In the 1950s, twenty years after the introduction of measures of protection and spurred by a world boom (which sustained the demand for Latin American exports of raw materials), governments discovered 'economic development' and the singular virtues of these necessities forced upon them originally by world slump.

Even then it was only the larger economies – with a fair degree of industrial development, and, in the Latin American case, raw-material export markets – that could afford the strategy. The minimum effective size in most industries was far beyond the smaller countries. For every Brazil, there were a dozen Costa Ricas. In other cases, exports flagged too early to keep up the pace of required imports. Countries without much industry could do little without severe short-term damage to local living standards and massive illegal imports by the rich. Yet those countries big and developed enough had striking successes – and apparently without cost to the government; the budget was not burdened with subsidies.

Yet there were costs in shutting out the competition of imports. The high prices (and low quality) of domestically produced goods, often exaggerated by an exchange rate that cheapened foreign exchange and made the domestic currency more expensive, made it almost impossible to export manufactured goods. Manufacturers and governments in import-substituting economies almost always suffered from 'export pessimism'. But they attributed this not to import substitution or overvalued currencies so much as to the impossibility of the less developed attaining the standards of efficiency of the more developed. Even some of the neoclassical economists were not exempt from this loss of optimism – Harry Johnson, writing in the sixties, turned cause and effect round, seeing import substitution as the consolation for inefficiency – 'in some cases, the prospects for genuine economic growth are so bleak that nationalism is the only possible means available for raising real incomes'.[1]

Nor was it clear that the means used to implement the strategy in fact did so. In the jungle of regulations, instructions, discretionary rulings, taxes and subsidies, the criteria for decisions disappeared. Some industries were protected because they were new and expanding; others because they were old and declining, conforming to Macario's 'inefficiency principle': 'protection for inefficiency, in accordance with the principle that the less capable an industry is of withstanding foreign competition, the more protection it deserves'.[2] And in all cases, there was the suspicion that products were protected because the businessman knew the brother of the Minister or was married to the sister of the President or some other personage with influence.

However, for those outside the circle of beneficiaries, the import-substitution strategy had a different significance. For it seemed to be the natural complement to national political liberation. This might not be the liberation of people, but of states and local capital, and not a liberation from oppressive colonial government, but from what was seen as the domination of the nineteenth-century world division of labour, forcing particular countries into roles which both guaranteed their poverty and frustrated the possibility of economic development. It was understandable that the global division of labour was seen as simply a thin disguise for the machinations of the Great Powers, who by this means divided up the world economy as they had shared out the world polity. Classical economic theory was thus no more than an economic rationale of colonialism. The attempt to establish an independent national economy was just as much an affirmation of self-determination as the struggle to throw out the imperialist powers. Development was no longer something to be awaited as the ultimate product of the working of an invisible hand but rather something that could be created by the intelligent action of the state. Paradoxically, the liberalism of national self-determination collided with the economics of liberalism.

It was this element of liberation, of self-emancipation, which in part recruited the left to import substitutionism[3] and reconciled them to the apparently unlimited growth of state power. Socialism became entirely encompassed by radical nationalism, even though nationalism and the belief in a strong state were by tradition part of the politics of the right. The concepts changed their meaning in subtle ways. Thus, 'exploitation', supposedly for Marxists a relationship between capital and labour, came to describe the relationships between governments or countries or groups of countries. In the more extreme cases, countries became homogenous classes, with 'proletarian nations' being exploited by 'bourgeois nations'.[4]

The Latin Americans favoured a more discreet terminology, although the emotional force of 'centre' and 'periphery' came close to that of 'capital' and 'labour'. The terms translated relationships of power and economy into those of geography, or physical space, and reduced to one single force market imperatives, competing capitals, and the institutions and policies of governments. In the old European empires there had been a close identity between the interests of government and capital, but even there there had been contradictory trends – and the market had still operated independently of state and national capital. In the post-empire world, the complexity of a world system was reduced to no more than the relationships between homogenous entities, countries. The domestic mirror-image of this struggle of political geography, embodied in the terms of trade between manufactured and agricultural goods, was a conflict between town and country.

The case might have seemed most plausible for the poorest primary-commodity producers. But, as it happened, there was no long-term deterioration in the terms of trade between primary commodities and manufactured goods. There was deterioration in the package of goods traded in 1870, but the deterioration was greatest for manufactured goods; in reality, the goods traded had changed so radically that comparisons were misleading. By the 1970s, North America exported more primary commodities than the less developed countries, and the majority of exports of the less developed countries, by the early eighties, were manufactured goods. The case fell apart.

Prebisch's argument also stressed the extraordinary position of the continental economy of the United States by comparison with that of Britain in the nineteenth century. The great dollar shortage that threatened to bring world trade to a halt did not occur. The United States government persistently issued more dollars than it took in, running a deficit in its external trade and obliging those who exported to the United States to accept its paper. Foreign exporters could thus export, as the theory said they could not. There was no permanent disequilibrium in that respect. Furthermore, new trading centres emerged – first Europe, and then Japan (which, contrary to some of the theory, made a successful transition from periphery to centre) – so offering a diversification of markets and therefore a reduction in dependence upon the United States.

If the problem had been incorrectly diagnosed, so also was the ultimate target. To be 'developed' was confused with economic independence. But were there any such countries? By what criteria could one judge 'independence'? Was an independent economy one which was self-reliant, growth being generated from within the domestic market rather than by external demand? There were occurrences of such conditions, but they were relatively rare and short-lived, and certainly did not provide a general pattern for economic development. In the 1930s, the United States government was just as incapable of ordering its domestic affairs so as to eliminate mass unemployment as were its poorer neighbours (indeed, as we have seen, in employment terms, the United States fared worse than the Latin American countries). There was no self-generating domestic market that kept the North American economy afloat while the rest of the world stagnated. The concept of a 'self-generating' economy seemed to be a myth, except for the most backward countries, at very low and vulnerable levels of income. On the contrary, the more advanced an economy, the less self-reliant it became. If 'dependency' indicated the economic relationship between a country and the world, the more developed the country, the more dependent it was – that is, the more domestic activity was determined by external relationships.

This was not at all to say that the powerful states of the world did not use their power to force weaker governments to make economic concessions. They oppressed, bullied, bribed, cheated, but these were not the *determinants* of the world economy, though they were painful for the countries concerned. Big companies also used their power to seek to bend the market to their advantage, but they were still subordinate to the world market. The governments of the more developed countries were competitors, and their competition undercut any united claims. The great division between Moscow and Washington was only the most obvious schism between the powerful; within each bloc, East and West, there were many rivalries that offered space for the weaker countries to survive. Neo-imperialisms there were, but they did not direct the world economy nor could they predetermine the outcome of competition.

The theory of 'unequal exchange' foundered upon this reality. The more developed countries did not hold a monopoly in the supply of manufactured goods such that they could determine and hold stable the prices of their exports; on the contrary, they competed fiercely with each other. Companies and states were not the same and had contradictory interests which only occasionally permitted united action. Wages were not the sole freely self-determining element in the system, nor – *pace* the endless editorials of ruling-class warriors fulminating in Western newspapers – were trade unions able to exploit a monopoly in the supply of labour to set wage and employment levels as they chose. Even if they had temporarily succeeded in doing so, there were always new supplies of labour to break the monopoly – women workers, immigrants, and finally workers in the less developed countries. Furthermore, wages were very far from being the determinant of the prices of industrial exports – the theorists of unequal exchange omitted to note the scale of past capital accumulation in the more developed countries which supported extraordinarily high levels of labour productivity. Nor, when the slump of the seventies afflicted the world, could the governments of the more developed countries guarantee full employment or a given wage level – wages and employment levels both fell. The more developed countries did not form a single block, nor was each of them an homogenous entity which could 'exploit' another country or group of countries. This vision of the world was a fantasy.

It was therefore quite wrong to pose either unequal exchange and robbery or autarky as the sole alternatives for the less developed countries. Nor was social reform, let alone revolution, required to accelerate capital accumulation. The processes of a capitalist world continued to operate with the same features as in the past.

The nationalist critique of export-promotion development was also flawed. It was said that exporting imposed excessive fluctuations on a backward economy, reflecting changes in overseas demand. This was true for all economies in the early 1930s, particularly for raw-material exporting countries, but, as we have seen, it was not true of the newly industrializing countries in the 1970s. On the contrary, the availability of diversified external markets allowed much greater stability in growth to exporting countries since they could move goods from declining to expanding markets. A higher ratio of exports to gross national product for newly industrializing countries seemed to correlate with *reduced* economic fluctuations.

Export dependence, it was also said, produced political dependence – the government of a backward country found itself the victim of the government of its major market. This was true if there was only one market and that market could be controlled by the government. But in an increasingly integrated world this was rarely the case. There were many markets, there was competition between buyers, and a mass of contrary interests separated governments and companies. The failure of most efforts by the governments of more developed countries to make economic boycotts or embargoes work showed how limited was their power to control the world market.

If countries became dependent upon exporting, it was also said, the advanced powers would sooner or later close their markets to imports. The case had a surface plausibility in the 1930s, the heyday of the identity between private capital and governments in more developed countries, but decreasingly so after 1950. In any case, there was not one market that could actually be closed, and it was inconceivable that the more developed countries could collaborate sufficiently to close all markets. In the seventies, in any case, the fastest growing markets were in the newly industrializing countries and the oil-producing countries. If all else failed, the world black economy had an insatiable appetite for goods outside the purview of official agencies.

It was not clear, in any case, that governments still retained sufficient power to control imports. They could inflict great damage in particular fields for short periods, but that was usually in part at their own cost (or rather the cost of their citizens) and within narrow limits. A Multi Fibre Arrangement, the most notorious set of restrictions governing a sector of international trade, prompted garment exporters to move their output into new lines or higher-value lines, to shift production to countries with unfilled quotas or to the more developed countries (or to organize part processing in many places), or to increase their subcontract work for companies located in more developed countries where such work escaped the regulations of the arrangement (as was the case in the European Common Market). In the end, it was quite unclear what had occurred. In other trades, too, great ingenuity went into defeating protectionism: when the import of leather shoes was regulated in the United States, they reappeared as imported uppers and soles, and then, when these too were regulated, as other leather goods, and so on; each time, the exporters stayed one jump ahead of the regulators. As we have noted, Japanese steel passed through the bleaching bath of Sweden to defeat West German restrictions. And if the legal channels failed, there was, it seemed, a growing volume of illegal movements; in July 1984, for example, a United States customs official alleged to a Congressional committee that nearly $20 bn worth of 'illegally shipped' textile and garment products had entered the United States in the preceding nine months. And if all else failed, capital itself moved.

Nor were the motives of the participants at all clear. Companies did not ship their profits to the United States unless the tax regulations were favourable. National loyalty could not be relied upon to ensure an identity of interest between the United States government and US-registered companies. Businesses manufacturing in the United States needed access to the cheapest inputs to production if they were to compete with foreign producers, whether in the United States market or abroad. It was General Motors and Ford who opposed in Congress a Bill to enforce a rule that a given proportion of the value of vehicles sold domestically should be manufactured there; they opposed it because they needed to import cheap components to ward off Japanese companies. Companies were thus equivocal – shoe-makers pressed for an embargo on imports, but shoe retailers pressed for an expansion of imports. Nor were governments any more clear, tacking between spasms of partial protection, when elections required some nationalism, and loud rhetoric about free trade. But all the time, the structure of the integrating world system was moving in the direction of free trade.

The case of the development economists of the 1950s was probably less of an obstacle to change than were vested interests. And the forces promoting liberalization were less theoretical arguments than *ad hoc* observations. Thus, the maintenance of an overvalued exchange rate to cheapen key imports for industrialization and also overseas borrowing, it was noted, also had the effect of pushing buyers to purchase imports rather than domestic substitutes. The maintenance of low interest rates, a 'cheap money policy', to encourage industrial investment, in fact encouraged excessive investment and capital-intensive production,[5] often with excess capacity – investment was wasted, and the number of jobs created was smaller than it might otherwise have been.

Some of these effects were exaggerated when governments built 'upstream' manufacturing, heavy industry. Here the capital intensity was high and often the optimum scale of plant was well beyond the size of the domestic market. Heavy industry – the 'commanding heights' or 'strategic sectors' of an economy, as they were called – exercised a particular fascination for planners and politicians. Its introduction supposedly symbolized the arrival of a fully developed and self-reliant economy, with a capacity to make the machines which made machines. In practice, heavy industry drew disproportionately on national savings to create an output over a relatively long period and usually at very high cost. If the prices were subsidized, the industries became a permanent drain on government funds. If they were not, the high costs were offloaded on downstream manufacturing, increasing their costs. Without competition from imports, the heavy industries tended to become technically obsolescent; not only did the prices of home and overseas heavy industrial goods diverge, their efficiency and their running costs also diverged. (Some observers attributed the slow growth of both China and India in the sixties and seventies to the very heavy burden of their respective heavy-industrial programmes.)[6] Heavy industry also made economies vulnerable in slump. As we have seen, five of the six economies we examined in Chapters 2 and 3 experienced severe strain through the combination of world slump and their respective heavy-industrial programmes.

There were other problems which we have noted earlier – the relative under-investment in agriculture, which was said to produce an underpricing of agricultural goods in comparison to industrial goods, and thus outmigration from rural areas. Subsidies to encourage exports produced expansion of commercial crops at the expense of basic foodstuffs, a process which culminated in a growing volume of imports of foodstuffs.

Limiting competition by excluding imports could not only lead to monopoly pricing and poor quality of local output, but also a tendency for local technology to stagnate. A number of estimates of the costs of protection were formulated. For example, Bergson assessed the costs of Brazilian import controls in 1967 as equal to between 8 and 10 per cent of the gross national product (arising from the misallocation of investment, monopoly profits and avoidable higher costs).[7] In a more dramatic presentation, Robert McNamara, then President of the World Bank, alleged that in 1965 the less developed countries spent $2.1 bn of domestic resources to manufacture automotive parts worth, on the world market, $800 m dollars; the 'loss' of $1.3 bn was roughly equal to World Bank lending in the preceding twenty-three years.[8] As we have seen earlier, in other cases goods manufactured under protection had a 'negative value added' – the world market price of the imported inputs was greater than the price at which the output could be sold; this was concealed by the bureaucratic structure of controls.

The discretionary power available to public officials in protecting particular companies and sectors inevitably tended to encourage corruption, 'to create', as Myrdal put it in the fifties, 'tumours of partiality and corruption in the very centre of the administration'.[9] But even without this feature, creating an industrial structure solely on the basis of the domestic market entailed producing an industrial output which exactly matched the existing distribution of income, which usually meant a bundle of retail goods strongly skewed towards upper-income consumption. Thus, as with basic foodstuffs in agriculture, mass consumption was sacrificed to the redistribution of profits towards industry.

Import controls, in essence, created a domestic monopoly for local producers. With a bias towards industry in general and selected sectors in particular, this redistributed resources from consumption and non-priority sectors to the favoured few. It was a mechanism for forcing the pace of accumulation in the selected sectors at the cost of the rest of the economy, and it is in those terms that it should be judged. For the orthodox school of economic theory allowed protection for 'infant industries' – industries just starting and unable initially to compete, but generalized import substitution protected all industries, most of which were, in relative terms, in less developed countries, infant. And for many, it worked. In the Brazil of the thirties, a surge of national growth in conditions of world stagnation seemed miraculous. Ambitions soared; policy seemed to make the difference between slump and boom. Governments were astonished and swiftly developed 'delusions of economic invulnerability fostered by the surprising early successes and rapid penetration of industry into a supposedly hostile environment'.[10] But the process could be checked with equal speed, as seemed to occur in Brazil in the early sixties. One commentator inferred – 'industries have moved rapidly from high profits and growth to precocious maturity, at which point they fall back to monopolistic quiescence with lower profit rates, reduced levels of investment and ageing plant and equipment'.[11] In fact, the judgement was premature, for there was still the great burst of growth of the Brazilian miracle to come. None the less, for a given historical period and for given countries, the strategy did work – it built industrial capacity and trained labour forces in industrial skills with great speed. It created the potential for an internationally competitive manufacturing sector. It is not clear that that potential could have been created by other methods in the sort of conditions prevailing and in the countries concerned. But that is not to say the same thing would work at other times.

The world of the 1980s is qualitatively different from that of the 1930s. Then the division of labour between manufacturing centres and primary-commodity-producing peripheries, as well as the political sway of multinational empires, enforced measures of economic isolation on the great economic blocs – the dollar, franc, sterling, mark and yen areas – and particular countries. Today, these simple divisions have disappeared. The impact of slump has been not to recreate the old empires, nor regional trading blocks, but rather to increase the integration of a multitude of independent powers. It is this emergence of a new set of geographical relationships underlying a new world system of production that has left the old import-substitution strategy on one side.

The Neoclassical Case

Neoclassical economists did not in general accept that the problems of less developed countries required a separate theoretical approach; they denied the relevance, validity or indeed possibility of a 'development economics'. The same economic logic was equally applicable in all fields. In the debate over the most efficient methods of economic development, as we have seen, the neoclassical case was increasingly influential, even among those who had earlier been its firmest opponents. This influence tended to be greatest in specific issues of policy, rather than in the general position, for in the latter it required more obvious distortions of reality to ensure consistency. We have noted the picture which was presented of the development of the Gang of Four which omitted the decisive and discriminatory role of the state and the public sector, and placed all emphasis on changes in policy.[12] Time, place and circumstance, the commodity composition of output at the starting-point of development and changes in external markets, all disappear. Thus, Professor I. M. D. Little boldly asserts of the Gang of Four that 'the success is almost entirely due to good policies and the ability of the people – scarcely at all to favourable circumstances or a good start'.[13] He goes on to list a series of favourable domestic factors, but no external ones. The conclusion is that any government in a less developed country is complete master of its fate; or in an analogous earlier form, the poor are poor only because of their own deficiencies; the rich man is rich solely because of his merits, and not his good fortune.

Such a case is essentially a moral one rather than a conclusion from scientific inquiry and, as such, inhibits the search for contrary cases. There was relatively little interest in the failures – only some countries, some companies and some commodities were at stake, and only in some periods of the past. Why did Hong Kong not industrialize before the fifties if growth was inevitable with the right form of governance? How did Australia – like Brazil and Mexico – maintain rapid growth over a long period behind high protectionist walls? Rather casually, Little observed that Australia was rich, unlike less developed countries,[14] which suggested export promotion was relevant only for poor countries. How did Brazil and Mexico not 'exhaust' import substitution, when South Korea was supposed to have done so in a mere five years? And what was to be made of Chile combining the most generalized liberalization with stagnation?

In any case, empirically the association of exports and economic growth varied widely. Countries which were more advanced – more industrialized – benefited most from liberalization. The relationship was virtually non-existent for the poorest countries.[15] But neoclassical economics could not accept differences between countries any more easily than it accepted the importance of the changing opportunities provided in different periods of historical time. The poorest countries could be offered only the same moral adjurations as were offered by the Victorians to their poor.

The failure to acknowledge the role of the state in the growth of the newly industrializing countries was symbolized in the neoclassical view of planning. We have noted earlier Little's irritation with planning in Taiwan. Bela Belassa – if correctly reported – took an even more curious position:

Experience indicates that countries which have not planned have had a much better economic performance than those that have relied on planning methods. Countries that have [not] planned include Taiwan, Korea, Israel, as well as Brazil; India has planned. Whereas the first group reached rapid rates of economic growth, relying largely on private initiative, in India, investment, production and import controls applied in the process of planning have constrained not only the growth of the private sector but also the growth of the entire national economy.[16]

Yet Belassa's non-planners, Taiwan, Korea, Israel and Brazil, did indeed plan, and did *not* rely 'largely' on private initiative. We must suppose that the Soviet Union did not grow swiftly in the 1930s, nor China in the first Five Year Plan period, nor Korea in the sixties. And presumably, contrary to all appearances, Chile, Uruguay and Argentina all grew swiftly in the seventies. The Cold War has overwhelmed common sense.

The alternative to planning was to seek to make individual projects or sectors efficient, on the assumption that if the prices were 'right' and markets competitive, the parts of the economy would spontaneously and mutually adjust to each other. Attempts to change the structure of the economy were doomed to increase the inefficiency of the economy, so that any gains would be more than nullified by the losses. The whole endeavour to force change was doomed, much as conservatives had always maintained concerning radical social intervention: the world was the best possible. Yet the specific criticisms of the operation of import-substitution policies did not support this position of conservatism; and the historical record, not least in the case of the Gang of Four, pointed in the opposite direction: governments had intervened and, from the perspective of the political leaders concerned, with considerable success.

As we have noted earlier, 'right prices' were required in order to permit the revelation of national comparative advantages. Although entrepreneurial flair might be accepted as a comparative advantage, this could hardly be stretched to include government efforts to use their privileged position in the market to create, as the South Koreans had done, a world-class shipbuilding industry.[17] The use of public muscle against the market was not consistent with allowing the market's invisible hand to find appropriate specializations from the correctly priced scarcities and abundances. If the South Korean government was to be admitted as an entrepreneur, almost anything was justified within the terms of the theory, including the value of monopoly. The state's monopoly of the use of power permitted it to transfer resources between lines of production and between consumption and production, apparently without regard to cost – governments seemed to have the power to guarantee success and avoid the costs of failure.

There were equal difficulties over the comparative advantage of cheap labour. For this might be the result, not of 'right prices' being charged – wages which reflected world scarcity or the abundance of local labour – so much as a particularly nasty government utilizing its monopoly of power to imprison or eliminate a sufficient number of potential or actual rebels to terrify all the rest into accepting wages and conditions inferior to those the unrestricted market might establish. The neoclassical economists were hypersensitive to the deleterious effects on markets of workers combining to try to protect wages and conditions, but cavalier when it came to governments interfering in labour markets to enforce low wages, regardless of whether these reflected real scarcities or the number of police truncheons.

The neoclassical emphasis on the importance of policy still omitted recognition of the decisive role of the public sector in all the newly industrializing countries regardless of the political persuasion of the regimes concerned. There was also a surprising myopia concerning the actual ends of government policy. I. M. D. Little acknowledged that governments were often corrupt and frequently had little interest in the welfare of their citizens, yet his arguments turn upon the assumption that governments can be persuaded to change policy if it can be shown that popular welfare could thereby be enhanced. But if a government's main preoccupation was the development of military capacity, then efficiency in the achievement of this purpose might or might not allow for welfare ends to be pursued. Import-substitution strategies might well be successful in the light of this consideration, even when unsuccessful relative to the ends favoured by neoclassical economists.

The inconsistencies of the neoclassical case arose from a prior political commitment just as much as did those of the development economists. Indeed, it was difficult to imagine a case which did not represent such a political position. If the development economists – like protagonists of import-substitution strategies – presented a case embodying the short- and medium-term interests of national capital (whether state or private) in countries which were backward, but had some industrial capacity, the neoclassical case stood four-square with the hypothetical interests of a world capital, the major part of which had powerful links with the more developed countries. In social terms, the dispute appeared to be between different segments of capital, not between the forces of reaction and progress, capitalism and socialism, or capital and labour.

The Missing Character

We are far from being able to offer a solid explanation of why, at a given moment in history and not before, a group of countries was able, through the rapid expansion of manufactured exports, to accelerate the rate of economic development to extraordinarily high levels. But, in this respect, the problem is no greater than that affecting any of the other great economic changes. Indeed, the more important the problem, the more economics is silent on the causes of the phenomenon, the factors governing its behaviour and the means appropriate to dealing with it. The arrival of slump or boom, of long-term growth or stagnation, inflation or persistent high unemployment are all equally lacking authoritative and demonstrated explanation.

Superficially, it seems easier to understand import-substitution industrialization than export expansion. In the first, the active forces appear to be domestic, more easily identifiable and subject to public influence. Long-term changes in exports open the stage to a world economy where the connections are much less self-evident, and there is no single public influence. One might explain particular commodities from particular countries to particular markets, but the aggregate trend remains as elusive as the movement of the stars.

None the less, some of the elements can be enumerated. For example, the great efforts made by many governments in less developed countries since the Second World War to develop the basic infrastructure and an educated labour force must have narrowed the gap slightly between more and less developed countries in terms of some of the conditions for modern production. The improvements made are concentrated in particular localities – in the big cities, industrial estates, export-processing zones, etc. – so that the narrowing of differences will be much greater than the aggregate national figures suggest. Furthermore, the new investment is frequently in the most modern facilities, when the more developed countries are still utilizing older infrastructure.

As a surrogate indication of the development of infrastructure (power, water, drainage, highways, sea- and air-transport terminals, etc.), take the figures for energy consumption per head of the population (bearing in mind the higher rates of growth of population of the less developed countries). In the twenty years to 1980, energy consumption in low-income countries increased from 218 (kilogrammes of coal equivalent) to 368, a 68 per cent increase. For middle-income countries, the equivalent figures were 462 and 987, a rough doubling of energy availability. Of course, the industrial-market economies (the more developed countries) remained far in advance – their consumption increased from 4,540 to 7,495, a 65 per cent increase; proportionately, the low-income countries increased from 4.8 to 4.9 per cent of the more developed countries' energy increase, the middle-income countries from 10.2 to 13.2 per cent. But, to repeat, the gap is much less than this when one takes account of the geographical concentration of the infrastructure and its modernity. For example, it is said that the telephone system of Brazil is more advanced than that of the United States, because it was introduced more recently as a complete system (whereas in the United States, no complete new system can be introduced because of the elaborate system already in place).

Second, standards of physical health in less developed countries have improved remarkably. Take, for example, the average expectation of life at birth (in years) between 1950 and 1979. They rose from 43 to 58 in less developed countries (ranging from 35–46 for low-income Africa to 51–64 for middle-income Latin America). Or take the decline in infant mortality (deaths per thousand children aged one to four years) from 28 to 12 (ranging from low-income Africa (from 44 to 27) to middle-income Latin America (from 23 to 8)). Furthermore, just as infrastructure is heavily concentrated, so also are the improvements in health – life expectancy among the better-off in less developed countries is now hardly different from the average in the more developed countries. For the urban working class, physical health is a precondition for attaining modern standards of labour productivity.

Education is also exceptionally important for high productivity in industry. Here the changes have been no less dramatic. The literacy rate for all the less developed countries rose from 33 to 56 per cent between 1950 and 1979 (with a low of from 17 to 29 and a high of from 57 to 78). The proportion of the relevant age groups attending secondary schools rose from 18 to 29 per cent (1960 to 1980), and in middle-income countries, from 14 to 39 per cent. Those in higher education increased from 2 to 4 per cent (from 3 to 11 per cent in the middle-income countries).

These were quite extraordinary changes in both some of the conditions of production (infrastructure) and the conditions for attaining high levels of labour productivity (physical health, education). There were also major direct efforts to industrialize, with investment programmes over long periods to increase the industrial inputs to manufacturing. And governments competed with increasing dedication to attract private industrial investment – with incentives, tax reliefs, cheap raw materials and many other concessions. In many of the less developed countries there was also a very substantial increase in domestic savings. In sum, for a major part of the less developed world there was a sustained effort to launch economic development which, in turn, had the effect of reducing the differences in the conditions for manufacture between localities in less and more developed countries.

All these were factors which could be influenced, to a greater or lesser extent, by governments in the less developed countries. But there were other important changes in the world at large. For example, the costs of transport and communications declined rapidly throughout the post-war period. Major investments in containerizing docks, developing new airfields and creating modern networks of motorways combined with changes in the technology of transport equipment and the declining weight of the goods moved to render the costs of movement a decreasing element in the price of goods. As movement became cheaper, the range of possible locations for production widened.

There have also been important and well-known changes in the conditions of international trade. From the autarkies of the 1940s, the more developed countries have increasingly liberalized their trading and monetary relationships. This has led to the integration of the industrialized countries with new patterns of interdependent specialization, creating, in an important sense, a single world manufacturing system located in many countries.[18] Less developed countries, or rather, that minority with the capacity to export manufactured goods, have been incidental beneficiaries of the liberalization, and have secured special rights through bilateral trade treaties, the general system of trade preferences, and special arrangements to admit imports to more developed countries that have been part-processed abroad.

However, all these factors, whether internal or external to less developed countries, were 'permissive' – that is, they would considerably facilitate the expansion of manufactured exports, but would not themselves produce it. If companies and buyers in more developed countries had not been impelled by the changing structure of the world market to seek lower-cost purchases (or lower-cost locations for manufacture) in new countries, the permissive factors would not have supplied the missing demand. Efforts by companies and governments in more developed countries to prevent the transfer of technology or manufacturing to the less developed were overwhelmed by the sheer scale of market demand. Once the buyers had stimulated the process, supply was reshaped – new companies learned skills and turned them to new commodities; a process that went far beyond its modest starting-point and could no longer be easily controlled, gripped many of the newly industrializing countries.

The historical moment when this process seems to have begun – in the late fifties and early sixties – coincided with the development of severe labour shortages in Western Europe. There, the labour markets were swiftly diverting workers from agriculture, attracting large numbers of women into paid employment and drawing in workers from abroad. Gender and nationality weakened before the scale of labour demand. The geographical extent of the European labour market widened – from the core of the Common Market to its periphery (in Italy) and beyond (to Spain, Portugal, Algeria, Yugoslavia, Turkey, Finland, and thence to the Middle East and West Africa). The more highly skilled the worker, the more extensive the geographical catchment area, to the point where the demand for highly skilled people – for example, doctors, engineers, airline pilots – came to encompass a global supply area. As Europe's demand extended, it came to meet an equally strong demand from North America, with the United States also attracting workers from Europe.

The drawing in of new sources of labour to labour-intensive sectors in the more developed countries – to agriculture, mining, parts of manufacturing (particularly garments, assembly work), domestic services, etc. – appears as part of the same process as the search by buyers and manufacturers from the more developed countries for new sources of cheap products in less developed countries. Initially, this concerned cheap, labour-intensive goods of low weight, of which garments, plastic goods and footwear were pre-eminent examples. Later, microprocessing and electronic goods were added, and, as transport costs declined, heavier engineering commodities.

This moment, at the end of the fifties and the beginning of the sixties, thus appears as the starting-point for a new phase in the perpetual process of the redistribution of manufacturing capacity and the manufacturing labour force, sorting out a new network of specializations. The redistribution abroad was not sufficient to prevent a continuing increase in wages in the more developed countries, and this supported continuing waves of relocation, of geographical dispersal of the manufacturing labour force of the world. By the late sixties, even increasing unemployment in the more developed countries could not check the process. Competition forced companies into the new mould. They were obliged to copy each other to stay competitive. Consultancies developed to advise them; governments became increasingly accurate in

wooing capital investment. New areas of technical ingenuity developed
to marry skill-intensive processes in a number of more developed countries to labour-intensive ones in a number of less developed countries,
organized by a growing supply of international managerial ability and
experience.

Once the complex learning process was mastered – buyers learning
methods to overcome supply problems in less developed countries,
suppliers learning how to relate production to fast-changing overseas
markets, governments learning about the preconditions for swift, reliable and cheap exports, managers learning how to relate diverse supply
points, mixing internal suppliers with subcontractors, and all the time
ensuring the stable quality and price of all parts – it had become part of
the structure of world capitalism and was no longer open to reversal
except at intolerable cost to world capital. Trade in some commodities
could be blocked, but usually only temporarily; there was no world
trade police to ensure that specifications and nationality were not
changed or that forgeries were caught and prevented. Technical changes
could shift locational advantages for particular goods back to more
developed countries, but it does not seem possible that the general process of dispersal and increased specialization could be frustrated.

Part of the education of buyers involved learning to expect that costs
in the new locations would rise after a period, and to move on to other
sites when this happened. The behaviour of buyers influenced each
other, those from Britain and Japan copying each others' new routes.
Those with most foresight cultivated a widening range of local agents
to monitor wage costs and quality performance, warning the overseas
purchaser when conditions were ripe to consider switching purchases
between countries.

It is an unstable process in detail, but highly stable in aggregate – the
locational advantages for particular commodities change swiftly, but
whole sectors disperse slowly. Take, for example, the garment trades –
on the one hand the trend is towards general location of production in
low-wage areas; on the other, technical innovations may make production of particular goods competitive in high-wage areas. Draper
Laboratories of Massachusetts have recently claimed that their automated garment manufacturing machinery will make American workers
(at – then – $5 an hour) competitive in some lines of clothing with
workers in Asia. In Britain, Ross Electronics has recently claimed that

its workers can make low-cost portable radios once more after twenty years of domination of the market by companies in east Asia. Perhaps it is true that only rapidly changing technology in the infant industry of electronic-chip assembly necessitated location in low-wage countries; once the technology becomes stable, automated production can replace labour and companies will then relocate in more developed countries. None of this affects the general trend, for as one commodity is pulled one way, another goes in the reverse direction. It becomes impossible to predict a systematic flow other than dispersal. Certainly, it seems impossible for governments to influence the overall structure, although they may shape particular locations in a process of continual reshuffling.

In sum, the combination of the changes in some localities of the more advanced of the less developed countries, in the nature of manufacturing and in transport systems, provided the context for the dramatic effects of changes in the labour markets of the more developed countries, the first small redistribution that was the ultimate source of the growth of manufacturing exports in the newly industrializing countries. This does not explain why it was the Gang of Four and other countries (such as Israel, South Africa, etc.) which led the way. But this is a less important question since, given the structural change in the world economy, one country or another would sooner or later have followed a similar path. However, it cannot be accidental that the place where the process started, Hong Kong, was alone in being a free-trade area with a relatively unlimited supply of cheap labour and a cadre, the exiled Shanghai textile capitalists and their skilled workers: a formula that combined competence and hunger without a domestic market large enough to absorb the potential output. The tiny open economy could be worked upon freely by world demand without official intervention. The needs of the world and of the merchants and makers of Hong Kong coincided. Once Hong Kong had blazed a trail, its relatives (sometimes the same people) in Taiwan could duplicate the process there, but now with strong state initiative and supervision. Combining the opportunism of Hong Kong with the long-term state planning imperatives of South Korea made possible new miracles of expansion.

These are speculations, but they combine some of the insights of the accounts offered by the neoclassical economists and by the left. The Gang of Four were created by the world economy. Policy and management were, for three of them at least, vital in that process, but without changes in the structure of the global system, their governments on their own could not have achieved that development.

De-industrialization

The growth of the manufacturing output of the newly industrializing countries, rapid as it was, was more an augury for the future than an indication of current substance. The share of global output held by the newly industrializing countries remained, in aggregate, small. Even in those sectors where their exports seemed to have had most effect, it was still small as a proportion of global production. Thus, even in textiles and garments, despite the decline in employment in the more developed countries and the increase in imports, in 1980 they still accounted for 65 per cent of the world output of textiles and 75 per cent of clothing (their shares of employment in these fields were 27 and 39 per cent).

The effects of the exports of the newly industrializing countries were trivial by comparison with those of the changes generated autonomously in the industrial sectors of the more developed countries. They would hardly figure on an historical scale that included such major ruptures as the impact of the coming of railways in Britain, the decline of the steam engine or the mechanization of textile manufacture or agriculture. In fact, the industrialization of the newly industrializing countries actually contributed to the growth of the more developed countries – the increase in their demand for machinery imports far outweighed the effects of their increased exports.

Industrial capitalism has always survived through ceaseless adaptation. Thousands of piecemeal innovations effect a continuing transformation of manufacturing output and so produce continuing changes in the labour force. There is scarcely a product where the technical specifications remain constant over even half a decade. As the commodity changes, the process of production is changed and the workforce is continually redistributed between activities within and between workplaces. It could not be otherwise in competitive capitalism. That background is far more turbulent than anything produced by the newly industrializing countries. In the twenty years in which the exports of the newly industrializing countries to the United States grew with great speed, the United States economy added twenty million new jobs (1950 to 1970), and then twenty million more in half the time (1970 to 1980), and then one and a half million in the first four years of the eighties. If imports destroyed jobs, the North American labour market had enormous capacity to more than compensate for the losses. In fact, it was not imports that destroyed jobs, but rationalization and slump.

Regardless of imports from newly industrializing countries, the economic structure of the more developed countries was in a process of major change – or rather, the change was persistent and was approaching a point where basic concepts needed to be revised. For the very idea of an 'industrialized' country was under threat. Take for example, a high-growth more developed country, Japan. Between 1970 and 1983, major industrial sectors of the economy declined – chemicals (− 20 per cent); steel (− 20 per cent, with − 40 per cent in employment); shipbuilding (− 25 per cent, and − 30 per cent in jobs); textiles (− 30 and − 50 per cent); coal (− 60 and − 75 per cent); and aluminium (− 90 and − 75 per cent). It was expected that these sectors would continue to decline for the foreseeable future, and that as a result, imports would increase to replace what was manufactured locally. But unemployment did not increase commensurately, given the strong growth of jobs in services. Japan was 'de-industrializing'.

From the 1970s, all the more developed countries experienced to some extent a decline in the proportion of the workforce engaged in manufacturing. It was not necessarily also a decline in the proportion of the national product contributed by manufacturing, although that also occurred. The jobs lost in the decade of slump and stagnation from 1974 were disproportionately concentrated in manufacturing (and especially in heavy industry), and the new jobs created were concentrated in services. De-industrialization was not the result of increased imports, and governments which limited imports on the pretence that it was, generally produced perverse effects on their economies.[19] De-industrialization was not the source of unemployment – it should be blamed rather on slump and a failure to generate a sufficient number of new jobs to match the growth of the labour force; de-industrialization *per se* was not the problem, although it provided the occasion for exaggerated discussion[20] and the creation of many scapegoats. There seemed to be no particular reason why a predominantly servicing economy should not provide sufficient employment as easily as a predominantly industrial one if it were possible to overcome slump.

De-industrialization concealed a common process involving both the more developed and the newly industrializing: increased specialization. The manufactured exports of the United States did not cease with the growth of services, but became increasingly concentrated in certain sectors (capital goods, chemicals, agricultural products, services), with particular strength in goods of high technology and those which used raw materials most intensively (while labour- and capital-intensive exports were declining). In an integrated world, comparative advantages cast each country in a specialized role, and de-industrialization was not so much the decline of industry as the decline in those sectors in the more developed countries that had little long-term viability. The process was the result of the decline in the peculiar monopoly of production in all fields that the more developed countries had held in the past.

Doubts remained. It seemed to defy common sense to suggest that all or even many less developed countries could expand their exports indefinitely without economic disaster in the more developed. There was no immediate prospect of such a dramatic change, and no prospect of it at all without a growth of world incomes capable of absorbing the increased production. From the standpoint of the less developed, the targets set for the growth of manufactured exports seemed heroic, but relative to the massive domination of world manufacturing by the more developed countries the targets were small. If world capitalism resumed its growth, there would be no difficulty in absorbing the high estimates of exports. There was no reason to expect these changes to be larger than those absorbed in the past – for example, the displacement of British manufacturing by that of the United States and Germany in the 1890s. Britain's relative position in manufacturing has declined consistently since that time, yet more people were employed, at higher incomes, in Britain in the 1980s than ever before (despite higher levels of long-term unemployment).

Thus, the exports of the newly industrializing countries, harbingers of a new manufacturing world order, were not the products of interlopers, but an integral part of the new structure, which was emerging, a global industrial system. Those exports could not be prevented, short of self-destruction. The periodic outcries against imports in the more developed countries attacked symptoms of change (and trivial ones at that), which were as irrelevant as the agricultural machines broken by the Luddites. It suited important political interests to divert attention from slump to the foreigner. President Reagan, for example, sought to re-establish the military superiority of the United States through rearmament, and to do so without increasing taxes. The results, high interest rates and a high-value dollar, made imports to the United States unusually cheap. It suited everybody to blame the foreigners and their wretched manufactures for the difficulties, rather than presidential warmongering. Similarly, it suited employers driven to lay-offs by their own new investments, made to maximize profits, to attribute the misery of unemployment to faceless foreigners. Without foreigners, it would have been necessary to invent them.

Import-substitution industrialization strategies were the offspring of world slump, as well as attempts to overcome slump. Their successes showed that, contrary to the prescriptions of neoclassical economists, governments could intervene in the process of capital accumulation by changing the relationship between the domestic market and the external economic environment. But, despite the vision of its protagonists, the strategies were not general prescriptions for development. Only some large countries could pursue such policies, and only for limited periods of time in given historical circumstances. Sooner or later, if growth were to continue, the domestic accumulation process – whether wholly or partially in the hands of the state – would have to be reintegrated in the world process.

With the benefit of hindsight, we can see that the strategies were applicable generally for a given period, roughly from 1930 to the late fifties. Their validity – despite the Brazilian miracle of the late sixties – came increasingly into question towards the end of this period as a new structure emerged in the world. These strategies were mechanisms in the larger and more industrialized poor countries to make a forced march to manufacturing capacity by manipulating the domestic terms of trade to grant a monopoly to particular industrialists. But the forced march was only a prelude to rejoining the world system on terms laid down by the system itself. The participants thought otherwise; the prelude to reintegration was identified as a rupture in the international division of labour (the economic dimension of a world dominated by imperialist states), a striking-out on an entirely new and heroic path to create a fully independent national economy. Even when the slump of the early eighties forced integration upon the reluctant, many still clung to the old vision. But realities were driving the tide in the opposite direction. Slump turned import substituters into export promoters, and export promoters into importers. There were still some governments that succeeded in protecting themselves against the pressures, partly because they had not enjoyed the great surge of growth in the sixties. The Soviet Union had made many changes relative to external markets, but it still clung to its relative isolation (sharing, however, vicariously in the more daring adventures of its East European associates).

The same was true of some of the less developed countries. Many of the low-income countries had no capacity to break away from their old role of exporting low-value agricultural goods. In much of Africa, incomes fell throughout the seventies. It was thought possible that by the end of the eighties, incomes per head there might be lower than in 1960. For television watchers, the faces of famine victims showed the cost of these bare statistics. The newly industrializing countries and the majority of the low-income countries have as little in common with each other as they had with the more developed countries. There was no longer a Third World. In so far as there had ever been, outside conference rhetoric, a common view and a common interest, it existed no longer. Nor did it help to identify these different 'Worlds' with different levels of poverty, saying there was now a Fourth World of the very poor. The very poor – like the very rich – existed everywhere, in all 'Worlds', and the responsibility for sustaining or changing poverty lay, not with different worlds, but with the one world of reality. The old vision that had united the less developed countries, a vision of a common process of national economic development that would support an ethic of humanity and peace, had become utopian. The less developed countries could grow now only on the same basis as the more developed countries, by contributing to a common world product.

6 = States and Economic Development

The process of accelerated economic growth in the newly industrializing countries appears to be everywhere associated with the expansion of the public sector and the role of the state. It has not been 'free enterprise' nor multinational capital which has led the process, but the deliberate and persistent efforts of governments. Foreign companies appear as formally invited – and often barely tolerated – guests at a feast organized, supplied and supervised by Ministers; not infrequently, the guests have been expropriated in the midst of the festivities.

This accelerated economic growth – whether of the type in Brazil (interaction between the will of the state and a domestic market, structured by a degree of income inequality sufficient to create a mass market for consumer durables) or of the type in South Korea (interaction between the will of the state and external markets) – is, as we have noted, just as much a triumph of state capitalism as are the achievements of the first Five Year Plans in the Soviet Union or the People's Republic of China. Neither type is, as many capitalists believed, a revival of an authentic private capitalism, or, if it is, the theory of private capitalism is in substantial error. There is only one tiny monument to the ancient virtues of *laissez faire*: Hong Kong. In its very marginality, it confirms the general thesis: in the period since the Second World War, sustained economic development has been part and parcel of the drive of the state to develop national power.

However, the growth of state power appears to be common both to those countries which grew swiftly and to those which did not, so that state power alone is not the source of growth. If this were so, all less developed countries would be growing swiftly. In fact, the power of the state has also grown in slow-growth countries. Take, for example, India: in the seventies, of the 101 largest companies (by value of assets), thirty were state-owned (including the nine largest), covering 60 per cent of the total assets. Tatas, the largest private group, with nine of the 101, had total combined assets worth under half that of the largest public corporation, Hindustan Steel. Of the 101, twenty-seven were registered as foreign-owned. The distinction between public and private was somewhat blurred for Indian private companies; through joint ventures and government credit, about 30 per cent of the equity of the three largest private companies was held by the government (and if all government loans were converted to equity, the public share would rise to 60 per cent).

Furthermore, the growth of the public sector seemed to be limited only by the liquidation of the private, and to cover all sectors of the economy (see Table 7). The growth was remarkable and, despite impressions to the contrary among businessmen, flowed from no ideological source nor from a strategy of economic development. In part, it reflected desperation, the use of the public sector as a hospital for 'sick industries' (as they were called). The growth of the public sector paralleled that of the bureaucracy of the state itself – when, in the thirty years to 1980, the growth of the gross domestic product averaged 3.6 per cent annually, 'Public administration and defence' grew by 6.9 per cent (and in the final decade, by 8.2 per cent).

Despite some impressions to the contrary, the Indian process was not the same as that in the more developed countries; see Table 8. The

Table 7. *India: Growth of the Public-sector Share of Employment in Organized Industry,* by sector, 1961, 1971 and 1981 (percentage)*[1]

	1961	1971	1981
Agriculture and allied industries	21.2	24.5	35.1
Mining and quarrying	19.0	29.2	86.3
Manufacturing	10.9	16.2	24.9
Construction	71.5	84.0	93.6
Public utilities	84.9	90.1	95.4
Transport and communications	95.6	95.6	98.1
Trade and Commerce	37.0	49.6	64.7
Services	92.5	85.0	85.8
All activities (average)	58.3	60.8	67.7
Absolute totals (millions)	7.05m	10.37m	15.48m

* Establishments employing 25 or more workers; the original figures include estimates of varying reliability and comparability, so the proportions are only rough approximations.

Table 8. *Employment Measures of the Size of the Public Sector, Selected Countries, 1980*[2]

	Number of public-sector employees per 1,000 population	Percentage share of non-agricultural labour force in the public sector	Public-sector wages as a percentage of national income
Jamaica	29	12	16
South Korea	27	10	16
Argentina	20	6	5
Kenya	20	28	11
Egypt	12	9	9
India	5	20	3
Belgium	49	19	9
Britain	41	10	9
Austria	39	10	3
United States	20	3	4
West Germany	11	2	3
Japan	10	1	3

Indian public sector appears on two of the measures in the table as among the smallest in this selection. The 'non-agricultural labour force' of the second column is the formal sector, and therefore a gross underestimate of the reality; a high proportion here is most misleading. More generally, there is little consistency in the table, which underlines the great variety of local peculiarities involved in the relative weight of the public sector. Furthermore, comparisons are most difficult. For example, the unusual size of the state in the first three more developed countries (lower half of the table) as measured against the size of population, disappears in the second column (where the very small size of the non-agricultural public-sector labour force becomes important). The final column suggests that the more developed countries generally have smaller public sectors than the less developed countries when compared to the size of the national income. A historical series might show that the size of the state declines proportionately by this measure as a country develops (excluding the centrally planned economies, that is).

The 'state' is not one standard thing in all countries, and even if it

were, 'countries' are not uniform. The public sector includes very different elements, products of peculiar histories, as well as items that change
with the phases of national economic development and different periods
of world history. There is no single prototype. In the twentieth century,
the government of the United States has exercised enormous power
over the rest of the world. In economic terms, Washington on its own
has the capacity to lift the world economy, and although this may be to
only temporary effect, it is not something any other government can do
alone. It makes no sense to speak of 'the state' as if all countries
followed the American model. The majority of governments have little
power over the important elements of their economic environment,
whether they are more developed or less developed (and the powers of
the larger less developed states are considerably more than those of the
smaller more developed states).

The relative power of states has several dimensions – relative to each
other, to their inhabitants and to the global economy. The first shows
considerable variations – the decline of Britain, the rise and decline of
the United States, the rise of West Germany and Japan. The second,
power relative to the inhabitants of the country concerned, seems to
grow continually. But the third appears to be declining in general, and
to decline as individual countries develop. Paradoxically, the power of
governments in economically backward countries is far greater in their
domestic economies than that of governments in economically advanced
countries, even though the latter, in world terms, are far more powerful
than the first. The state's original power derives from the control of
part of the world's population, resources and territory, and of access to
a market. Yet the more industrialized the country, in contemporary
conditions, the more the condition of continued growth of the wealth
and power of the state depends upon permitting the integration of the
local with the world economies, the integration of local capital, labour
and market with the international. The more industrialized the country,
therefore, and the more powerful the state in the world, the less it
controls its local economy. In the 1930s, it was backward Brazil that
could shake off slump, not advanced United States.

We have already slipped back into the error of speaking of 'states',
despite all caveats. We shall continue to do so in order to simplify
issues, without repeating the vital reservations and qualifications
every time. Here, 'state' implies the combined entity of government,

central and local administrations, and the public sector; not, as it occurs in some traditional contexts, the entirety of a country in its political or official guise, nor, as in others, merely government.

Economic Development

Once rulers come into contact with each other through trade or warfare, they are obliged to demarcate their territories and the populations which owe them allegiance. When the European states extended their military powers in support of their commercial activities, other rulers were obliged to copy the form of power of the Europeans in order to defend themselves and also formed states. States, then, come to constitute a system of competitive agencies, each alone or in a group of allies, striving to expand in political, military and economic terms at the expense of its rivals, or at least to ward off the threats of other states. The competition forces, to a greater or lesser degree, measures of uniformity upon the competitors; if one government acquires a new and more powerful weapon, its nearest rivals are obliged to follow suit in order to defend themselves.

Once industry becomes part of national power (both in terms of the wealth it brings to a government and in terms of direct control of the production of weapons and military equipment), all governments are under some pressure to industrialize in order to compete. Thus, the motivation for national industrialization (as opposed to the simple making of profits from industrial activities) is always necessarily a governmental one, not a private capitalist one. There is a direct connection between the imperatives forced upon states by a competitive environment, the governmental efforts to industrialize, the relative domestic growth of state power and the form of forced industrial growth, control of borders, imports and exchange rates (elements central to governmental powers). The connection is even stronger where heavy industry is involved. Not only does this usually require state investment to launch – for the potential rate of private profit is initially too low to induce investment – but also states usually seek to control heavy industry directly, on the assumption that it is of strategic significance (both through its leverage over the rest of the economy and its role in military production).

These points can be abundantly illustrated from the history of industrialization. The insecurity in Europe in the seventeenth and eighteenth centuries produced the first efforts at systematically stimulating economic development. In France, under Colbert, or Portugal, under Ericeira or Pombal, for example, the control of imports was a key element in attempts to increase national investment. In Britain, as Marx notes, at the end of the seventeenth century, the key elements – the colonial system, the national debt, the form of taxation, and protectionism – had been brought into alignment to force growth: 'These methods depend in part upon brute force, for example, the colonial system. But they all employ the power of the state, the concentrated and organized force of society, to hasten, hothouse fashion, the process of transformation of the feudal mode of production into the capitalist mode, and to shorten the transition.'[3]

Government military ambitions – whether expansionist or defensive – were intimately interwoven with the striving for development. The threat of foreign conquest or domination also gave the government the justification for demanding special efforts of the population, for diverting resources from consumption to investment. Already in the eighteenth century, the militarily inspired need for industrialization had profound effects on the metallurgical and chemical industries, shipbuilding and transport; through those industries, influences flowed into the rest of the economy.

Take again the British example. In the period when the industrial revolution took place, between 1688 and 1815, some 127 years, England was engaged in major wars for roughly seventy years.[4] In the closing phases of this period, there were 350,000 men under arms (1801), and half a million in 1811 (that is, between 9 and 10 per cent of the labour force), with many other hundreds of thousands more engaged in keeping them supplied with arms, clothing, foodstuffs and transport. The government demand for goods was accordingly a key factor in reshaping the pattern of national output. For some fifty years (1780 to 1830), government consumption was larger than the value of exports, so that this was a process of government-led, rather than export- or market-led, growth. By 1801, gross public expenditure may have been equal to over a quarter of total national expenditure. The state thus imposed a 'permanent arms economy', which raised and sustained aggregate demand, reshaped the pattern of output, evoked a level of investment higher than would otherwise have been the case, and had the incidental side-effect of flattening the fluctuations that arise from ordinary patterns of growth (an early example of what later became part of Keynesian macroeconomic strategies). The curtailment of manufactured imports from Europe and the increased demand as a result of expanded war production forced an increased utilization of labour and capital; in addition, more waste land was brought into cultivation than ever before (three million acres were the subject of parliamentary Enclosure Acts between 1793 and 1816, and an even larger, although unknown, acreage was privately enclosed). The overall process, a vast speed-up in forced growth, seems also to have involved some redistribution of income between classes, and of resources from consumption to profits – 'the bulk of the increased indirect taxation necessitated by war seems to have been borne by consumers rather than producers, and the new direct taxes touched the mercantile and manufacturing classes relatively lightly'.[5]

This was a classic case, combining general commercial rivalries, political and military insecurity and warfare. There were other cases with less dramatic ingredients. Take for example, Egypt and its temporary disentanglement from both the Ottoman Empire and British and French control. Under Muhammed Ali (1805 to 1849), the government introduced the control of imports as one of the means of industrializing, in order to underpin temporary political autonomy with industrial strength. The government assumed a monopoly of domestic agricultural trade and of all industrial production. Land reforms were introduced as well as a considerable extension of irrigation. Muhammed Ali brought technicians and machinery from Europe to develop factory production; by 1830, the country was manufacturing textiles of cotton, wool, silk and linen, as well as sugar, paper, glass, leather and sulphuric acid and other basic chemicals. A foundry was set up to manufacture arms, and some elements of machine fabrication were created. Total employment in manufacturing has been estimated at 30,000 to 40,000 (in a population of 3 to 4 million). The apparatus of the state must have been enormously expanded by this remarkable effort. In 1841, the experiment was terminated when the Great Powers forced a reduction in the size of Egypt's armed forces and the enforcement of the 1838 Anglo-Turkish Convention, opening all Ottoman possessions (including Egypt) to free trade. The government of Egypt did not again attain sufficient political autonomy – control of tariffs and taxes – to undertake this kind of process of forced growth until after the Second World War.[6]

If the strategies appear very similar to those we have discussed earlier as import-substitution industrialization, some of the social implications were also parallel. Vested interests grew up around tariff controls, turning the response to temporary necessity into a long-term virtue. We noted this phenomenon in the case of Mexico and South Korea, where some sections of business resisted efforts to liberalize imports. During the Napoleonic Wars, the Continental Blockade cut off supplies of British manufactured goods to European markets, a form of involuntary protection which stimulated the manufacture of domestic substitutes. David Landes notes that, when hostilities ceased and British goods became available once more, the return to free trade was not always smooth: 'For every substitute that died quietly . . . another remained as a vested interest . . . [and] mechanized textile manufacturing in central Europe, essentially a product of wartime shortage, made a strong effort to convert monetary advantage into permanent privilege with some success.'[7]

As industrialization spread eastwards in Europe, it tended to re-produce the same features. The extension eastwards of the power of the advanced countries of Western Europe forced the Tsars from the time of Peter the Great, to seek to increase industrialization and to do so by attempting to control imports. From the seventeenth century, Trotsky comments, through policies of deliberate protectionism, 'the state strove with all its power to accelerate the country's natural economic development. New branches of handicraft, machinery, big industrial capital, were, so to say, artificially grafted on the natural economic stem.' He adds, 'Capitalism seemed to be an offspring of the State.'[8]

If military insecurity forced the Tsars to pursue industrialization, later innovations in military technology had important ramifications for the scale and type of industry to be introduced. In the late nineteenth century, the Tsar's decision to expand and modernize the imperial army evoked from Engels the comment:

From the moment warfare became a branch of the *grande industrie* (iron-clad ships, rifled artillery, steel-covered bullets, smokeless powder, etc.), *la grande industrie*, without which all these things cannot be made, became a political necessity. All these things cannot be had without a highly developed metal manufacture. And that manufacture cannot be had without a corresponding development in all other branches of manufacture, especially textiles.[9]

Imperial Russia was less successful in its chosen course than the country that directly threatened it, imperial Germany. Bismarck's Germany was seen in its day as the prototype for forced growth through the control of imports. Once Germany was unified, it became possible to employ national protection throughout the territories of the Reich. For the first time, the policy mix became known as 'socialism', albeit Bismarckian imperial socialism. Cheap North American wheat and cheap British manufactured goods were said to be affecting German production in the 1870s. In 1879 a tariff act was passed covering the import of agricultural goods, iron and other industrial products (including textiles). The tariff levels were low by later standards (and also by the standards of the times as represented in tariffs in the United States, France and Austro-Hungary), but were said to have been sufficient to limit competition and support efforts to cartelize sections of German business in the hands of large banks. Furthermore, the state intervened to support efforts to expand industrial production, particularly in mining and heavy industry. The railways were nationalized, public utilities municipalized, and the banks subjected to greater public supervision. The central drive was Germany's increasingly intense competition with Britain and France in the domination of both Europe and Africa.

All relative latecomers to the process of deliberate national capital accumulation seem to have been required to exaggerate the processes of state intervention. Thus, those samurai who assumed power in Japan after the Meiji Restoration – in response to the threat of the United States and the European powers – deliberately employed the new state to force industrialization (with a particular military bias). In the Soviet Union, the tactics were the most extreme so far, with the state control of all industry and, ultimately, all agricultural activity. Partial Western boycott as well as the drying up of Russia's traditional exports forced the country into defensive import controls, which, in time, would be advanced as a hallowed theoretical principle. In the late twenties, the threat of Western military intervention, 'capitalist encirclement', was the pretext of Stalin's vastly accelerated process of capital accumulation in the first Five Year Plan period. An important component, incidentally, in the theoretical consideration of this process was the manipulation of the terms of exchange between agricultural and industrial goods, the early preoccupation of Prebisch, as we have seen, now explored in the work of Preobrazhensky and Bukharin. The Russian experience also introduced for the first time the prime importance of heavy-industrial development as a means of 'leaping over' the traditional stages of development, also, in practice, giving the state immediate access to heavy-weapons production.

The Russian case provided a theoretical basis for forced development in the hands of the state. Up to that time, the economic thought of the leading capitalist power, Britain, with its emphasis on free trade – which always favoured the most advanced power – had been predominant. Most of the thinkers who had amended this line of thought – among them, Alexander Hamilton (in *Report on Manufactures*, 1791) and Friedrich List (*National System of Political Economy*, 1841) – had, after Adam Smith, done so as a marginal adjustment to free trade, not as an alternative case. Protection was permitted for 'infant industries', manufacture at its beginning; once strong enough to compete, it should be submitted to free competition. The Russian case now produced a fully fledged nationalist alternative based upon the elimination of most imports and the creation of a state demand that forced the expansion of the whole economy. Others, while not embracing such an extreme form, also began to formulate principles that rejected free trade entirely. In the conditions of inter-war slump, a school of economists in Eastern Europe developed parallel to the work of Prebisch in Latin America. Like Latin America, Eastern Europe exported raw materials to its very powerful neighbour, in this case Germany. Market relationships were always strongly interwoven with geopolitical links between one very powerful country and a number of much weaker ones. The slogan of free trade in such circumstances naturally seemed a piece of hypocrisy designed to conceal Great Power domination.

Thus, in the late forties, at the birth of a worldwide effort of many countries to undertake development, the record of practice was already rich, and pointed to the key roles of import controls, state investment (especially in heavy industry) and national planning (whether acknowledged formally or not). What was new was not the practice of many less developed countries, but the fact that there was now some theoretical rationale. Perhaps the theory – or the lateness of the process – exaggerated its features, for, leaving aside the special case of the Soviet

Union, tariffs were set much higher than before, quotas were employed more generally, exchange controls were made tighter and state intervention was more pervasive and comprehensive.

Protectionism in the late forties, however, was no longer a marginal question in a world where general free trade supposedly prevailed, as in the nineteenth century, but was the norm among even the industrialized countries.

More Developed Countries

With the benefit of hindsight, we can see that in Europe, and to a lesser extent North America, the three decades between 1930 and about 1960 are dominated in political thought by preoccupations concerning the economic role of the state, by one or other version of state capitalism. This concern was not with basic capital accumulation, as in countries undertaking industrialization, but with the fighting of two world wars and the worst slump in the history of the world. National autarky was the norm in political conceptions, and implied import controls, exchange control, large public sectors, and state planning. In the British case, in the late forties, the political perspective which united the Labour government and Conservative opposition was temporarily described as 'social democracy', the heart of which was the idea of a state-managed economy, directed along a course of stable growth with full employment; the intellectual underpinnings were derived from the work of Keynes. By the seventies, there was no such confidence in the capacity of governments to control their domestic affairs; the market, the invisible hand of a benevolent economic deity, was everywhere seen as the only means of allocating resources efficiently; economic growth and high employment were seen as the gift of the world market, not of domestic management. For a supposed science, it was a quite remarkable transformation – from the world of Macmillan's *The Middle Way* (1938), Crosland's *The Future of Socialism* or Shonfield's *Modern Capitalism*, to the neoclassical and supply-side economists of President Reagan's government.

Elsewhere I have identified the set of assumptions concerning a state-organized economy in Britain in the 1930s and 1940s as 'corporatism'. Official politics oscillated between a 'pluralist' version, favoured by the

Conservatives, and an '*étatiste*' version, stressed by Labour, but neither side was consistent in excluding the other. The first was characteristic of established business interests, seeking state protection against competition – a simple defensism. The second was associated with new large-scale modern corporations, exercising a monopoly or quasi-monopoly within the domestic market and seeking to use the state to plan the domestic economy on functional lines to secure both steady expansion (with the elimination of the declining competitive sectors) and the integration of national efforts to contest for international markets. Protagonists of the first position tended – although not invariably – to oppose state ownership as reducing the area of their activity; those of the second were either neutral or greeted extended state ownership as underpinning their own activity (by supplying cheap services or raw materials) and increasing the area of large-scale order, so making possible more effective planning. However, both sides agreed that the domestic economy must be organized by the state to reduce or eliminate competition, whether by voluntary trade associations, cartels, statutory monopolies (the Conservatives experimented with such forms in the thirties) or public ownership. Both supported tight import controls as the means to reorganize the domestic economy and protect a domestic monopoly of the market (it was argued that while foreign producers could compete freely in the domestic market, there was no possibility of domestic firms being persuaded to collaborate) and exchange controls to force British finance into investment in Britain.

The overall case was in part a rationalization of existing practice. The British economy that emerged from the First World War was already much more state-organized than it had been earlier, as a result of focusing national efforts on warfare. The Ministry of Munitions was the largest employer in the country, and the state had taken over the railways, directed cotton and jute trading, and laid down the conditions for private business. There was some unwinding of the system after the war, but no proper return to 1914. The railways were returned to private ownership, but in the form of four functionally organized (rather than competitive) divisions. The government subsequently nationalized the electricity generating system, civil aviation and broadcasting. Most of the measures were undertaken by Conservative governments (with some business grumbling), and on technical grounds – to attain a minimum scale of operations, to enhance national prestige, to eliminate 'wasteful' competition. After the great crisis of 1931, the government introduced import and exchange controls, and subsequently, a 'cheap money' policy, subsidies to exports, schemes to reorganize key sectors affected by slump (steel, shipbuilding, cotton, fishing, wheat, etc.). In 1938, a Conservative government even went so far as to try to begin the process of nationalizing the coal industry.[10]

The shift in emphasis between the period before the First World War and the 1930s could hardly have been greater. The model of a national economy had become transformed – from a market to a functional machine directed by the state. An observer of the thirties in the United States detected something similar in the change of terminology there:

For a short period ... New Deal and business spokesmen wrought a virtual revolution in popular symbolism. 'Competition' became 'economic cannibalism', and 'rugged individualists' became 'industrial pirates'. Conservative industrialists, veteran anti-trusters and classical economists were all lumped together and branded 'social Neanderthalers', 'Old Dealers' and 'corporals of disaster'. The time-honoured practice of reducing prices to gain a larger share of the market became 'cut-throat' and 'monopolistic price slashing', and those engaged in this dastardly activity became 'chisellers'. Conversely, monopolistic collusion, price agreements, proration, and cartelization became 'cooperative' or 'associational' activities; and devices that were chiefly designed to eliminate competition bore the euphemistic title, 'codes of fair competition'.[11]

The emerging new order appealed to a very varied audience; at one extreme, there were those of a tradition, often linked to Catholic social thought, which saw in the order of medieval estates an ideal of harmony that had been broken by the Reformation in religious terms and the French Revolution in political terms. The doctrines, expressed most clearly in France by De Maistre, were explicitly counter-revolutionary (where the revolutions were both bourgeois and proletarian). At the other extreme were socialists who saw the new 'industrial feudalism' as deriving from a tradition of the scientific reordering of society to eliminate conflict, a St Simonian and technocratic tradition; much of the charm for some intellectuals of the rhetoric, if not the practice, of Stalin's planned economy arose from a similar source. In sum, it seemed to all anti-capitalists that the age of the market and of private capital was coming to an end; in the future, economies would be directed as if they were machines by trained and professional managers, and the distinction between public and private would disappear.

Some were not convinced of the intellectual validity of the new case, however. In Britain, *The Economist* grumbled:

We are within measurable distance of setting up a new feudal system, with the market, instead of British land, parcelled up among the barons.[12]

The Conservative party programme, the journal argued later, perpetuated

a set of notions that sees its ideal of an economic system in an orderly organization of industries, each ruled feudally from above by the business firms already established in it, linked in associations and confederations, and at the top meeting, on terms of sovereign equality, such other Estates of the Realm as the Bank of England and the Government.[13]

Public opinion in 1939, at the beginning of the Second World War, was very different from that in 1914. The mark II war economy was introduced with great speed and with much greater consistency than the sum of *ad hoc* responses between 1914 and 1918. The economy was converted, at least in theory, to a war-making machine with a single directing centre in the government. The 'war economy' became one of the models of economics, and it was thought that it could be directed not solely at war, but also at poverty or economic development (and indeed the imagery of war was a reiterated theme in Russian planning efforts). And after the war, the *étatiste* speculations of Labour and Conservative radicals of the thirties became the driving force of the Labour government. The initial aim was to create a new order of society through the nationalization of basic industries, business cartelization, a national minimum welfare standard and a national plan. It was the high point of opposition to the 'anarchy of the market', now replaced by the guidance of experts and professional managers.

It was a brief triumph. From 1947, contrary to most anticipations, the world and British economies began to grow with unexpected speed, and did so for longer than anyone could have expected. The controls intended to protect against slump turned to inhibitions of potential growth. Within a remarkably short time assumptions were being reversed, until the government could contemplate, almost without trepidation, the return to the convertibility of sterling.

However, that is a different story. For our purposes, the important point is that in the forties, at the foundation of the aspiration to sustained economic development, the more developed countries had a much more limited notion of free enterprise than that which came later. Roosevelt's New Deal and the Monnet Plan in France were not very far from the planning conceptions that inspired the Indian Second Five Year Plan. Indeed, the colonial era had not been unaffected by the *étatisme* of the thirties – it was colonial governments which undertook the first measures of state planning. The historian of planning in India notes of the 1945 British Government of India *Second Report on Reconstruction Planning* that 'one may look in vain for any fundamental objective or method of the Five Year Plans of the 1950s [in independent India] which is not foreshadowed in this remarkable documentary product of the later days of British rule'.[14] In the late forties, what later became 'development economics' was the dominant mode of thought in both more and less developed countries. What was to be derived from the need to develop was equally derived from the need to defend against slump and to wage war.

There was a junction between the fashionable corporatist speculation of the thirties and the concerns of geopolitical domination and national economic development, between what became the more and the less developed countries. As we have mentioned, this occurred in Eastern Europe, and perhaps, as Harry Johnson once noted, it is not accidental that the postwar founding fathers of development economics were often of East European origin – Mandelbaum, Rosenstein-Rodan, Balogh, Kaldor, etc. A Romanian economist writing in the thirties, Mihail Manoïlesco, made the link between a critique of the externally imposed character of economic backwardness, and the means to overcome it, a functional national economy organized by the state, with controlled imports. His *Le Siècle du corporatisme*[15] argued the case for autarky under state direction of all economic activity, as the method by which countries exporting agricultural products could escape from an exploitative international division of labour (a theory which he called an intellectual swindle created to hide the ways in which rich countries exploit poor ones).

The corporatist tradition, which many in the thirties saw as the most fruitful area for political speculation about the means to overcome the crisis of those times, was buried in the discredit of Italian fascism. Conservatives lost an intellectual pedigree. Thereafter, what had been called corporatism came to be known as socialism in one of those curious ironies with which history deludes us. But *étatiste* corporatism, whether in its Russian or Stalinist guise, or in the milder Keynesianism of Western managed economies, was the tradition of which Third Worldism was a descendant.

The State

In sum, then, the imperatives and the traditions that flowed into Third Worldism are apparent. On the one hand, a climate of political, economic and military insecurity and competition impelled the less developed countries, depending upon their initial endowment, to industrialize. Whether the country was newly free of colonial domination or, as in the Latin American case, had long possessed formal independence, it was the state which alone could exercise leadership in this process, forcing the rest of society (including private capital) to conform. With decolonization, the removal of a former imperial ruling order (as in much of Asia and Africa) vested unprecedented power in the hands of the new states. It is scarcely to be wondered that, as Trotsky observed in tsarist Russia, 'Capitalism seemed to be an offspring of the state.' And governments showed little compunction in nationalizing industry or curbing private capital as they saw fit, even to the point, as with Chiang Kai-shek in Republican China, of aiming to eliminate all private capital in industry.[16]

Thus, the decisive role of the state in the development of the newly industrializing countries is in no way peculiar; on the contrary, it appears to be the norm. As we have noted, in the cases of South Korea, Taiwan and Singapore, the strategy of development was even related mainly to military concerns. Indeed, perhaps part of the exceptionally energetic intervention of the state in these three cases reflects the desperate struggle for survival in a militarily unfavourable environment. Despite the staggering burden of arms spending, the incentives to industrialize were even greater.

In these early phases, the state operates as a virtually autonomous agency. It is not 'representative' of business classes, and is certainly not simply a coordinating agency. In Brazil, for example, one of the more advanced newly industrializing countries (that is, where private capital is of considerable social weight), what Cardoso calls the 'pact of domination' – the alliance of high officials of the state, heads of the subsidiaries of multinational corporations in Brazil, owners of large Brazilian business groups and sectors of the middle class [17] – was firmly directed by the government. Whether bullying or bribing its recalcitrant allies, the government reserved to itself the exclusive right to define the growth strategy for Brazil and pursue it with whatever means it identified as appropriate. The judgement of the government, even when reached through consultation, was its own, not the summary of other forces, and constituted a singular gamble about what the interests of Brazil were and how they could best be prosecuted. This was far from being the lowest common multiple of the interests of private capital.

In South Korea in the sixties, as we have seen, the power of the government, and of Park within it, was even more extreme. An observer of the Korean and Japanese patterns drew out an interesting contrast, which again illustrates how the state grows relatively less powerful *vis-à-vis* capital as a country industrializes:

In Japan, the business community can dismiss most politicians by withholding support in an election. In Korea, the business community could dismiss Park only by shutting down operations and ruining themselves in the process. Conversely, the Korean government can ensure the failure of any businessman should it care to do so.[18]

The crisis of 1980 in South Korea was identified here as marking the emergence of a powerful business class, so that it was no longer possible for the government to behave as freely as it had done in the past.

What appears as the result of relative economic backwardness, the dominating role of the state, also seemed true in the heyday of managed capitalism in the more developed countries. Then the common wisdom seemed to accept that capitalism had become 'the offspring of the state' – had been adopted, even if not born to this parentage. Galbraith expressed the view sharply: 'In notable respects, the mature corporation is an arm of the state', but then he almost immediately reversed the emphasis: 'the state is, in important respects, an instrument of the industrial system'.[19] Shonfield, the other distinguished theorist of the modern 'social-democratic' state, pushes Galbraith's formulation to the point where the state almost absorbs private capital:

> The state controls so large a part of the economy that a planner can, by intelligent manipulation of the levers of public power, guide the remainder of the economy firmly towards any objective that the government chooses.[20]

In retrospect, such confidence was heroic, for when it was advanced the thesis had not been tested – and was not tested until the seventies. Then it became increasingly clear that, in the more developed countries, the state did not control the domestic economy. The powers within its gift were relatively small in economic terms, if not in military or other ones. By the late seventies, aspirations for public power in Europe and North America had become much more modest, whatever the political party concerned.

The left remained one of the last to hold to the more ambitious conception of state power. For some, it seemed the state could create and sustain the economy as it wished. As we have suggested, the more backward an economy, the greater the power of the state to influence domestic affairs; then its limit is sheer resources rather than recalcitrant social influences. There might be scope for great change there, but not in the state's relationships to the world system. The left in both more and less developed countries retained a view that almost anything was possible if the state were under socialist control. But the power of the state was, in all circumstances, constrained. The external context imposed one set of limits – the government's credit rating, import capacity, strength of currency, trade and capital balances. Domestically, there was a different set, ranging from the less important material endowments to the more important social structure. But then the state itself, as we have noted, was not one single entity which could have a single will. The agencies of the state competed as fiercely within the public domain as states competed outside it, and that 'anarchy of the public market' frustrated consistent action and forced budgets to be far larger than was justified by the job in hand. There was also the black economy, operating as corruption within the state, that bent high public purposes to private ends. In such circumstances, it was rare for most governments to be able to establish a strategy and pursue it single-mindedly over the medium term. To have faith in the institution in general was to substitute pure ideology for reality – in political mythologies, states supposedly embodied the aspirations of peoples when private capital did not, so therefore support for the state was support for popular power.

The Change of Direction

By the end of the seventies, the role of the state in virtually all the less developed countries was large, far larger in most cases than the role of foreign capital. In 1979, public sectors accounted for between 15 and 25 per cent of the value added in gross domestic products, and over half of total investment. Nationalized corporations alone accounted for about 10 per cent of gross domestic products, ranging from between 2 and 3 per cent in the Philippines to just under 40 per cent in Ghana and Zambia. As a proportion of gross fixed investment, nationalized industries invested nearly 70 per cent in Algeria (1978–81); 45 per cent in Pakistan (1978–81); 36 per cent in Venezuela (1978–80); and 23 per cent each in Brazil (1980) and South Korea (1978–80).[21] And the number of non-financial public corporations had grown substantially in the preceding two decades – thus, for example, Brazil's, just over a hundred in 1960, had become just under five hundred in 1980. In the newly industrializing countries, state capitalism was apparently everywhere supreme.

The motives for this expansion were diverse. Theory proposed the state should initiate activity where the starting costs for the minimum efficient scale of production were high and the cumulative investment large at low rates of return, but the contributory long-term effects large (in economese, where the maximization of social returns did not coincide with private profitability), but few governments had access to the appropriate data, let alone motivation to find it, in order to make such calculations. Rather, behaviour was governed by conventions and the aspiration to create a self-sufficient national capacity, to secure basic supplies – of, for example, steel, chemicals, heavy industrial products. With these went large-scale public works in power generation, highways, dams and irrigation works. As we have seen for the newly industrializing countries, many, on the basis of the successes of the sixties, launched upon state-initiated heavy-industrial programmes in the seventies at just the time of greatest worldwide difficulties in these sectors.

In practice, there were many other motives for operations taking place in the public sector, from local convention (as in the case of Korean and Japanese public tobacco monopolies) or political accident, corruption or favour (as with the Mexican government's holding in Cuernavaca cemeteries). Businessmen were sometimes punished by expropriation; some, facing bankruptcy, were rescued by friends in the government (as in the Philippines – part of the 'cronyism' system); we have noted the state as hospital for 'sick industries' in India. Sometimes the public were supposedly to be protected from 'natural monopolies' – railways, public utilities, communications. Some industries just starting were expropriated in order to accelerate development and achieve a large minimum scale of output. Some were taken in order to rationalize them and inject new capital. Minorities were punished by nationalization, as happened to Uganda's Asians, or to foreign companies generally. Malaysia used the public sector's expansion to lower the share of Chinese in private capital ownership. In 1982, President Lopez Portillo nationalized the banks of Mexico (catching in his net at the same time a shoal of associated manufacturing companies) in order to guarantee the security of their overseas debts; the Mexican left demonstrated in support of the measure, presuming, quite wrongly, that it showed an advance in popular power. Some nationalizations, in revolutionary conditions, were conservative means to defend the status quo – as when the Portuguese government nationalized the banks in order to prevent them being seized by bank workers. Yet others were occasions for spoliation; an observer of the Indonesian government, for example, noted that 'one cannot ignore the influence that is inevitably being exerted on industrial development policy by the military/bureaucratic network whose economic fortunes are being (or have prospects of being) advanced by the establishment and operation of large-scale state enterprises'.[22] Indonesia's giant state oil corporation, Pertamina, like its Mexican equivalent, Pemex, was notorious for financial scandal.

Whatever the immediate motives, expropriation quite often provided the opportunity for the government to create a corporation with a scale of production capable of competing in the local market with multinational corporations, or at least, while supplying such companies, re-taining an area under local control.[23] Protection was vital in the short term in order to secure a monopoly of the market for the state company. If the government then relaxed, it was likely to end with an inefficient high-cost operation, forcing a redistribution of resources towards this activity. Or with persistent application, it could create a public-sector corporation with capacity sufficient to operate abroad and become a small multinational.

In the seventies, as we have seen, the climate of opinion changed dramatically. The public sector came to be seen less and less as the basic instrument for national industrialization, and the volume of criticism of nationalized industries reached unprecedented levels. It was too easy for governments to use their corporations to pursue purposes, private and public, quite other than the production of the goods and services they were supposedly directed to produce. The prices of their output could be held down in pursuit of an anti-inflation policy, and the resulting deficits then became a burden on the public exchequer (and a pretext for accusations of inefficiency). Political appointments to management often produced incompetent direction; there was much corruption and overstaffing. The output as a result was high in cost; in many cases, far from contributing to national savings as had been intended, public-sector companies became permanent pensioners, a net drain on savings. Many despaired of staunching the losses, and the public sector became identified as tolerated waste.

Often it was politically too difficult to reform them while growth continued. But the difficulties of the late seventies and eighties made the problems insupportable. The deficits soared, threatening to swamp national treasuries. The World Bank and the International Monetary Fund exercised strong pressure to reduce public-sector deficits as a condition of lending. Sometimes public-sector borrowing was part of the growth of external debt. The heavy-industrial programmes, high in cost and with very long gestation periods before any useful output was available, exaggerated the financial vulnerability of governments. As we have seen, Taiwan was obliged to make radical cuts in the public sector to protect public finances, and South Korea, Mexico and Brazil came under close external scrutiny which forced the balancing of the accounts of state companies.

Short-term financial exigencies combined with long-term changes in opinion (related to changes in the structure of the world economy) to produce a quite astonishing cult of 'privatization', a catchword to summarize both denationalization of public companies and efforts to subject the public sector to competitive market measures. It went with a no less remarkable revision of attitudes towards foreign capital (governments now competed to attract it, rather than being preoccupied with minimizing or controlling it) as well as to external trade.

In late 1985, a Hong Kong journal summarized moves afoot to denationalize sectors of activity in various Asian countries as follows:

1. Telecommunications – Japan, Bangladesh, Thailand, South Korea, Malaysia, Sri Lanka.
2. Airlines – Thailand, Singapore, Bangladesh, Malaysia, South Korea, Turkey.
3. Shipping and shipbuilding – Singapore, Bangladesh, Sri Lanka.
4. Railways and buses – Japan, Thailand, Sri Lanka.
5. Highways – India, Malaysia.
6. Banks – South Korea, Singapore, Bangladesh, Taiwan, Philippines.
7. Oil and petrochemicals – India, South Korea, Philippines, Turkey.
8. General industry (especially textiles, engineering, chemicals) – Sri Lanka, Philippines, Pakistan, India, Singapore, Bangladesh, Turkey.
9. Hotels – Singapore, Philippines.[24]

The government of India had just announced a new policy to ban the takeover of 'sick industries', to shut down twenty-six of the hundred textile mills held by the government and to sell others; private directors were to be put on public boards, and much more public-sector activity subcontracted to private companies. The Singapore government publicly limited its future intervention; it proposed that all state companies should be open to private share purchase on the stock exchange and that all minority shares should be sold off. In Brazil, a programme was promised for the disposal of up to seventy-seven state corporations.

The pre-eminent motivation was not an economic strategy so much as a series of emergency financial measures, but as with all such *ad hoc* reactions, the sum effect constituted a strategy, whether conscious or not. For beleaguered governments, the changes seemed to make pre-eminent sense; as the World Bank pointed out, a 5 per cent cut in public-corporation costs in Tanzania and a 5 per cent increase in revenue would produce government surpluses capable of meeting the cost of national health spending; the Mexican government let it be known that the losses on the railways in Mexico also nearly equalled health care spending. But it was also the case that the point of many public-sector activities seemed to have disappeared. The South Korean government said that up to 1972 nationalized industries had played a decisive role, but since then private companies had increasingly developed the capacity to replace them. In an integrating and liberalizing world, the distinction between public and private became blurred, and the arguments for nationalization tended to grow weaker. The rigidities of nationalized corporations (frequently restricted to one activity by statute, unlike private companies that could move between sectors), the problem of corruption and state intervention, and, above all, their political vulnerability rendered them less and less useful in open economies. The changes in the People's Republic of China – selling public companies to private shareholders, privatizing housing and medicine, opening sectors to competitive joint ventures with foreign companies – were only remarkable in the speed with which the changes were introduced and the contrast with past Chinese history; the Chinese were part of an apparently universal move back to a private capitalist world.

Privatization was part of the process of relinquishing the aim of *national* economic development. That aim had made necessary large public sectors as the prime instrument of national purposes. If development now meant the growth of the world product, with different countries playing specialized roles within it, a redefinition of the role of the state was required. Nationalized industries were either not required or, if they remained, needed to operate in all essential respects as if they were private companies, simple competitors on a world market.

The role of the state in propelling rapid development in the newly industrializing countries joined both a phase in the world system, that stretching between about 1930 and the 1960s, and phases of growth of individual national economies. The phase of state capitalism in world growth declined in Europe in the fifties. In the less developed countries, its decline is still far from complete although everywhere the public sector is under threat. For particular economically backward countries, state capitalism has virtually invariably been a feature of accelerated industrialization since the industrial revolution. Sustained world growth from the late 1940s to the 1970s offered an external context highly favourable to growth in the newly industrializing countries, regardless of the specific tactics of the governments concerned, whether leaning to export promotion or comprehensive import substitution. And finally, for those countries emerging from colonial empires, the state inherited unrivalled power in a context of weaker social rivals – the urban middle-class leaders of nationalist movements owed little either to landed inter-est or to the weak forces of private capital. Thus, all factors favoured the forced development of state-dominated economies.

In the seventies, this state domination would perhaps have tended to decline, as private capital expanded disproportionately quickly. But state-initiated heavy-industrial programmes leaned in the opposite direction, until the second slump of the early eighties forced either curtailment, postponement or pruning of these ambitions. In retrospect, perhaps the late seventies were the last time when the newly indus-trializing countries could have attempted to repeat the traditional pattern of economic development, building independent, fully diver-sified, industrialized economies. The slump ended that, forcing a much greater degree of integration in the world system at exactly the same time as the same processes forced a radical pruning – and enhanced specialization – upon the more developed countries. The debt crisis, the decline in world trade, and what was misleadingly called 'de-indus-trialization' in the economically advanced countries, were directed at the same end, the precipitation of a much more sharply defined world economy as a bundle of national specializations.

Contradictory imperatives were imposed upon the governments of the newly industrializing countries: on the one hand, a nationalist ori-entation to reduce dependence upon the rest of the world system and to develop economic and military self-reliance through full diversification of activity; on the other, to expand the income and power of the state and country concerned by increased interdependence and increased specialization. While there were some states that were able to cling to the first perspective (even if with amendments) – such as the Soviet Union – most were bent towards the second by the sheer need for survival. National economic independence was becoming an expensive luxury few could afford – and the richer they were, the less they could afford it.

Thus, the more successful the governments of newly industrializing countries were in pursuing growth, the more powerful private capital at home and the more closely integrated with external markets and world capital abroad, the more the power of the government to shape the domestic economy declined (or, more accurately, the more governmental power, to be effective, had to follow the trend of the market). The weaker an economy was, the less important it was for the world system, other things being equal, the greater the power of the government to shape the domestic economy (but also, of course, the more pressing the problems of external constraints and dearth of resources). The changes in both more developed and newly industrializing countries thus promised the continuing erosion of the foundations of the economic power of the states concerned, the basis of any revival of state capitalism. Privatization – and its theoretical underpinnings in neoclassical economics – was the ideological and practical recognition of this emerging new world order.

This did not mean the decline of the state, but rather a redefinition of its role. For governments remained fundamental to the system; they supervised the territories and inhabitants of the world; provided the necessary conditions of production in terms of infrastructure; guaranteed the stability of exchanges – and therefore, of the forms of value without which the system had no meaning – and of rights to property and management; their police and armies guaranteed the order and safety of the participants; they ensured the quality, physical, educational, emotional and psychological, of the labour force. Without these there could be no capital accumulation, nor indeed simple profit-making. If capitalism seemed to be 'the offspring of the state' in the early phases of national accumulation, in the great broad ocean of the world system the world's states were clearly the offspring of world capital, heterogenous though that entity might be. And that was true even for the giant states that dominated the world political order, those of the more developed countries.

7 = Sociologies

An ideology is a distinct group of beliefs about the social and political world and is a vehicle for the defence or advance of the interests of a social group. Members of the group and their associates are enabled to understand their experience and act by means of the distinct set of beliefs which, at least in theory, links interests to perception and behaviour. Thus, to say that what we have called 'Third Worldism' is an ideology is not merely to identify a distinct set of beliefs about the world – we also have to say what social group created or sustained this set of beliefs. We need to test the beliefs not only empirically – did the way the world developed confirm or contradict the propositions – but also sociologically – how effective was Third Worldism in embodying and advancing a set of social interests?

It is a difficult exercise, for there are no clearcut criteria by which political statements can be attributed to given social groups aligned with given social interests. How indeed can we even identify the effective social groups satisfactorily? It is not enough to examine the social origins of the leadership, for very often, they are different from the social groups they lead; indeed, quite often outsiders are better equipped to articulate the interests of a group than the members of it, for they are immersed in social practice while the outsider has the advantage of detachment. Nor is it always evident from the speeches and writings of the leaders what his or her followers regard as being of the highest importance. In the case of Third Worldism, we deal with a world movement, so that the social group becomes very heterogenous; the data required to go beyond the merely speculative or anecdotal is vast and far beyond the scope of this work.

There is a further problem in the exercise. Some social groups and classes have stability over long periods of time – the owners of land as opposed to cultivators, labour and capital. Others are in continual change, rising and falling with the economic evolution of the system. The sets of ideas they espouse likewise change, rise and fall; furthermore, ideas are the property of all, so ideas that begin as an expression of one set of social interests can be taken over and employed in the service of another – or can join that great cultural compost heap from which all of us draw notions for the purpose in hand. The faster capitalism changes, the greater the fluctuation in social groups – new industries rise, old ones decline and disappear; great industrial clans follow the same trajectory, and the expressions of their interest can rise to the point of dominating both the ruling order and the society at large, and then disappear. Changes in institutional arrangements likewise produce social strata with their own characteristic culture and programme. As we have noted earlier, import-substitution programmes created and sustained a set of interests that gained from the arrangements, supporting the ultra economic nationalists; and those interests resisted efforts to liberalize. The introduction of import substitution likewise displaced groups of interests; Hirschman notes that in Latin America, importers, often ethnic minorities (Lebanese, Jewish, Italian, German) or foreign companies, were displaced to the advantage of native manufacturers;[1] business, national, ethnic and racial elements were interwoven in the battle to control imports. Resistance there is, but in general, it is difficult for any subsidiary group – as opposed to whole classes – to withstand the continual reorganization imposed upon society by the operation of the domestic and world markets. As we argued earlier, changes in the structure of the world economy obliged most governments to reduce import substitutionism almost universally. However, in earlier pre-capitalist times, it was more possible to resist, producing in certain circumstances 'the common ruin of the contending classes'.

The Middle Classes

The Bandung generation, the leaders of the Third World in the 1950s, with their extensive following and sympathizers in the more developed countries, claimed to represent the mass of the people of the less developed countries, the world's poor. The condition of these millions of poor was contrasted with the world's rich, those inhabiting the more developed countries. The one had robbed the other, greedily monopolizing a common inheritance of world resources. However, the leaders

of the Third World, whether leaders of movements for national independence in the colonial empires of the European powers or radicals in the
independent states of Latin America, were themselves rarely drawn from
the poor, and when they came to office, rarely implemented programmes
which could unequivocally be identified as advancing the interests of
the mass of the poor. The movements and parties for independence and
for national liberation were led, organized and most passionately
supported by members of the urban middle classes and, more narrowly,
those with a Western education (quite often in conditions where Western
education was itself a mark of no ordinary privilege).

The term 'middle classes' is a most slippery one, that varies in definition with speaker and context. Today, in the more developed
countries, virtually the whole population identifies itself with the social
middle, from high officers of state and of the armed forces, police chiefs
and even chiefs of major companies (who would in general regard the
term 'capitalist' with distaste) to the mass of working people. Furthermore, 'middle class' is also an accusation among the middle classes,
something of which we should be ashamed. Thus, scientific classification
frequently disappears into posturing, claiming upward mobility or
condemnation.

It is a pity, for in the twentieth century, the 'intermediate strata',
those who are neither capital (or land) owning, nor labour, have been
the social groups in the more developed countries which have grown
most swiftly. The social structure has been changed decisively by this
disproportionate growth. It represents the enormous concentration of
wealth and power in very large public and private organizations and
the decline in employment in direct production. The white-collar
occupations – ranging from lower managers, foremen and supervisors,
to clerical and other office staff, teachers, and the personnel of the
public sector – have grown since the turn of the century at a much
swifter rate than other groups.[2] Today, with the disproportionate
growth of services, as opposed to industry, this trend is exaggerated,
and no longer necessarily related to the disproportionate growth of
large organizations (the small-scale sector of services is no less white-
collar). The change – along with many others – has transformed the
social climate, making almost all political discussion part of the 'middle
ground'.

A comparable process took place in the less developed countries, although the proportions were very different there. The creation of a group of clerical and bureaucratic employees of the state, whether the government was the instrument of an imperial power or an independent administration, changed the urban social structure. In the nineteenth century, the clerks had worked in privileged positions in small numbers. The new white-collar occupations were engaged in large numbers, organized as a mass. As the numbers increased, the status of the old middle classes declined; quite often today, the incomes of the clerical staff are no better than those of the manual working class. The tension between traditions of privileged status and actual lack of status provided one thread in the trade unionism associated with mass white-collar employment and collective discipline. The colonial clerical staff in the European empires also faced blockages in the path of upward social mobility from the presence of the foreigners who held the most senior positions.

The new white-collar class was far removed from the old '*petite bourgeoisie*' of nineteenth-century Europe. Marx wrote extensively about these social strata, identifying them as consisting of shopkeepers, small businessmen, rich and middle peasants and other small property owners, and the local functionaries of the government in provincial towns. This heterogenous collection of groups was bound together by a common hostility to big business and to trade unions or urban labour, and by a loyalty to small property and economic independence. While this set of groups remains socially important in less developed countries today, it is quite different from the new middle classes. Like labour, the white-collar workers are concentrated in the big cities, collectivist by the nature of their occupations and lacking any commitment to private or small property ownership; in one sense, with occupational identification with the state, they might be considered naturally 'socialist': a propertyless proletariat, but with education. By contrast, the urban working class proper was, in the forties, quite small, and the class of native capital very small. The major social and political forces in society were two: the rural and small-town *petite bourgeoisie* and peasants, and the urban middle classes.

The inherited political categories did not fit such a social structure. The stage in intellectual terms was dominated supposedly by the collisions between landowner or landlord and peasant, between capital and labour; the second dichotomy, stemming from the social structure of the more developed countries, frequently overwhelmed all others, even though it concerned only a very small part of the population. Mao Tse-tung in China noticed this disjuncture between concepts and reality in the early 1940s – 'Chinese society', he observed, 'is a society with two small heads and a large body; the proletariat and the big landlords and capitalists are minorities, the broadest group is the middle class.'[3] Unknown to Mao, the same phenomenon had arisen earlier both in economically backward Germany, during Marx's life, and in economically backward Tsarist Russia, during Lenin's. In both cases, both leaders had argued that workers' interests must be expressed in the party programme with the maximum clarity, so that if the 'middle classes' wished to support the workers' party, they could do so on terms laid down by the workers and without compromising the workers' position. For Marx, what he called 'the democratic *petite bourgeoisie*', the liberal leadership of the movement against the emperor's rule in Germany, was a constant danger to the workers' party, threatening to replace workers' interests with their own.[4] Mao's inference from the situation in China was the precise opposite:

If the policy of any political party does not look after the interests of the middle classes, if the middle class does not gain its proper place, if the middle class does not have freedom of speech, if it does not have clothes to wear, food to eat, work to do, books to read, national affairs cannot be well managed.[5]

Thus, the majority of the Chinese, the combination of the rural *petite bourgeoisie*, the peasants and the urban middle classes, constitutes the force that should determine an important part of the party's programme. The party, be it noted, is not the expression of one clearcut class interest, but rather makes concessions to a coalition of forces. Mao's view is a clearcut rejection of the views of Marx and Lenin, and an expression of populism: for the middle classes, as so defined, constitute the 'people'.

The heart of the nationalist movement was the 'people', but its cadre consisted of the children of the urban middle classes, privileged by origin, with the education of their colonial masters, but without a secure place or path of advancement in society. In fact, the entry of new educated unemployed upon society was not a new phenomenon. Historians of the English Puritan revolution and civil war have noted the important role of a suddenly expanded newly educated stratum upon the established Church and society. Others have discussed the Narodnik movement in Tsarist Russia in the 1860s and 1870s in the same terms. Marx himself grumbled in the 1870s about the invasion of the German workers' party by rootless young people, 'declassed bourgeois youth' with nothing but their brainpower to sell.[6] And, in our own times, the sudden expansion of higher education in the 1950s has been linked to the radical turbulence of the late 1960s when the Cultural Revolution in China seemed to spark off movements in universities as widely apart as Berkeley, Nanterre and the London School of Economics.

In the European empires in Asia and Africa, the children of the urban middle classes who had mastered the education and culture of the imperialists were still denied entry to power and authority on terms of equality with the foreigner. All around, poverty and corruption seemed to be the result of foreign rule, and the wealth of the metropolitan countries seemed self-evidently to have been stolen from the colonies (as indeed, part of it had). In the twentieth century, an unprecedentedly severe slump afflicted the raw-material-producing colonies most grievously. And, furthermore, the Europeans inflicted upon the world an apparently endless series of catastrophic wars – the next was being prepared before the wounds of the first had been bound up. Everything testified to the exhaustion of any useful role empire might once have been thought to fulfil. To the brutality of the foreigner, his inability to keep the world from war, was added the cruel indifference of his market and his capitalism. The new revolutionaries offered an alternative way of life: an end to the robbery – the draining of resources out of the country – the transformation of society and, through the mechanism of state planning, the economic and social advance of all.

There were more mundane purposes. The exclusion of foreigners from the administration at last opened up high office to local aspirants. The exclusion of foreign goods promoted the interests of domestic producers, both in agriculture and industry. Settling issues with the foreigner meant also a settlement with those who had supported them, often large landowners or the old rulers; there was an opportunity for land redistribution. The expulsion of the imperialists was, like the exclusion of imports, a once-and-for-all diversion of opportunities to local competitors, the creation of a monopoly of jobs for the minority of educated people. The style was infectious and continued into the postcolonial era in continuous efforts to exclude groups of natives who could be identified as foreigners. In India, linguistic agitation in the fifties aimed to exclude those who did not speak the local language from jobs in the provincial administration. A commentator at the time noted the beneficiaries:

It is the middle-class job hunter and place seeker and the mostly middle-class politician who are benefited by the establishment of a linguistic state, which creates for them an exclusive preserve of jobs, offices and places, by shutting out, in the name of the promotion of culture, all outside competitors.[7]

Even today, the same reactions continue – with attempts by Assamese to exclude Bengalis, of Sikhs to exclude all. The nationalist ethic now afflicts the integrity of the new countries from within.

If the cadre were from the educated urban middle classes, the leadership was almost always of much higher social status. The Nehrus belonged to an aristocracy of wealth, Gandhi was a London-educated lawyer, Sukarno one of the few engineers of the Netherlands East Indies and from the aristocratic *priyayi* class. The leadership of the Chinese Communist Party were not quite so grand – Mao and many of the others were the children of landlords who became students at Peking and other universities; Chou En-lai, child of a mandarin, was one of a group who had studied in France. In the 1930s, Nym Wales collected biographical details of some seventy leading members of the party to show that they were overwhelmingly of the *hsüeh-cheng* (families of 'small farmers, merchants and even aristocratic official families'). To her surprise, the Kuomintang leadership were of almost the same social origin.[8] In Calcutta, the leaders were *bhadralok*, the respectable folk, with a deviation among Communist leaders towards the brahmin caste. In Egypt, the nationalist leadership was closely associated with state employment, for the majority of the educated were employed in public or military service in the early fifties.[9]

In society at large, to be from such social origin gave prestige but no broad appeal. In any case, the urban sector was small. The children of the middle classes needed to create coalitions of classes as the basis for disciplined movements, vehicles for achieving power – whether the army (as in Egypt and many others), a party and an independent army (as in China, Vietnam, Algeria, Indonesia, Mozambique, Angola, Zimbabwe), a social movement (as in India), a guerrilla army, or a base in the organized trade unions (as in parts of the West Indies).

The Class Coalition

The leadership had a vision of an independent state and of the creation of national power. It was a perspective with much appeal for those likely to inherit what the foreigners left behind – whether land, businesses or official positions. For them, nationalism summarized a powerful material interest. But for the majority who would not necessarily benefit directly, but without whose support power could not be won, more tangible benefits were needed to secure willing support. On the other hand, if class movements of revolt developed, they could rapidly go beyond the control of the existing leadership, raising issues which were not part of the demand for political independence from the colonial power and which, in colliding with other interests, might promote the destruction of the coalition. It was a constant besetting problem in a number of independence movements: to retain full control in the hands of the leadership and yet offer enough to a wide enough segment of the population to sustain a politically significant movement.

For the Indian National Congress, the existence of a Communist party appealing directly to factory workers constantly complicated the equation. In China, the early Kuomintang, with Communist support, sought to distinguish action by workers against foreign employers from action against Chinese employers. Sun Yat-sen explained it to Cantonese workers in somewhat unpersuasive terms:

The difference between the Chinese worker and foreign workers lies in the fact that the latter are oppressed only by their own capitalists and not by those of other countries ... The Chinese workers are as yet not oppressed by Chinese capitalists ... They are oppressed by foreign capitalists.[10]

The truth was exactly the opposite, as an American observer noted in the thirties:

Exploitation in [Chinese-owned] enterprises was generally greater than in foreign-owned industries; the technique backward and relatively undercapitalized. Chinese firms were able to compete only by such methods.[11]

Workers were of decreasing significance in the turbulent history of the 1930s in China, and the Communist party found it possible to make only the minimum concessions in terms of its programme to them.

This was not true of the peasantry. Not only were they the overwhelming majority of the population, the heterogeneity of interests involved made it very difficult to offer concessions to one group without simultaneously provoking the opposition of another. In India, there seems to have been quite often some indifference to the appeals of nationalism in rural areas; agricultural tenants were less concerned with the nationality of the government than the nature of the landlord and the conditions of tenure. In his study of Orissa in the 1930s, Bailey notes the poor results of Congress's rural agitation until the time when a local leader promised that, in settling with the British, Congress would have to settle with those who supported the British – the landlords and rajahs; that would mean land redistribution, security of tenure for the tenants and rural reform. Suddenly, the movement began to develop swiftly.[12] India was not alone. The same link – between nationalism and land reform – was frequently noted as a key factor in creating the social basis for the National Liberation Front of Vietnam in the sixties (in opposition to the United States backed regime of Ngo Dinh Diem and his supporters of northern Catholic landlords).

In China, for much of the time, the peasantry were no more susceptible to the appeals of nationalism than elsewhere, although the savageries of the Japanese occupation of parts of rural China produced a stream of recruits for the Red Army. 'Mass nationalism', Meisner observes,

was not something that welled up from the elemental forces of the countryside and eventually reached Mao Tse-tung and his associates. It is more historically accurate to say nationalism was brought to the peasants from without by an ardently nationalistic elite bent upon shaping history in accordance with its ideals.[13]

Nationalism had to be laced with material interests. Up to the 1935 Seventh Congress of the Comintern, this could be the simple promise of the expropriation of landlords and gentry. But the Congress laid down the new line that the Chinese Communist party must ally with the Kuomintang (the voice of capital and landlords in party theory) in a united front against Japanese invasion. It was straining credibility to call for the expropriation of landlords while seeking to ally with them. The party programme was revised to eliminate the call for land reform and limit demands upon 'patriotic landlords and enlightened gentry' to rent reductions. Mao was to insist on rent reductions in subsequent years, since otherwise, he observed, 'the masses in the newly liberated areas will not be able to tell which of the two parties, the

Communist party or the Kuomintang, is good and which is bad'.[14]

For reasons which remain obscure, the party made a radical shift in this position in the autumn of 1947. The leadership for the first time urged the peasants themselves to seize the land rather than remaining content with limited rent reductions. Whether it was a tactic to increase peasant support for the party and recruitment to the Red Army, or was designed to expropriate an important segment of Kuomintang support, the party nearly lost control in the mass movement of land seizures that resulted. It was a vivid illustration of the dangers to the leadership of loss of control in the face of popular initiative. By December, the party leadership had swung hard into reverse to re-establish control. Mao wrote:

> There has been an erroneous emphasis on doing everything as the masses want it done, and an accommodation to wrong views existing among the masses, one-sidedly proposing a poor-peasant/farm-labourer line . . . that the democratic government should listen only to workers, poor peasants and farm labourers while no mention at all was made of the middle peasants, the independent craftsmen, the national bourgeoisie and the intellectuals.[15]

Henceforth, as it was expressed later, 'spontaneous struggle by the peasants must be firmly prevented in agrarian reform'.[16]

An Independent Leadership

The issue at stake in the 1947 peasant movement in China was a continuing one wherever the independence movement was required to struggle over a long period of time. It was expressed most clearly in China, for Communist parties were much more explicit in their political calculations. There had always been a strong emphasis on the need for the working class to identify its interests with the maximum independence of other classes (as we have seen earlier in the discussion of the relationship of the middle classes to the German workers' party), and once the link between the party and workers had been broken, as it was in China in the late twenties, the defence of the independence of the party was substituted (although the party was always described as 'the leadership of the proletariat', which preserved some semblance of consistency).

A high order of dexterity was required to promise enough to secure support yet not enough to incite spontaneous mass initiative that might supersede the existing leadership. It was the genius of Mahatma Gandhi in India to provide the most striking examples of the politics of flirting with most interests, but marrying none. It was a triumph of equivocation on the major social issues, with complete, not to say ruthless consistency in preserving his own independent role of leadership. Gandhi regretted the poor treatment of agricultural labourers, but did not espouse land reform. He deplored low wages for hard work, but proposed nothing concerning the distribution of power in industry. He attacked the ill-treatment of untouchables (and invented a new name for them, Harijans) but did not oppose the caste system. He regretted the abuse of women, but supported the social organization of genders. He was not a pacifist, since he supported the British war effort in the First World War. He was in favour of non-violence for unofficial movements, but did not support Indian troops who refused to obey their British officers and fire on Indian demonstrators. ('A soldier who disobeys an order to fire breaks the oath which he has taken and renders himself guilty of criminal disobedience. I cannot ask soldiers to disobey; for when I am in power, I shall in all likelihood make use of these same soldiers. I should be afraid they might do the same when I am in power.')[17] Gandhi strove to be all things to all men and women, both in order to create the broadest possible movement of Indians, but also to avoid becoming committed to one or other social interest and thereby reducing his own power of manoeuvre.

Gandhi operated in a politically fluid situation, tacking one way and another between the power of the British Raj and that of the complex movement he led. His performance was a public one and in the centre of the stage. Mao on the other hand operated with his own military forces based in separate 'liberated areas'. The guarantee of the independence of the party leadership from the social classes of China was vested in the party's armed power rather than in political dexterity. That independence then became embodied in the overwhelmingly dominant position of the former Kuomintang state machinery, which the Communist party took over in 1949. Now the relative independence of the state permitted it to eliminate landlordism and transform the distribution of land into giant publicly directed communes virtually without reference to peasant interests; it was also able to end the private ownership of industry, the private capitalists who had been erstwhile allies, and impose upon urban labour an austere regime of work. By contrast, no independence was vested in the Indian National Congress nor in the state of which it assumed direction; or rather, it could behave relatively freely with weak private capital, but it could not afford to tamper with the rights of the dominant peasant castes.

The history of the Chinese Communist party has other points of particular interest for the themes discussed here. For it crosses the transition in the history of the Soviet Communist party (and the Comintern) from a party which began in aspiration as an international-ist movement of revolutionary urban and industrial workers in 1917 and ended as a nationalist agency of state officials, operating independently of the social classes of the Soviet Union and dedicated to the national economic development of Russia. The ideology created in this process, Stalinism, is an amalgam of the rhetoric of proletarian internationalism and the interests of the propertyless middle classes and functionaries of the state. The party could thus go some way to retaining the loyalty both of those who wished to abolish the state and of those who wished to absorb the whole of society in the state. In so far as the rhetoric of Marxism was transmitted to Third Worldism (along with an admiration for a heroically simplified account of Russia's economic development), it was by means of Stalinism, with its emphasis on a militarized '*blitz-krieg*' process of capital accumulation.

This account has been concerned mainly to discuss examples of the decolonization of Asia and, more narrowly, India and China. It is easier to see the processes there because of the sharp discontinuity of the ending of imperial power. However, the changes in the social structure also affected those less developed countries which were not part of the European empires. In Latin America, the successive waves of nationalist domination and in particular the processes of the late thirties and forties which brought to power, in a number of countries, populist dictators often based upon worker and peasant movements and opposed to an 'internationalist' landowning class was one area where the urban middle classes had a crucial role to play. Much later these issues became interwoven with renewed struggles to end American domination on the basis of an indigenous tradition of guerrilla warfare. The ambitious educated youth, less burdened than those in Asia with Stalinism, none the less embraced politics of a comparable kind. The theoretical tra-dition might be lacking, but again the independence of the revolutionary leadership (and, later, the state) was a continuing preoccupation. Con-

sider Regis Debray's summary of the views of Fidel Castro: 'The guerrilla force is completely independent of the civilian population in action
as well as in military organization; consequently it need not assume the
direct defence of the peasant population.'[18] Amid the thorny ortho-
doxies of Stalinism, Mao would not have dared to enunciate such an
apparently elitist principle. Gandhi would not have thought in that way
although his practice, if we allow for a metaphorical sense to military
defence, always conformed to the general principle.

In sum then, the propertyless middle classes – or rather, in Asia and
Africa, their Western-educated sons and daughters – played a peculiarly
crucial role in mobilizing a coalition of forces to oppose imperialism.
That this opposition came from a particular source and possessed a
particular set of distinct social interests does not invalidate the
movement. For the first time they identified the issue of mass poverty
and affirmed the possibility of overcoming it, while showing vividly the
role of the Europeans in creating and maintaining that poverty. But the
aspirations of the new ruling orders also meant that, once in power, the
issue of overcoming mass poverty became subordinate to the growth of
national power. Class issues disappeared in national ones. The great
historical clash that filled the minds of the left – between nationalist
private capital and an internationalist industrial working class – was
refracted in a much narrower dispute, between the holders of small
property (in Russia, the NEP men and the kulaks) and the bureaucrats,
between a version of private capitalism and state capitalism. The concepts of socialism and popular liberation (from the exploitation of
labour as much as foreign domination) became entirely absorbed by
those of state power, the liberation of governments. Echoes of the old
debate continued in the Indian Congress – between, we might over-
simplify, the middle peasants and traders of Gujerat and the propertyless middle-class nationalists of Bombay and Calcutta, effective voices
of right and left.

But in so far as the new state was successful in creating and fostering
industrialization, it created a new class of private industrial capital, that
slowly grew in power and influence. The Indian government found itself
increasingly influenced by the same type of ruling order as in the more
developed countries, and the propertyless urban middle class was
effectively eased out of influence. The old state-capitalist Indian left
went into decline, even as the classes that had for so long played

such an important role in its fictional dramas, capital and labour, emerged.

The debate – between peasant and bureaucrat – could be seen in many countries in the post-independence years. Even in fully state-capitalist China, the echoes continued in the debate in the party after the Great Leap Forward. And the authentic anguish of the hungry and propertyless educated youth can be heard loudly in the Red Guard movement of the Cultural Revolution, the supposed embodiment of the left. The right, the NEP men and the kulaks of China, rejoiced at the downfall of the Red Guards on the death of Mao.

The nationalists expropriated the concepts of the left, and the left became dominated by nationalism. The social basis for revolutionary change became equivocal. The vehicle for the emancipation of the world had been, for Marxists, and even for many other socialists, the industrial working class. But in the post-war period, especially in countries where the industrial working class was still scarcely a credible social challenge, the agency of change became different things at different times – the people, the poor, the peasantry, even the lumpenproletariat; sometimes students, ethnic minorities, and many others. No wonder the left became confused. It affected even those who claimed to be leading theoreticians; the well-known Marxist, Paul Sweezy, in the excitement of the Chinese Cultural Revolution, decided that the honorific term 'proletarian' should apply to whomsoever he chose:

Only 'natural' bearers of values espoused by Marx and Lenin, which centre on the imperatives to eliminate all real inequalities (although not of course, all individual differences) are real proletarians, who have no privileges or special interests and on whom, therefore, the responsibility falls to carry on the struggle against *all* privileges and special interests.[19]

The combination of naïveté, special pleading and apparent innocence in the tradition Sweezy claims to uphold is matched by the upside-down view of class politics. For the revolutionary leader no longer embodies the aspirations of a class; he – or she – graciously bestows the accolade of 'proletarian' on whomsoever he nominates; all independent power is now in the leader's hands, not in the hands of the class he chooses to lead.

Ideologies

In the period from 1945 to the sixties, new states were created on an unprecedented scale. New ruling classes were created, fitting uncomfortably into the tight suits and large cars of state power. The newcomers mixed anger at their earlier exclusion from power, at the discrimination exercised over them and at the cruelty imposed upon them, with eager attempts to emulate those who had formerly ruled. The governor's palace became the presidential residence.

The creation of so many states, the arrival of so many new ruling orders, could not fail to change the world's social structure. The sheer novelty of this extraordinary process has now been largely forgotten, but it is, in retrospect, hardly surprising that it changed the perceptions of the world. The newcomers created changes of style and culture no less striking than, in the past, those effected by other groups of new entrants to national ruling classes – when the Manchus or the Mongols conquered China or the Franks Gaul. In this modern process, the social, political and economic coincided – a rising social stratum, Sukarno's 'newly emergent forces' that came to conquer or inherit state power, new states, and the definition of new economic units extracted from the integrated form of the old imperial economies. Third Worldism offered a theory, a tradition and culture, and a forward perspective: through state power, countries could be transformed to achieve the economic basis for national dignity and a tolerable way of life.

As we have seen, the new ideology was constructed both from Stalinism and from *étatiste*–corporatist conceptions dominant in Western Europe in the thirties (and to a much lesser extent, in North America), the product of slump and an era of world wars. It began as a radical critique of the existing distribution of power and wealth in the world, and in that form won adherents on the left in the more developed countries. It inspired a substructure of academic studies, from development economics through all the social sciences to the new 'area studies'. In Europe and North America, the social stratum that responded was that which created Third Worldism – the propertyless middle classes of the big cities, now an international social stratum. And when the young and educated broke with their parents in the Cultural Revolution in China, it was the same people who responded in Nanterre and Berkeley.

What is surprising is not that this major change in world social structure took place, but the astonishing speed with which it was absorbed. The new ruling order was swift to abandon their cheap suits and the austere style of life of the Bandung years. They discovered Savile Row, the Sheraton style and the values of a world order, and did so even when the process of national liberation was incomplete – Central America continued in turmoil. The educated children of the urban middle classes, with high hopes and extreme nationalist views, settled into their new roles as rulers, and quickly grew inured to supporting the burdens of great local poverty. The critique of a world order dominated by the Great Powers and their inexhaustible predilection for warfare, a critique with its distant echoes of Lenin, faded into the rhetoric of haggling over commodity prices, the national egotisms of relations between states, and irritable grumbling about neo-imperialism. Just as the dark-suited ladies and gentlemen who ran France still retained on their coat of arms, 'Liberty, Equality and Fraternity', the cry of the oppressed in 1789, so the ruling orders of some of the less developed countries still bore the insignia of the revolutionary oppressed of the 1950s. In Indonesia, the doctrine of Bandung, Pansila, is still taught as the ideology of the state even though its author, Sukarno, and the order he ruled has long since been disgraced and overthrown. In the same way, in China – and, even more curiously, in Russia – the walls sport an unlikely ikon, portraits of a hairy Victorian gentleman, Karl Marx. One should not be misled by these affectations.

Marx might have enjoyed the irony of becoming an ikon, provided the explosive power of this decoration was not eliminated. He might also have been struck by the irony that Third Worldism, supposedly a radical break in the traditions of the world, the theory of the emancipation of the poor majority by means of a third alternative, was in fact only the prelude for a new type of reincorporation in the world economy. Temporary seclusion and isolation of the national economy permitted the manipulation of the terms of trade to give a monopoly to industry and thus accelerate 'primitive accumulation'. This was not the basis for independence, but rather the springboard for the fledgling capitalists of the leading less developed countries to learn to spread their wings. An incidental byproduct of the process was that the left, in the name of socialism, was subverted, and bent to the tasks of supporting and defending the process of national capital accumulation in the name of national liberation.

It was a harsh process, and required radical terminology to conceal it. When elementary accumulation was complete, the ruling orders, willingly or not, returned to the global market. Everywhere the politics were required to change – from Sukarno to Suharto, from Nasser to Sadat, from Mao to Deng. Some were not flexible enough to evolve, or the social order of which they were chiefs resisted the overthrow implied in the new strategies: Nkrumah, Ben Bella and Sukarno made exits as dramatic as those of Allende and Goulart in the ruin of their ambitions. Others had the good grace to die before the need to overthrow them became insupportable (and thereby earned a cherished place in the national pantheon of heroes, translation to the status of ikons).

The poor, who had supposedly been the object of all this agitation, remained poor, the landless without land, the workers still the creatures of the wage system, states still divided and hostile. New divisions appeared, new national liberation struggles emerged, but pitted now against what used to be the newly independent governments. The new orders were obliged to behave in ways not dissimilar to the old. The former idealists turned to the old weapons – truncheon and bayonet – to maintain order, and to old arguments. Some tried to stretch the old talk of Third Worldism to cover the class interests of the new ruling orders, much as social democrats in Europe endeavoured to use elastic concepts of rebellion to cover defence of the status quo. Consider the striking elision in Kenneth Kaunda's speech to Zambian workers in 1969:

Now government is yours, industries are yours, the whole economy is yours . . . to run and manage effectively and successfully . . . it is as this background . . . that I find it imperative in the interests of the nation as a whole to announce a wage freeze until further notice and . . . an embargo on strikes.[20]

8 = The End of National Reformism

The history of capitalism – like that of its unlovely child, nationalism – is one of geographical spread, the slow colonization of the globe by the market. From Lancashire, we might say with some licence, to England and north-western Europe, from North America to Latin America, south and then east Asia, from south-east Asia to Africa. In the 1950s, the same process continued, now transforming itself where it had already arrived. The commodity composition of the flows of trade between the different geographical components of the system were transformed – the patterns of skills and productivity, networks of interdependence and collaboration, physical distributions, urbanization, income distribution and social structure, all were remarkably changed. But in terms of the brute undifferentiated capacity to produce, colonization continued. From the old exchanges of raw materials for manufactured goods between the less and more developed countries, the pattern changed: the more developed countries now produced a growing volume of raw materials and agricultural goods, highly sophisticated manufactured goods, and a vast array of advanced services, while the less developed exported a growing volume of manufactured goods and some raw materials. The categories are blunt, and within each crude sector there were thousands of varied and changing networks of exchange that defied the simple formulae that passed among the uncritical for theory. In the crude sense, the second half of the twentieth century was no different from earlier periods of dispersal; in the specific and disaggregated sense, the changes overturned the inherited notions of what those exchanges constituted.

Nationalism was one of the main exports of the new capitalism of Western Europe. To protect a people against the depredations of the market and conquest by European states required the creation of a state, with a centralized and disciplined body of armed men capable both of warding off outsiders and dragooning the population to the tasks of accumulation. The Americas struck out first to defend themselves against the European empires, then East Europe. In the post-war period, Asia and then Africa followed suit, until all the world had acquired the machinery of local defence and work discipline, as well as the decorative forms of independent states. Up until the Second World War, it had seemed that this was progress, and that the creation of the democratic republic provided the cradle for the infant of free enterprise – the one must entail the other. Lenin noted that in Prussia this conjuncture had not occurred – the junkers from their feudal estates had created the Kaiser's state for German capitalism. Others observed that the Japanese samurai had followed suit. The democratic republic was not needed to build capitalism.

Others argued that capitalism had exhausted its capacity to spread. The Bolsheviks considered advanced capitalism had become so tangled in its contradictions that it could no longer pursue the progressive transformation of the rest of the world. It had produced imperialism, which in turn had allied with those 'feudal' forces which opposed the spread of capitalism. As we have seen, others detected in the system new features which destroyed any symmetrical development of centre and periphery. Modern capitalism, others said, had become an intensive system, swiftly increasing productivity in its historical heartlands but without needing to extend beyond them. The market could no longer be trusted to ensure either the spread of the system or, indeed, the survival of capitalism itself – the rationale for the Keynesian management of national economies flowed from the same postulates as development economics and, indeed, the economics of the centrally planned economies.

None the less, despite the pessimism that had been bred in the inter-war slump and continued into the post-war era, capitalism did spread. More of the dispersal would have been noted if it had not been concealed in the simple dichotomy of more and less developed countries. Somehow the incorporation of Japan or Italy or Spain, or in North America, of the deep South, in the group of more developed countries did not disturb the theoretical complacency of the immovability of capital. By the seventies, as we have seen, many more were involved. The change promised to be ultimately very large, but in the eighties was still quite small. In comparison to the great accumulation of manufacturing capacity in the more developed countries, the share of the less developed was still slight. Where there had been a measure of redistribution between the two, it affected only a minority of the less developed countries and, within them, an even smaller minority of their inhabitants. The anxieties and fears in Europe and North America ought perhaps to have concerned trends and the future, not what had already been accomplished. There was no way that slump, a worldwide phenomenon, could be attributed to the newly industrializing countries, nor unemployment laid at their door; they were in sum still far too small to lift or lower the world profit rate; there was no way they could overcome the depressing weight of the great overhang of capacity in the more developed countries. As most studies showed, imports in general, and imports from the less developed countries in particular, had had very slight effects on employment in the more developed countries; rationalization and declining demand as the result of slump were the sources of unemployment. Indeed, it is more truthful to see imports as the result of industrial decline rather than the cause.

However, even if imports could have been identified as more significant than this, there is doubt as to whether the governments of the more developed countries could do much to stop imports at an acceptable cost to themselves. As we have noted earlier, the more advanced a country, the more powerful generally the state that administers it, but the less the power of the government to determine domestic economic activity. For the price of great political and economic power in the world is integration in a world economy, which, perversely, then makes it almost impossible to separate domestic and external activity. Of course, governments can wreak havoc with particular commodities, either directly, by defying the conventions and institutions supposedly regulating world trade, or, more likely, through covert manoeuvres, intrigue or cheating, or some form of so-called 'voluntary' self-restraint. However, the effects are usually temporary – the flow of black goods or goods from third countries compensates; or other flows of goods are affected (a British ban on imported garments from Indonesia produced a decline in Indonesian imports of British aircraft). Import controls furthermore raise the costs of inputs to domestic production, resulting in a loss of exports and a weakened competitive position in domestic markets relative to imports.

The perverse effects of import controls are seen at their most dramatic in the case of agricultural production, particularly in Europe, with the notorious Common Agricultural Policy. But even with a much slighter set of import controls, the Multi Fibre Arrangement covering textiles and garments, the effects are very difficult to justify. In the long period in which the Arrangement (and its predecessor) have operated, there is no evidence that any employment has been saved, but much evidence that prices have been kept much higher than would otherwise have been the case. Buyers of clothing have thus paid an extra tax on their purchases in order to sustain the profits of textile and garment companies. It has not stopped imports, and now large retailers are frequently dependent upon imports for their main trade. It is from this quarter that the main opposition to import controls derives, and it is now sufficiently large to overturn the Arrangement sooner or later. It is also possible that the periodic trade wars in agricultural goods between Europe and Japan on the one hand, and the United States on the other, will ultimately result in a decline in the protection of agriculture, to the great gain of food exporters in the less developed countries. In the United States, it is the users of cheap imported components or supplies – the big car manufacturers, shoe retailers, steel sellers and users, machine-tool traders – who provide the main safeguard against import controls.

The generalized control of all imports overcomes some of these difficulties. But then the entirety of domestic output becomes relatively expensive, and exports suffer unless subsidized (which in turn involves redistribution of income between different sectors). Whole lines of production become profitable because of the creation of a domestic monopoly, and the consumer is obliged to pay heavily to keep domestic capital in operation. A general relative impoverishment must ensue, with a relative decline in technical advance as the byproduct of monopoly. This analysis leaves out the possibility of a retaliatory trade war with the country's main trade partners, which adds unmitigated disaster to the other problems. In the field of imports, the power of state intervention is that of a blind Samson: it can pull down the temple on the heads of the unfortunates within, but has no power to raise a new temple, to guarantee existing employment and incomes on a nationally self-sufficient basis.

All this concerns the capacity for deliberate intervention by the government of a more developed country. In practice, as we have noted, those capacities vary enormously, from the power of the government of the United States, able to borrow over $200 bn in a single year, to that of a small country that has less weight in the system than many of the less developed countries. The capacity for deliberate intervention does not exhaust the role of governments. The combined effects of fiscal, monetary and trade policies of the more developed countries have a decisive impact in the world system, but within any one country these policies are not determined by a single aim, and for the more developed countries to be able to align all governments in all three areas for a single end would be unprecedented. Even with limited management – as when the more developed countries tried to prevent the floating of the dollar in 1971 – they fail. While the system consists of competing states, it is impossible to conceive of circumstances where a sufficient number would have sufficient common interest to override their differences. Thus these enormous powers are, in terms of the global system, blind; they cannot be the subject of combined and conscious action.

Governments are fully aware of the limits upon their capacity to intervene. But they also recognize that the ideological basis of their power implies that they must intervene to protect and enhance the position of their inhabitants, and that it is the tradition of every country to blame foreigners for whatever domestic misfortunes occur. Protectionism is cheap for the government – for it is the buyers of formerly imported goods who pay. So it is easy to understand that, no matter how disastrous long-term import controls may be economically, in political terms they are a cheap method of seeking votes. Even governments, like that of President Reagan, whose claim to fame is a defence of free competition, flirt endlessly with protectionism and, in the preparation for elections, can be persuaded to go further. But the controls cannot be generalized or made permanent without damaging the system that generates the wealth and power of the dominant states themselves. The remedies are worse than the cure.

In any case, the arguments for alarm are not necessarily correct. The central problem of the world economy today is the phase of slump and stagnation, not change; change is part of the intrinsic nature of the system in boom or slump, and has been since its inception. It is always easier to see the negative effects of such change, even though historically it is the benefits which have loomed larger. Thus, for example, since 1880 two thirds of the jobs in more developed countries have been lost, but during the same period total employment has increased three times over. In European agriculture, 90 per cent of the jobs have been lost over the past century as the result of mechanization – the proportion of the labour force engaged in agriculture has fallen from about 50 to between 4 and 5 per cent – yet total employment as well as agricultural output have continued to expand. If slump and stagnation could be overcome, there is no reason to believe that employment would decrease whether from relocation of capacity or as a result of technical innovation. Of course, what is true for the labour force as a whole is not true for individual workers – a redundant fifty-year-old coal-miner cannot get new employment as a computer programmer. But if increased output is the result of rationalization, resources will be available to ensure the former miner need suffer no hardship. That, rather than defending an increasingly obsolete structure of employment, is the heart of the problem.

Is the growth of output in the newly industrializing countries a temporary phenomenon? The change in the structure of the world economy, integrating the activity of the more developed countries, is the source of the growth of output of the newly industrializing countries. That change, the product of the successive measures of post-war liberalization, has created a set of interdependent specializations, and governments cannot now return to the status quo ante except at intolerable cost to their domestic economies. Once the internationalized core was created, the effects spread outwards, involving increasing numbers of less developed countries, so that now there are new newly industrializing countries – it is a continuing process. It seems inconceivable that the general trend could now be reversed, although the detail is in constant change. Particular countries loom larger or smaller in the spread at different times; activities move back and forth between different groups of countries. But the overall change appears so deep-rooted in the emerging structure of the system that it is now permanent. Although originally a product of the rapid and sustained growth of the system, it is now no longer dependent upon that; as we have seen, slump and stagnation can now intensify the process of dispersal even though it may also reduce the rates of growth of some of the newly industrializing countries.

The process is helped by the disaggregation of manufacture, so that product parts can now be made in specialized locations relatively remote from each other, and the finished product assembled somewhere else. This division of labour creates geographical patterns of high skill, which both enforce interdependence and give some temporary stability to the territorial distributions. On the perimeter of these networks of specialization, buyers, driven by competition, continue to search for new, lower-cost sources of output. It is these buyers who provide the means of raising and standardizing the quality and price of output; they provide the means to sellers to conform to world standards and the incentive to do so (by providing access to important markets). By now there can scarcely be a country where buyers have not explored the possibility of purchase, calculating on the proverbial back of an envelope how far price and quality of local output are competitive or, if not, under what conditions they might be. These are the explorers of the new world empire, the buyers of handicrafts and carpets and woven goods, providing the first market possibilities in the great broadening highway that leads to machine tools, ships and vehicles.

Because the process is now part of the structure, it no longer depends on those countries that are currently newly industrializing. Of course, there is a strong presumption that, once started, countries continue on the same path, changing and upgrading output as industrialization deepens (and other newer competitors take over the lower-value lines of output). But this is not necessarily so – the front-runners can fall back, become trapped in one particular specialization and stagnate there. Nor would this necessarily be the fault of the government, for the possibilities of public initiative grow weaker as the process continues. And indeed, the market can be ingenious in overcoming the obstacles put in the way of the process by the interests of government – as happened in South Korea in 1979 and 1980, when the ambitions of General Park were defeated. Despite the alarms of the early eighties, the threats from purely economic or financial sources to the newly industrializing countries did not seem unmanageable. Mexico's debts loomed dangerously large in 1985, and Singapore's growth sank to zero; no doubt others would also face turbulence. But despite vulnerabilities and dangers, general dispersal continued. Only sudden shock seemed dangerous, but that could affect a more developed country just as much as a newly industrializing one; for example, the bankrupting of a major company could begin to unravel the nets of finance uniting Wall Street and the European bourses. That was not a special feature of the redistribution of manufacturing.

The medium-term threat to the possibility of continued growth in the individual newly industrializing countries (as opposed to general geographical dispersal) came not so much from crises generated in the financial or trading system as from politics. Lebanon and Iran were awful warnings – of the possibilities of dismemberment of an established state in the case of the first (one that might, otherwise, have been included in the list of newly industrializing countries), and of the retreat to an archaic and reactionary social order in the case of the second. In some of the newly industrializing states, the class struggle posed the main threat to the ambitions of the local ruling order. Hitherto we have been concerned to evaluate part of world capitalism by the criteria of the system itself – the size and durability of the rate of economic growth, the structural changes of the economy, the changing composition of output and employment. Little attention has been devoted to the growth of incomes and consumption, to income distribution and inequality, to what happened to the poor; from the perspective of the accumulation of capital, these are extraneous elements, accidental byproducts of the process, even though for most of the participants these are the most vital questions. In reality, the dazzlingly high rates of growth of output, year in and out, were not achieved by magic, nor by governments, nor by management; they required the muscle, brain and discipline and the unremitting toil of millions of collaborating workers. This is the character omitted from the drama, the character required to create the output, but in conditions of political and social passivity, not to say apathy. The 'flexibilities' and 'structural adjustments' that sound so comfortingly remote from people, so sterile of moral content, are in fact attributes of workforces. The 'adjustments' are imposed in countries where one of the most massive and continuing sources of subsidy to the growth of capital derives from a failure to pay the full costs of the process, as seen in the workers' conditions of housing and nutrition, water and drainage, in pollution, in the exhaustion of labour, in all the casual savageries of police regimes.

The newly industrializing countries are unstable precisely because of the disciplines and sacrifices which the frenetic pace of growth has imposed upon the workforce. The condition of maintaining what stability there is now requires the continuation of high rates of growth. At each check to growth, there is some sense of foreboding in the ruling order that it could produce an explosion of popular rage. Remedial action in Brazil and Mexico was long delayed, both because their governments refused to postpone their dash for growth, their attempt to enter the world order of powerful states, and because they feared the possibility of rebellion, particularly in the run-up to national elections (in July 1982 in Mexico and November 1982 in Brazil). The continuing fears of the Seoul establishment were vindicated in the anger that swept the country, in the strikes and occupations and popular seizure of Gwang-ju in 1980; 1984 saw a more modest repetition, with some measures of political liberalization and eager popular response, followed by renewed repression in 1985, and a new wave of revolt in 1986.

The transition to a modern economy is not simply measured by the composition of the output or the skills of the workers. The mechanisms required to enforce involuntary sacrifices at a primitive phase of the growth of capital inhibit, if they do not make impossible, accumulation in a more sophisticated phase. The first can be planned by the state in detail; it is measured in crude, undifferentiated output – of coal, iron ore and steel, fertilizers. Here the state can overshadow all. Import-substitution industrialization often fits such a phase, and it does not require the conscious participation of most of the labour force. A regime whose main instrument to enforce conformity is terror for the majority and bribes for the few can keep up an impressive rate of growth of crude output regardless of what the workforce thinks – as was done in Britain in the nineteenth century, or Russia in the 1930s and 1940s (and sporadically thereafter). The cost is very high, but it can be done. However, the more variegated the output becomes, and the more intensive the skill and technology required, dependent upon continuous technical innovation and the creative participation of the workers, then the more the operation of the economy requires the deliberate, conscious and rational participation of millions of people, with their psychological involvement and responsibility. No planning system can substitute for this, and the imposition of a single centre of authority turns the system into chaos. Thus, the pursuit of growth itself forces a different kind of 'liberalization' from the one we have hitherto considered. How to make the transition from the old to the new system of production is a problem perpetually besetting Eastern Europe and Russia, for there the old system created the dominant institutions and they will not now simply allow themselves to be adjusted away.

There is one known and one hypothetical way to ensure mass involvement. The known way is by means of an elaborate, detailed and changing structure of incentives and incomes that relates changing market priorities to the detail of production; the final sanctions for failure in making the right adjustments are unemployment and bankruptcy. The state may intervene to seek to ensure certain outcomes, but it also is ultimately dependent upon the independent operation of the market. It is a feature of such a system that none of the participants can completely determine the general outcome of the market, nor even predict it; it is also important that the incentives and sanctions remain powerful, lest people refuse to work or to change (and possess the resources to escape the penalties). The hypothetical system – which has on occasions operated in certain circumstances – is one in which workers control the process of production in detail; output is determined by the immediate producers, and, in aggregate, the composition of the total output is decided collectively. Such a system is determined entirely by the participants; demand and supply are fused in one. It implies a democratic, collective decision-making process to ensure the proportionalities are maintained.

Hitherto, it has been the aim of the governments of the newly industrializing countries to do all in their power to frustrate the growth of the most modest forms of worker involvement embodied in independent organization and bargaining, the first steps in the incorporation of workers in the conscious direction of the process of production. Worker involvement is seen simply as praising the government, waving flags when Ministers tour factories, a walk-on stage army to ratify the fantasies of the rulers. Yet, independent trade unions are vital for the operation of advanced economies. Everywhere in the newly industrializing countries they are banned or neutralized, from the tame CGT of Mexico and the yellow unions of Brazil (although both Mexico and Brazil also have some independent unions) to the government-controlled NTUC in Singapore and the explicit legal prohibition on the intervention of 'third parties' (that is, national trade unions) in South Korean industrial disputes. Thus, governments seek to prevent the development of just those forms of organization demanded by the operation of mature capitalism.

Even the limited forms allowed often prove incompatible with the greed of capital or the ambitions of governments for total conformity. Both South Korea and Singapore are moving towards the dissolution of national unions in favour of plant unions where each isolated group of workers is exposed to the full power of employers and state without the legal possibility of help from other workers (in Taiwan, unions are already limited to single companies and single local administrative districts, which in effect makes national unions illegal). Strikes have been illegal in Taiwan since 1949, and Singapore has effectively made them illegal. In South Korea, General Park's 1971 ban on strikes was abrogated by his successor, General Chun, in 1981, only to be replaced by a statute stipulating that no collective bargaining was to be started without government approval (strikes are banned for employees in government, national and local, in state-owned companies and in defence industries). Covertly, government and employers collaborate to frustrate organization, to imprison, silence or kill militants. It is here that the 'low-wage competition' in imports to Europe and North America begins, but the governments there show strange fortitude in tolerating the treatment of workers in newly industrializing countries while being eager to curb their imports.

Such regimes make for fewer labour disputes, for the illusion of national unanimity is based upon the enforced silence of the majority, but they pose severe obstacles to moving on to a modern economy. They also mean that when disputes occur, they prove more intractable and violent, more swift to move on to political opposition. The 1975 dispute at Hyundai's Ulsan shipyards swiftly changed to riots; the 1980 miners' dispute led to the seizure of the town of Sabuk; the disputes in Gwang-ju led to the seizure of the province. Terrorizing the workforce so as to maintain very low wages and long hours has declining returns with a maturing economy. Liberalizing imports will not touch this problem, nor will political liberalization which stops at the gates of the factory. In fact, the emerging forces of the economy oblige employers to defeat the law if production is to proceed – as South African employers have for long been obliged to evade the apartheid provisions so that they can employ skilled black workers or negotiate with *de facto* associations of black workers. There are reports that foreign employers in Taiwan have already reached national agreements with illegal proto-unions as the only means available of easing the supply of skilled labour and standardizing incentives.

Without a relaxation of the repressive conditions governing labour and society at large, it will prove increasingly difficult to make the transition to a modern economy. The growth of capital will be punctuated by explosions of the frustrated fury of the workers, simultaneously called upon to play an increasingly responsible role but denied the legal means to do so. The selfsame problem afflicts many countries, including the Eastern European countries and South Africa. If only one of these explosions were to spill over into revolution, it would completely change the terms of reference of the argument concerning repression.

A comparable point concerns the problems thrown up by the process of the geographical dispersal of manufacturing capacity from the more developed countries. For although this is not the cause of unemployment, it is the source of a radical reduction in the power of organized labour to limit the depredations of capital. The mobility of capital means that it can escape from a national context which appears unfavourable (whether that is the result of an unsympathetic government or of strongly organized trade unions). An integrated system of manufacturing also creates a single global labour market, moving towards one price for labour in each skill grade regardless of whether the countries are more or less developed (of course, restrictions on the movement of labour inhibit this process of generalization, but only to a limited degree). This implies that groups of workers in different countries compete with each other for employment, offering employers the lowest price at a given level of labour productivity. The power of trade unions to influence this bargain without the support of the state is limited in a national context; in the international, it hardly exists for most occupations.

Hitherto, trade unions in the more developed countries have had a more or less explicit alliance with government to seek to stabilize employment and incomes, to damp down competition between workers and to create legal defences for workers against the competitive drive of employers. Often this has led to a legal framework for the regulation of the labour market (from the legal recognition of unions and collective bargaining and minimum wage, safety and health regulations to welfare provisions). In the post-war period, governments often agreed to concede such collaboration in return for the political loyalty of the union leaderships and the majority of their members to the status quo. In its heyday, the welfare state in Britain summarized the long-term and institutional character of this alliance between the state and labour; it was embodied in the social-democratic state and the common approach of the two dominant political parties, Conservative and Labour (defined in what was seen as a common political perspective, 'Butskellism', named after the Chancellors of the Exchequer of the two parties, Butler and Gaitskell). It was assumed by both the government and labour that capital was immobile and therefore in essence national. The state could accordingly guide and shape the behaviour of capital; a tripartite coalition was possible, and was explicit in many of the institutions governing the economy. That possibility is immediately jeopardized by the capacity of capital (as finance or profits, rather than as factories) to move, and to do so not only without loss but with the possibility of enhanced profits. If the state cannot control capital, it has little interest in an alliance with labour. On the contrary, it now needs to enforce conditions on labour which will persuade capital to invest in the country (or stay there if it is already operating there). The machinery of the welfare state and the political concessions embodied in nationalized industries become redundant; social democracy loses its *raison d'être*.

Although capital can go international, this is much more difficult for labour. It took many decades to create national trade-union structures with some power to curb competition between workers, and that was almost invariably achieved with some political assistance from the state in its own interest. Without a state and on an international plane, the task becomes daunting. Yet without measures to curb competition, the power of employers is enormously increased. They can play off groups of workers in many different countries against each other; they can organize an auction in which the lowest paid – at a given level of productivity – win, and do so in secrecy, since the competing workers have no way of knowing what the other bids are. The penalty for those who fail to work for the lowest world price of labour is unemployment. It is here that the fears in the more developed countries are most justified. After more than a century and a half in the long, slow struggle to establish order in the national labour markets, suddenly it seems world capital can escape and, furthermore, can force the reversal of all those gains. Capital has stolen a march, and labour is still far from understanding the implications of that, let alone beginning to create the appropriate institutions to counter it.

*

The Third World is disappearing. Not the countries themselves, nor the inhabitants, much less the poor who so powerfully coloured the original definition of the concept, but the argument. Third Worldism began as a critique of an unequal world, a programme for economic development and justice, a type of national reformism dedicated to the creation of new societies and a new world. It ends with its leading protagonists either dead, defeated or satisfied to settle simply for national power rather than international equality; the rhetoric remains, now toothless, the decoration for squabbles over the pricing of commodities or flows of capital.

The conception of an interdependent, interacting, global manufacturing system cuts across the old view of a world consisting of nation-states as well as one of groups of countries, more and less developed and centrally planned – the First, the Third and the Second Worlds. Those notions bore some relationship to an older economy, one marked by the exchange of raw materials for manufactured goods. But the new world that has superseded it is far more complex and does not lend itself to the simple identification of First and Third, haves and have-nots, rich and poor, industrialized and non-industrialized.

Yet the world order is still dominated by the culture, politics and ideology of the old pattern, a world of national egotisms where states determine what is important. Indeed, the global manufacturing system can only be identified through the prism of national shares of output; the interests of states take priority over understanding the technical geography of production. The concepts of nationalism thus organize our perception and our consciousness, and so predetermine our view of what is reality. It will be a long time before the identification of the world catches up with the reality.

The simple dichotomies of the past, First and Third World, imposed their own gross distortion. Poor and rich were never properly defined by different countries. Even the so-called poorest country has its clutch of millionaires living in the same lifestyle as their peers in the richest country. Each so-called rich country has, trapped in the cruel interstices of its economy, thousands of hungry and poor. The division between rich and poor is represented in each microcosm of the system; poverty at the global level was never a territorial concept. The 'geopoliticalization' of inequality illuminated in the first instance, but finally obfuscated. The poor of the United States were defined out of existence. The rich of India were carefully concealed from view.

The case deflected attention to geography. The stereotypes and the impassioned reformism attracted a generation of idealistic young people. Those on the left absorbed an enormous amount from Third Worldism and a version of the experience of the less developed countries. It seemed for a long time the only part of the world where men and women still struggled to be free, still had the capacity to dream and strive for a different world. When the more developed countries seemed sunk in apathy, selfishness and materialism, the old aspirations seemed still to exist in a Third World – as well as the energy to achieve them, to leap the stages of what seemed bureaucratically defined history. States became the surrogate for all those unknown millions of poor, and the rhetoric of national politicians stood proxy for the yearnings of silent masses. It was a nonsense to conceal the emergence of new classes, relating to the majority in much the same way as they did everywhere else.

Capitalism remained the same. The market remained the market. Only for a short time did it seem that the state had conquered the economy – to guarantee full employment in one part of the world, to force perpetual growth in the other. The period was long enough to soak into popular consciousness and the social sciences on both left and right. Conscious reform by the state, it was supposed, now replaced the blind transformations of the market. It was a half hint of socialism, a human order determined by need, but without the precondition – power in the hands of the majority. In place of popular democratic control of the means of production, much of the Third World offered old-fashioned dictatorship, the one-party state or the revolutionary military junta. The majority could not be trusted to exercise power.

National reformist aspiration grew weak as the new orders settled more comfortably into power. The old issues became less urgent. But, also, the needs of accumulation limited the potential for social reform. Furthermore, an increasingly integrated world system lays down narrower and narrower limits to the possibility of local eccentricity, including reform. In a competitive system, holding down the price of labour takes precedence over protecting it, and the domestic economy becomes increasingly a spin-off of a wider order. Such a prospect causes understandable alarm. If the state cannot control domestic affairs, regulate and order the growth of incomes and employment, and propel self-sufficient economic growth, all, it seems, becomes dangerously random. It is little consolation to repeat that we can always perceive the losses in what is declining, rarely the gains in what is rising. Nor is it much comfort to observe that if the old aspiration was utopian, then to stop believing it is the precondition for identifying the grounds for real optimism. One of those sources of optimism is in the weakening of the drive to war; as capital and states become slightly dissociated, the pressures to world war are slightly weakened. Furthermore, there promises to be some decrease in the belief that killing foreigners is a good thing. The process of dispersal of manufacturing capacity brings enormous hope to areas where poverty has hitherto appeared immoveable, and makes possible new divisions of labour and specializations which will vastly enhance the capacity of the world to feed everyone. Above all, the realization of one world offers the promise of a rationally ordered system, determined by its inhabitants in the interests of need, not profit or war. Of course, it will not be won by waiting. The world of states will not wither away of its own accord; old orders cling to their power with increasing vigour as they grow obsolete, particularly when they continue to have privileged access to the surplus generated in the system. Great battles will be required against states to win the new world; but the possibilities of doing so are now much enhanced by the changes that are under way.

It is particularly painful for the left to detach itself from the fate of states. If trade unions needed national governments to curb the competition of workers and so limit the drive of capital, the left needed the state to introduce reforms, even if that meant overthrowing the old government by national revolution and creating a new state. In the last two great waves of the struggle for national independence – the first when empires in Europe broke up in the first twenty years of this century; and the second when the European empires in the rest of the world disintegrated after the Second World War – the cause of socialism became swamped by the politics of nationalism and national liberation. Indeed, straightforward revolutions that did not involve expelling a colonial power became none the less 'national liberation', symbolizing how far the interests of creating a new state had overcome any interest in abolishing states. Nation and state replaced class. And the world of states was thereby preserved from challenge, for the warriors against imperialism contributed to maintaining it. That issue is now nearly over. The world consists of independent states, threatened by revolts of national liberation movements – the Tamils of Sri Lanka, the Sikhs of India, the Mindanao Muslims. These issues are far removed from the great unfinished question of world history: the freedom not of minorities, nor of states, but of the majority.

Select Bibliography

The field covered in the book is wide, and the reading listed below is therefore restricted to works giving an access to different areas of study. It is limited to books published in English (excluding articles, reports and monographs cited in the notes), and works that are relatively easy to obtain. The country report series of the World Bank provides the best up-to-date source of material for any particular developing country, but these are supposedly confidential to governments and so difficult to obtain. (However, some of the more substantial reports have finally been published.)

Agarwala, A. N., and S. P. Singh, eds., *The Economics of Underdevelopment*, New York, Oxford University Press, 1963.

Ahluwalia, Isher Judge, *Industrial Growth in India: Stagnation since the Mid-sixties*, Delhi, Oxford University Press, 1985.

Bairoch, Paul, *The Economic Development of the Third World since 1900* (transl. by Cynthia Postan), London, Methuen, 1975.

Batchelor, R. A., R. L. Major and A. D. Morgan, *Industrialization and the Basis for Trade*, London, National Institute of Economic and Social Research/Cambridge University Press, 1981.

Belassa, Bela, *Policy Reform in Developing Countries*, New York, Pergamon, 1977.

The Newly Industrializing Countries in the World Economy, New York, Pergamon, 1981.

Development Strategies in Semi-industrialized Economies, Baltimore, John Hopkins University Press, 1982.

and others, *The Structure of Protection in Developing Countries*, Baltimore, World Bank, John Hopkins University Press, 1971.

Bennett, Mark, *Public Policy and Industrial Development: the Case of the Mexican Auto Parts Industry*, London, Westview, 1984.

Bergson, Joel, *Brazil: Industrialization and Trade Policies*, London, OECD/Oxford University Press, 1970.

Bhagwati, Jagdish, *Foreign Trade Regimes and Economic Development: Anatomy and Consequences of Exchange Control Regimes*, Cambridge, Mass., National Bureau of Economic Research/Ballinger, 1978.

Booth, Anne, and Peter McCauley, *The Indonesian Economy during the Soeharto Era*, Kuala Lumpur, Oxford University Press, 1981.

Cheng Tong Yung, *The Economy of Hong Kong*, new ed., Hong Kong, Far East Publications, 1982.

Cole, D., and P. N. Lyman, *Korean Development: the Interplay of Politics and Economics* (Studies in the Modernization of the Republic of Korea, 1945–75), Cambridge, Mass., Harvard University Press, 1971.

Emmanuel, Arghiri, *Unequal Exchange: A Study of the Imperialism of Free Trade*, New York, Monthly Review Press, 1972.

Falkus, Malcolm E., ed., *Readings in the History of Economic Growth*, Nairobi, Oxford University Press, 1968.

Galenson, Walter, ed., *Economic Growth and Structural Change in Taiwan: the Postwar Experience of the Republic of China*, London, Cornell University Press, 1979.

Geiger, Theodore (with Francis M. Geiger), *Tales of Two Cities: the Development Progress of Hong Kong and Singapore*, Washington, National Planning Association, 1973.

Gersowitz, M., and others, *The Theory and Experience of Economic Development: Essays in Honour of Sir W. Arthur Lewis*, London, Allen & Unwin, 1982.

Harris, Nigel, *Competition and the Corporate Society, British Conservatism, the State and Industry, 1945–1964*, London, Methuen, 1972.

India-China: Underdevelopment and Revolution, Delhi, Vikas, 1974.

The Mandate of Heaven: Marx and Mao in Modern China, London, Quartet, 1978.

Of Bread and Guns: the World Economy in Crisis, Harmondsworth, Penguin, 1983.

Hasan, Parvez, *Korea: Problems and Issues in a Rapidly Growing Economy*, Baltimore, John Hopkins University Press, 1976.

Ho, Samuel P. S., *Economic Development of Taiwan, 1860–1970*, New Haven, Yale University Press, 1978.

Jones, Leroy, and Il Sakong, *Government, Business and Entrepreneurship in Economic Development: the Korean Case* (Studies in the Modernization of the Republic of Korea, 1945–75), Cambridge, Mass., Council on East Asian Affairs/Harvard University Press, 1980 (other volumes referred to as 'Studies').

Kate, Adriaan ten, and Robert Bruce Wallace, *Protection and Economic Development in Mexico*, Farnborough, Gower, 1980.

Kidron, Michael, *Capitalism and Theory*, London, Pluto Press, 1974.

Kreuger, Anne O., *Foreign Trade Regimes and Economic Development: Liber-*

alization Attempts and Consequences, Cambridge, Mass., National Bureau of Economic Research/Ballinger, 1978.

Kuo, Shirley W. Y., Gustav Ranis and John C. H. Fei, *The Taiwan Success Story; Rapid Growth with Improved Distribution in the Republic of China, 1952–1979*, Boulder, Colorado, Westview, 1981.

Kuznets, Simon, *Modern Economic Growth: Rate, Structure and Spread*, London, Yale University Press, 1966.

Lee, Eddy, ed., *Export-led Industrialization and Development*, Bangkok, ILO, 1981.

Leys, Colin, *Underdevelopment in Kenya*, London, Heinemann, 1975.

Little, I. M. D., Tibor Skitovsky and Maurice Scott, *Industry and Trade in Some Developing Countries: a Comparative Study*, London, OECD/Oxford University Press, 1970.

Economic Development: Theory, Policy and International Relations, New York, Twentieth Century Fund/Basic Books, 1982.

Mason, E. S., and others, *The Economic and Social Modernization of the Republic of Korea* ('Studies'), Cambridge, Mass., Harvard University Press, 1980.

Meier, Gerald M., *Leading Issues in Development Economics*, new ed., New York, Oxford University Press, 1964.

and Dudley Seers, eds., *Pioneers in Development*, New York, World Bank/Oxford University Press, 1984.

Mukerhjee, Santosh, *Restructuring of Industrial Economies and Trade with Developing Countries*, New Delhi, ILO/Concept, 1978.

Ranis, G., ed., *Government and Economic Development*, New Haven, Yale University Press, 1977 (see also Kuo).

Roos, Daniel, Alan Altshuler and others, *The Future of the Automobile* (Report of the MIT International Automobile Program), London, Allen & Unwin, 1984.

Seers, Dudley, and Leonard Joy, eds., *Development in a Divided World*, Harmondsworth, Penguin, 1970 (see also Meier).

Streeten, Paul, *Towards a New Strategy for Development*, New York, Pergamon, 1979.

Supple, Barry E., ed., *The Experience of Economic Growth: Case Studies in Economic History*, New York, Random House, 1963.

Turner, Louis, Neil McMullen, and others, *The Newly Industrializing Countries: Trade and Adjustment*, London, Royal Institute of International Affairs/Allen & Unwin, 1982.

Tyler, William G., *The Brazilian Industrial Economy*, Lexington, Lexington Books, 1981.

Vries, Barend A., ed., *Export Promotion Policies* (World Bank Staff Working Paper 313 – mimeo), Washington DC, World Bank, January 1979.

Warren, Bill, *Imperialism: Pioneer of Capitalism* (edited by John Sender), Verso, New Left Books, 1980.

Westphal, L. E., and K. S. Kim, *Industrial Policy and Development in Korea* (World Bank Staff Working Paper 263 – mimeo), Washington DC, World Bank, 1977.

Yung W. Rhee and Gary Parnell, *Korean Industrial Competence: Where It Comes From* (World Bank Staff Working Papers 469), Washington DC, World Bank, July 1981.

Winter, J. M., ed., *War and Economic Development, Essays in Memory of David Joslin*, Cambridge, Cambridge University Press, 1975.

World Bank, *World Development Report*, Washington DC, World Bank, various years.

You Poh Seng and Lim Chong Yah, eds., *The Singapore Economy*, Singapore, Eastern Universities Press, 1971.

Notes

Chapter 1

1. Paul Samuelson, 'International trade and the equalization of factor prices', *Economic Journal*, 58, June 1948, pp. 163–84.

2. See in particular: Economic Commission for Latin America (ECLA), *The Economic Development of Latin America and its Principal Problems*, New York, United Nations, 1950; *Economic Survey of Latin America, 1949*, Part 1, New York, United Nations, 1951, reproduced in *Economic Bulletin for Latin America*, 7, 1, Santiago, February 1962; *Problemas teóricos y prácticos del crecimiento económico*, New York, United Nations, 1952; *International cooperation in a Latin American development policy*, New York, United Nations, 1954 (especially Chapter 4).

   For a most useful account of Prebisch's intellectual development, see Joseph L. Love, 'Raúl Prebisch and the origins of the doctrine of unequal exchange', *Latin American Research Review*, 15, 3, 1980, pp. 47–72.

3. *The Economic Development of Latin America*, op. cit., p. 1.

4. See Thomas Balogh, *Dollar Crisis: Causes and Cure*, Oxford, Blackwell, 1949, and G. D. A. MacDougall, *The World Dollar Problem*, London, Macmillan, 1957.

5. *The Economic Development of Latin America*, op. cit., p. 65.

6. See Hollis Chenery, 'Interactions between industrialization and exports', *American Economic Review* (Papers and Proceedings, 92nd Annual Meeting, 1979), 70, 2, May 1980, p. 281; and United Nations, *Relative Prices of Exports and Imports of Underdeveloped Countries*, Department of Economic Affairs, Lake Success, New York, 1949, p. 7.

7. Hans Singer, 'The distribution of gains between investing and borrowing countries', *American Economic Review* (Papers and Proceedings), 40, May 1950, pp. 473–85. See also his 'Problems of the industrialization of underdeveloped countries', *International Social Science Bulletin*, 6, 2, 1954. The role of trade in the nineteenth and twentieth centuries is examined by Ragnar Nurkse in *Equilibrium and Growth in the World Economy*, edited by Gottfried Haberler and Robert M. Stern (Harvard Economic Studies 118), Cambridge, Mass., Harvard University Press, 1961; see also Irving

B. Kravis, 'Trade as a handmaiden of growth', *Economic Journal*, December 1970, pp. 850–72.

8. *Economic Survey of Latin America*, op. cit., p. 3.

9. Santiago Macario, 'Protectionism and industrialization in Latin America', *Economic Bulletin for Latin America*, 9, New York, ECLA, United Nations, 1964, p. 63.

10. *The Wealth of Nations*, vol. 1, edited by E. Cannon, London, Methuen, 1950, p. 367.

11. *Imperialism, the Highest Stage of Capitalism*, in *Selected Works*, vol. 5, London, Lawrence & Wishart, 1936.

12. A case which combined a thesis of Rudolf Hilferding, in *Finance Capital, A Study of the Latest Phase of Capitalist Development*, edited and introduced by Tom Bottomore, London, Routledge, 1981 (original edition 1910), and M. N. Roy – see his *Memoirs*, Bombay, Allied Publishers, 1964, and *Documents of the History of the Communist Party of India*, vol. 1, edited by G. Adhikari, New Delhi, People's Publishing House, 1971.

13. *North–South, A Programme for Survival* (Brandt Commission Report), Report of the Independent Commission in International Development Issues, London, Pan, 1980.

14. 'National development policy and external dependence in Latin America', *Journal of Development Studies*, 6/1, October 1969, p. 37.

15. See, for example, Paul Baran, *The Political Economy of Growth*, New York, Monthly Review Press, 1957; A. Emmanuel, *Unequal Exchange: A Study of the Imperialism of Free Trade*, New York, Monthly Review Press, 1972; Samir Amin, *Accumulation on the World Scale: a Critique of the Theory of Underdevelopment*, New York, Monthly Review Press, 2 vols., 1974; A. Gunder Frank, *Dependent Accumulation and Underdevelopment*, New York, Monthly Review Press, 1979, and numerous other works; see also F. M. Cardoso and L. Faletto, *Dependency and Development in Latin America*, Los Angeles, University of California Press, 1979.

16. Thus, the relatively slight differences in long-term growth performance between India and China up to the mid seventies suggested that the underlying material constraints were similar despite different political systems – cf. Chapter 10 in my *India–China: Underdevelopment and Revolution*, Delhi, Vikas, 1974.

17. London, Weidenfeld & Nicolson, 1968.

18. In E. A. G. Robinson, ed., *Economic Consequences of the Size of Nations*, London, International Economic Association/Macmillan, 1960.

19. Michael Kidron, *Capitalism and Theory*, London, Pluto, 1974, pp. 108–9.

20. Ibid. See also his 'Memories of development', republished in ibid. For a summary of the contingent factors at stake, see my *The Crisis of Development*

(World University Service Symposium, Ibadan, Nigeria), mimeo, Geneva, 1972.

21. For example, see P. T. Bauer and B. S. Yamey, *The Economics of Underdeveloped Countries*, Chicago, Chicago University Press, 1957; Jacob Viner, *International Trade and Economic Development*, Oxford, Clarendon Press, 1953; and Gottfried Haberler, *Terms of Trade and Economic Development*, Cairo, National Bank of Egypt, 1959. The neoclassical case was developed in: I. M. D. Little, T. Skitovsky and M. Scott, *Industry and Trade in Some Developing Countries*, Development Centre, London OECD/Oxford University Press, 1970 (with associated studies of Brazil by Bergson; Mexico by Kingl; India by Bhagwati and Desai; Pakistan by Lewis; Taiwan and the Philippines by Hsing, Power and Sicat); Anne O. Kreuger, *Foreign Trade Regimes and Economic Development: Liberalization Attempts and Consequences*, Cambridge, Mass., National Bureau of Economic Research/Ballinger, 1978, and in the same series, Jagdish Bhagwati, *Foreign Trade Regimes and Economic Development: Anatomy and Consequences of Exchange Control Regimes*, 1978; B. Balassa, and others, *The Structure of Protection in Developing Countries*, Baltimore, John Hopkins University Press, 1971, and *Development Strategies in Semi-industrial Economies*, Baltimore, John Hopkins University Press, 1982; I. M. D. Little, *Economic Development: Theory, Policy and International Relations*, New York, Twentieth Century Fund/Basic Books, 1982. For a polemical summary, see Deepak Lal, *The Poverty of 'Development Economics'* (Hobart Papers), London, Institute of Economic Affairs, 1983.

22. *Political Economy of Growth*, op. cit., p. 249.

23. See, for example, Pierre Jalée, *The Pillage of the Third World*, 1968, and *The Third World in World Economy*, 1969, both Monthly Review Press, New York.

24. Most elaborately explored in Emmanuel's *Unequal Exchange*, op. cit.; cf. also Christian Palloix, *L'Économie mondiale capitaliste*, Paris, Maspero, 1971; and Emmanuel and others, *Imperialismo comercio internacional: el intercambio desigual*, Cordoba (Argentina), Pasado y Presente, 1971.

25. *Accumulation on a World Scale*, op. cit., pp. 83–4 and pp. 89–90.

26. Fernando H. Cardoso, 'The originality of a copy: CEPAL and the idea of development', *CEPAL Review*, second half, 1977, p. 26.

27. *Political Economy of Growth*, op. cit., pp. 194–5.

28. The literature is voluminous, but among the best examples and discussions might be included: Colin Leys, *Underdevelopment in Kenya*, London, Heinemann, 1975; Anibal Quijano, *Nationalism and Capitalism in Peru: a Study in Neo-imperialism*, New York, Monthly Review Press, 1971; Thomas Biersteker, *Distortion or Development? Contending Perspectives on*

the Multinational Corporations, Cambridge, Mass., MIT Press, 1979.

29. Among other factors enumerated in *Towards a Dynamic Development Policy for Latin America*, New York, United Nations, 1963, p. 71. See his much later, *Capitalismo periférico: crisis y transformación*, Mexico City, Fondo de Cultura Económica, 1981.

30. Prebisch, in Gerald H. Meier and Dudley Seers, eds., *Pioneers in Development*, Washington, World Bank/Oxford University Press, 1984, p. 189.

31. *Political Economy of Growth*, op. cit., p. 225. See also his 'On the political economy of backwardness', *The Manchester School*, January 1952, republished in A. N. Agarwala and S. P. Singh, *The Economics of Underdevelopment*, New York, Galaxy Books, 1963, pp. 75–92.

32. Arthur Lewis, 'Economic development with unlimited supplies of labour', *The Manchester School*, May 1954.

33. By P. C. Mahalanobis; see his 'Some observations on the process of growth of national income', *Sankya*, 12 (Indian Statistical Institute, Calcutta), September 1953, pp. 307–12.

34. Sir Arthur Lewis, in Meier and Seers, *Pioneers*, op. cit., p. 129.

Chapter 2

1. See Leroy Jones and Il Sakong, *Government, Business and Entrepreneurship in Economic Development: the Korean Case* (Studies in the Modernization of the Republic of Korea, 1945–75), Cambridge, Mass., Council on East Asian Studies/Harvard University Press, 1980, p. 297. On the dominant role of the state, see also E. S. Mason and others, *The Economic and Social Modernization of the Republic of Korea*, same series and publisher, 1980, pp. 471–2.

2. Gilbert T. Brown, *Korean Pricing Policies and Economic Development in the 1960s*, Baltimore, John Hopkins University Press, 1973, p. 265.

3. The 1981 value of South Korea's exports was $21,254m or $546.38 per head of the population. This figure multiplied by China's then population of 991.3 millions produces an export value of $541,626.5m (compared to the actual value in that year of $21,560.1m); multiplied by India's population of 690.2m yields an export value of $377,111·5m (acutal $8,064m) – derived from Tables 1 and 9, *World Development Report 1983*, Washington DC, World Bank, 1983, pp. 148–9 and 164–5.

4. Pal Yung Moon and Byung Seo Ruy, *Korea's Agricultural Policies in Historical Perspective* (Working Paper 7704), mimeo, Korea Development Institute, April 1972, p. 60.

5. The source of the first item is D. C. Coleman and P. N. Lyman, *Korean Development: the Interplay of Politics and Economics*, Cambridge, Mass.,

Harvard University Press, 1971, p. 43; the second, Charles R. Frank, Kwang Suk Kim and Larry E. Westphal, *Foreign Trade Regimes and Economic Development: Korea*, New York, National Bureau of Applied Economic Research/Columbia University Press, 1975, p. 239.

6. Shin Byung Hyun, Deputy Prime Minister and Minister of Planning, Address, 13th meeting, International Economic Consultative Organisation for Korea, 16 July 1984, included in *Economic Bulletin*, Seoul, Economic Planning Board, July 1984, p. 12.

7. 'There are still a large number of Korean businessmen who are reluctant to do business in accordance with the rules of free competition' – Kim Kihwan, 'Korea's external economic policies in a new phase of development', ibid., p. 20.

8. ibid., p. 18. See also In Yong Chung (vice-minister), 'The economy is already too big to be managed in the old way by heavy-handed Government bureaucrats' – ibid., p. 21.

9. Leroy Jones, op. cit., p. 296. See also M. K. Datta-Chaudhuri, 'No state, outside the socialist bloc, ever came anywhere near this measure of control over the economy's investible resources' – 'Industrialization and foreign trade: the development experience of South Korea and the Philippines', in Eddy Lee, ed., *Export-led Industrialization and Development*, Bangkok, International Labour Organization, 1981, p. 56.

10. Cited in *Financial Times*, 31 October 1984, p. 18.

11. Leroy Jones, op. cit., p. 213.

12. 'Korea provides an almost classical example of an economy following its comparative advantage and reaping the gains predicted by conventional theory' – I. E. Westphal and K. S. Kim, *Industrial Policy and Development in Korea* (World Bank Staff Working Paper 263), mimeo, Washington DC, World Bank, 1977, p. 5.

13. Frank, Kim and Westphal, op. cit., p. 239.

14. Yung Chul Park, 'Export-led development: the Korean experience, 1960–78', in Eddy Lee, ed., *Export-led Industrialization*, op. cit., p. 111.

15. Cited by I. M. D. Little, 'An economic reconnaissance', in Walter Galenson, ed., *Economic Growth and Structural Change in Taiwan: the Postwar Experience of the Republic of China*, Ithaca, NY, Cornell University Press, 1979, p. 464.

16. Calculated from L. E. Westphal, Yung W. Rhee and Gary Purnell, *Korean Industrial Competence: Where It Came From* (World Bank Staff Working Paper 469), mimeo, Washington DC, World Bank, July 1981, p. 33.

17. See annex II of United Nations Commission on Transnational Corporations, *Transnational Corporations in World Development*, Third Survey, New York, United Nations, 1983, p. 29.

18. 'An economic reconnaissance', in Walter Galenson, ed., *Economic Growth*, op. cit., p. 448.

19. See Chiang Kai-shek, *China's Destiny*, London, 1947, p. 173.

20. Samuel S. Ho, *The Economic Development of Taiwan, 1860–1970*, New Haven, Yale University Press, 1978, p. 108.

21. See 'Agrarian Reform in China', in my *The Mandate of Heaven: Marx and Mao in Modern China*, London, Quartet, 1978, pp. 134–45.

22. See the speech of the Finance Secretary, Sir John Cowperthwaite, 1978 budget debate, on an accounting system for the colony: 'We might even be right to be apprehensive lest the availability of such figures might lead, by a reversal of cause and effect, to policies designed to have a direct effect on the economy. I would deplore this' – Information Department, *News Release on the Budget Debate*, Hong Kong, Hong Kong Government, 1978.

23. Deepak Nayer, *Economic Journal*, March 1978, cited by *The Economist*, Special Survey of Foreign Investment in Asia, 23 June 1979, p. 4.

24. *Financial Times*, Special Survey, 22 November 1982, p. 1.

Chapter 3

1. On Brazil, the basic data source used here is *Anuário estatístico do Brasil 1980*, Brasilia, Secretaria de Planejamento da Presidéncia da República (Fundação Instituto Brasileiro de Geografia e Estatística), 1980; see also *Pequeno documentário estatístico 1963/79*, Brasilia, IPEA (Secretaria de Comunicação Social da Presidéncia da Republica), 1980.

2. Banco de México SA, *Producto interno bruto y gasto 1960–1977* (Serie de Información Económica), Mexico City, 1978; see also *Informe annual 1978*, Mexico City, 1979.

3. Secretaria de Programación y Presupuesto, *Sistema de cuentas nacionales de México*, Tomo 1, *Resumen*, Mexico City, SPP, n.d.

4. *Censo industrial, resumen general 1976*, Mexico City, Secreteria de Programación y Presupuesto, Coordinación General del Sistema Nacional de Información, 1976.

5. Albert Fishlow, 'Brazilian development in a long term perspective', *American Economic Review*, 10/2, *Papers and Proceedings*, 92nd Congress of the American Economic Association, 1979, May 1980.

6. Centro de Contas Nacionais (Fundação Getulio Vargas), *Conjunturas econômicas*, 25 September 1971 and 26 February and 27 August 1972. See also Pedro S. Malan and Regis Borelli, 'The Brazilian economy in the seventies: old and new developments', *World Development*, 5, 1/21, January–February 1977, p. 31.

7. 'Incentives to import substitution have increased substantially more than

incentives to export' – Bela Belassa, 'Incentive policies in Brazil', *World Development*, 7/11–12, November–December 1979, p. 1036. This, he says elsewhere, 'increased the bias against exports that had existed already in 1973' – 'Policy responses to external shocks in selected Latin American countries', *Quarterly Review of Economics and Business*, 21/2, Summer 1981, pp. 131–64.

8. *Visão*, 'Quem é quem na economia Brasileira', various issues; cf. also William G. Tyler, 'Dependent growth and multinational firms in Brazil', *Ibero Americano*, 7/11, 1977, and *The Brazilian Industrial Economy*, Lexington, 1981.

9. See Tyler, 'even into the eighties, it was one of the most closed economies in the world', *Brazilian Industrial Economy*, op. cit., p. 47. Or Fishlow: 'the model never corresponded to a free enterprise stereotype' – op. cit.

10. 'Individual government agencies have the persisting power through their ability to grant or deny incentive concessions, to make or break individual business enterprises. The profitability of an individual firm is as much dependent upon its governmental relations as it is upon its productive efficiency' – Tyler, *Brazilian Industrial Economy*, op. cit., 1981, p. 59.

11. 1969–71, calculated from series, 1966–77, in *Consumos Aparentes*, Dirección General de Economia Agricola (Secreteria de Agricultura y Recursos Hidrolicos); 1979–81, calculated from series, 1978–81 (1981 figure is an estimate), unpublished official data. See also to 1979, *Las actividades económicas en México, manuales de información basica de la nación*, Secreteria de Programmación y Presupuesto, tomo 3, 1980, pp. 47–52.

12. *Two Years of Revolution, 1848 and 1849*, 1850, in Karl Marx and Frederick Engels, *Collected Works*, vol. 10, London, Lawrence & Wishart, 1979, p. 361.

Chapter 4

1. A. W. Clausen, President, World Bank, *Global Interdependence in the 1980s* (Remarks before the Yomiuri International Economics Society, Tokyo), Washington DC, World Bank, 13 January 1982.

2. Extracted, calculated and rearranged from *The World Development Report*, various issues, Washington DC, World Bank, (tables 3, 8 and 10). Taiwan data from *Taiwan Statistical Data Book 1983*, Taipei, Council for Economic Planning and Development, Executive Yuan, 1983, table 1, section 3, p. 21, and table 8, section 10, p. 189.

3. 'Low-income countries' – the World Bank classification for those countries with an income per head below $410 in 1980 (thirty-three countries, with 49 per cent of the world's population, producing 1.6 per cent of the world's

manufactured exports or 0.3 per cent of 'machinery and transport equipment' and 1.9 per cent of 'other manufacturing').

4. 'Middle-income countries' of the less developed countries in 1980 had an income per head of the population of between $410 and $4,500 (sixty-three countries with 26 per cent of the world's population, producing 13.2 per cent of world manufacturing exports, or 7.9 per cent of 'machinery and transport equipment' and 14.2 per cent of 'other manufacturing').

'Industrial-market economies' are those with, in 1980, an income per head over $4,500, but excluding both high-income oil exporters and the countries of the Eastern Bloc ('non-market industrial economies' or 'centrally planned economies'). The group had 16.2 per cent of the world's population.

5. Calculated from *World Development Report 1983*, Washington DC, World Bank, 1983, table 3, p. 152. For alternative estimates, cf. table 8 in Chad Leechor, Harinder S. Kohli and Sujin Hur, *Structural Changes in World Industry: A Quantitative Analysis of Recent Developments* (World Bank Technical Paper), Washington DC, World Bank, 1983, p. 31.

6. GATT Secretariat, *Textiles and Clothing in the World Economy*, Geneva, GATT, 1984.

7. Source: International Steel Institute.

8. The Organization for Economic Cooperation and Development, Paris, the association of twenty-four non-Communist more developed countries (but including also Turkey and Greece).

9. Source: R. Blackhurst, R. Marian and J. Tumlir, *Adjustment, Trade and Growth in Developed and Developing Countries* (GATT Studies in International Trade No. 6), mimeo, Geneva, GATT, 1978.

10. *Dynamic Products in the Export of Manufactured Goods from Developing Countries to Developed Market Economy Countries, 1970 to 1976*, Geneva, UNCTAD, 1978 (ST/MD/18).

Chapter 5

1. H. G. Johnson, ed., *Economic Nationalism in Old and New States*, London, Allen & Unwin, 1968, p. 15.

2. Santiago Macario, 'Protectionism and industrialization in Latin America', *Economic Bulletin for Latin America*, IX, New York, Economic Commission for Latin America, United Nations, 1964, p. 77.

3. Many of those who claimed to adhere to Marxism on the question of free trade remained surprisingly innocent of Marx's settled views, summarized in: 'We are for Free Trade, because by Free Trade all economical laws, with their most astounding contradictions, will act upon a larger scale, upon a greater extent of territory, upon the territory of the whole earth; and because,

from the uniting of all these contradictions into a single group, where they stand face to face, will result the struggle which will itself eventuate in the emancipation of the proletarians.' – Speech of Dr Marx, 'Protectionists, free traders and the working classes' (prepared for the Free Trade Congress, Brussels, 16–18 September 1847), in Karl Marx and Frederick Engels, *Collected Works*, Vol. 5, *1845–1847*, London, Lawrence & Wishart, 1976, p. 290.

4. An idea favoured by some right-wing nationalists in Italy after 1918, it re-appeared in China as part of the talk on the Kuomintang Right – cf., for example, Tai Chi-t'ao. A suggestion of the same idea occurs in Russian propaganda (the Cold War was thus a contest between a proletarian Soviet Union and a bourgeois United States). The concept serves the function of subordinating all domestic class conflict to external national rivalries. On Tai, see Maurice Meisner, *Li Ta-chao and the Origins of Chinese Marxism*, Cambridge, Mass., Harvard University Press, 1967, p. 177.

5. The World Bank notes in Indonesia that the capital intensity of production in import-competing sectors was four times greater than in exporting sectors – see Note 1, *Indonesia: Financial Resources and Human Development in the Eighties* (Report No. 3795, IND), mimeo, Jakarta, East Asia and Pacific Regional Office, 3 May 1982.

6. Harry T. Oshima, 'Asia's contribution to world economic recovery in the eighties', *Asia Development Review* (Studies of Asian and Pacific Economic Issues), Manila, Asian Development Bank, 1/1, 1983, p. 49.

7. Joel Bergson, *Brazil: Industrialization and Trade Policies*, London, OECD/Oxford University Press, 1970, Appendix 4, pp. 259–66.

8. *Address to the Annual Meeting of the World Bank and the International Monetary Fund*, 29 September 1969, Washington DC, World Bank, 1969.

9. Gunnar Myrdal, *Development and Underdevelopment*, Cairo, National Bank of Egypt, 1956, p. 283.

10. Albert O. Hirschmann, 'The political economy of import substitution', *Quarterly Journal of Economics*, February 1968, p. 12.

11. David Felix, 'Monetarists, structuralists and import-substitution indus-trialization', in W. Baer and I. Kerstenetsky, eds., *Inflation and Growth in Latin America*, Homewood, Illinois, Irwin, 1964, p. 384.

12. A more polite formulation has it that, 'It is not so much by neglecting the government's presence that the neoclassical picture manages to project the illusion of an economy ruled by the market. Rather, it is by arranging what is placed in the foreground, and in selecting the details that are nudged into the background that a curious transformation of Korea's economy can be achieved.' – Shahid Yusuf and R. Kyle Peters, *Prices, Plans and Investment: the Case of Korea*, mimeo, draft, Washington DC, East Asia Programmes Dept., World Bank, September 1984.

13. I. M. D. Little, 'The experience and causes of rapid labour-intensive development in Korea, Taiwan province, Hong Kong and Singapore, and the possibilities of emulation', in Eddy Lee, ed., *Export-led Industrialization and Development*, Bangkok, ILO, 1981, p. 25.

14. I. M. D. Little, *Economic Development: Theory, Policy and International Relations*, New York, Twentieth-Century Fund/Basic Books, 1982.

15. See M. Michaely, 'Exports and growth', *Journal of Development Economics*, 4, 1, 1977, pp. 49–53. See also Bela Belassa, 'Exports and economic growth', ibid., 5, 2, 1978, pp. 181–9, and William G. Tyler, 'Growth and export expansion in developing countries: some empirical evidence', ibid., 9, 1981.

16. The text seems to have been very poorly proof-read, and may have had a less ludicrous sense originally – cf. Belassa's comments on a paper by Daniel Bitram, 'The export of manufactures in Mexico and its promotion policies', in *Export Promotion Policies* (World Bank Staff Working Paper No. 313), prepared by Barend A. Vries, mimeo, Washington DC, World Bank, January 1979.

17. 'No conceivable calculations on the principle of static comparative advantage can justify these priorities', Datta-Chaudhuri, in Eddy Lee, ed., *Export-led Industrialization*, op. cit., p. 48.

18. This argument is explored in more detail in my *Of Bread and Guns: the World Economy in Crisis*, London, Penguin Books, 1983.

19. Cf. OECD, *Costs and Benefits of Protectionism*, Paris, OECD, 1985.

20. Well refuted in Robert Z. Lawrence, *Can America Compete?*, Washington DC, Broakings, 1984, pp. 72–5.

Chapter 6

1. Calculated from data of the Ministry of Labour (Director-General of Employment and Training), New Delhi, Government of India, n.d. See also Ministry of Finance (Bureau of Public Enterprises), *Annual Report on the Working of Industrial and Commercial Undertakings of the Central Government, 1980/81*, New Delhi, Government of India, 1982.

2. Figures rounded from *Government Employment and Pay: Some International Comparisons* (IMF Occasional Papers No. 24), Peter S. Heller and Alan Tait, Washington DC, International Monetary Fund, 1983.

3. *Capital*, translated by S. Moore, Moscow, Foreign Publishing House, n.d., p. 751.

4. Phyllis Deane, 'War and Industrialization', in J. M. Winter, ed., *War and Economic Development, Essays in Memory of David Joslin*, Cambridge, Cambridge University Press, 1975, p. 91.

5. ibid., p. 97.

6. Charles Issawi, *Egypt, an Economic Analysis*, London, Royal Institute of International Affairs/Oxford University Press, 1963, pp. 21–4.

7. David S. Landes, 'Technological change and development in Western Europe, 1750–1914', in H. J. Habakkuk and M. Postan, eds., *Cambridge Economic History of Europe*, vol. VI, Cambridge, Cambridge University Press, 1966, p. 373.

8. L. D. Trotsky, *Results and Prospects*, 1906, translation and publication with *The Permanent Revolution*, London, New Park, 1962, p. 173.

9. Friedrich Engels, letter to Danielson, 22 September 1982, No. 223, in *Correspondence of Marx and Engels* (Vol. 9, Marxist-Leninist Library), London, Lawrence & Wishart, 1936, p. 49.

10. See my *Competition and the Corporate Society: British Conservatives, the State and Industry, 1945–1964*, London, Methuen, 1972, Chapters 1–4, pp. 23–74.

11. E. W. Hawley, *The New Deal and the Problem of Monopoly*, Princeton, New Jersey, Princeton University Press, 1966, p. 54.

12. 2 April 1938.

13. 15 June 1942.

14. A. H. Hanson, *The Process of Planning*, London, Oxford University Press, 1956, p. 38.

15. Paris, Felix Alcan, 1934.

16. Chiang Kai-shek, *China's Destiny*, London, Dobson, 1947, p. 173.

17. F. H. Cardoso, *Autoritarismo y democratizaçhão*, Rio de Janeiro, Editora Paz e Terra, 1979, p. 215.

18. Leroy P. Jones and Il Sakong, *Government, Business and Entrepreneurship in Development: the Korean Case*, Cambridge, Mass., Harvard University Press, 1980.

19. J. K. Galbraith, *The New Industrial State*, London, Hamish Hamilton, 1967, p. 296.

20. Andrew Shonfield, *Modern Capitalism: the Changing Balance of Public and Private Power*, London, Royal Institute of International Affairs/Oxford University Press, London, 1965, p. 231.

21. Peter Short, *Appraising the Role of Public Enterprise: an International Comparison* (IMF Occasional Paper), Washington DC, International Monetary Fund, 1983.

22. Clive S. Gray, 'Survey of recent developments', *Bulletin of Indonesian Economic Studies*, xviii/3, November 1982, p. 49.

23. 'State-owned corporations have become powerful factors in the world economy. In recent years, the fastest growing state-owned enterprises have been those in certain developing countries where they act as competitors, suppliers, customers, and partners of transnational corporations in the local economy;

some of them have expanded their operations to other countries' – United Nations Commission on Transnational Corporations, *Transnational Corporations in World Development, Third Survey*, New York, United Nations, 1983, p. 11.

24. *Far Eastern Economic Review*, Hong Kong, 25 July 1985, pp. 63–70.

Chapter 7

1. A. O. Hirschman, 'The political economy of import substitution industrialization in Latin America', *Quarterly Journal of Economics*, 82/1, February 1968.

2. See the interesting discussion of the rise of 'the new middle classes' (an 'unfortunate term', R H) by Rudolf Hilferding in 1910, in *Finance Capital, a Study of the Latest Phase of Capitalist Development*, translated and republished, London, Routledge & Kegan Paul, 1981, pp. 347–50.

3. 22 December 1941, 'Address to the Shensi-Kansu-Ninghsia Border Region Assembly', translated in Boyd Compton, *Mao's China, Party Reform Documents, 1942–1944*, Seattle, University of Washington Press, 1952, pp. 247–8. The same passage has been heavily edited and differently translated in the official version, Speech at the Assembly of representatives of the Shensi-Kansu-Ninghsia Border Region, November 21, 1941, in *Selected Works of Mao Tse-tung*, vol. 3, Peking, Foreign Languages Press, 1965, p. 32.

4. Marx's attitude is expressed in his advice to the Communist League in the late 1840s:

Far from desiring to transform the whole of society for the revolutionary proletarians, the democratic *petty bourgeoisie* strive for a change in social conditions by means of which the existing society will be made as tolerable and comfortable as possible for them . . .

As far as the workers are concerned, it is certain above all that they are to remain wage workers as before; the democratic *petty bourgeoisie* only desire better wages and a more secure existence for the workers and hope to achieve this through partial employment by the state and by charity measures; in short, they hope to bribe the workers by more or less concealed alms and to sap their revolutionary vigour by making their position tolerable for the moment . . .

For us, the issue cannot be the alteration of private property but only its annihilation; not the smoothing over of class antagonisms but the abolition of classes; not the improvement of the existing society but the foundation of a new one.

 – Address of the Central Authority to the Communist League, March 1850, in *Collected Works*, vol. 10, London, Lawrence & Wishart, 1979, pp. 280–81.

5. Boyd Compton, *Mao's China*, op. cit., p. 248.

6. Letter to Sorge, 19 October 1877, in *Correspondence of Marx and Engels, Selection, 1846–1895*, London, Lawrence & Wishart, 1934, p. 350.

7. K. Mukherji, *Reorganisation of Indian States*, Bombay, Popular Book Depot, 1955, p. 31.

8. Nym Wales, *Inside Red China*, New York, 1939, p. 335.

9. See Charles Issawi, *Egypt in Revolution*, London, Royal Institute of International Affairs/Oxford University Press, 1963, p. 99.

10. Cited by Harold Isaacs, in *The Tragedy of the Chinese Revolution*, London, Secker & Warburg, 1938, p. 71.

11. Israel Epstein, *Notes on Labor Problems in Nationalist China*, mimeo, New York, 1949.

12. F. G. Bailey, *Politics and Social Change, Orissa in 1959*, Berkeley, Calif., University of California Press, 1963, p. 166 passim.

13. Maurice Meisner, *Li Ta-chao and the Origins of Chinese Marxism*, Cambridge, Mass., Harvard University Press, 1967, p. 266.

14. Mao Tse-tung, 'Correct the "Left" errors in land reform propaganda', 11 February 1948, in *Mao Tse-tung, Selected Works*, vol. 4, Peking, 1965, p. 197.

15. ibid.

16. General Report, Peking Municipal People's Government on Agrarian Reform in the Peking Suburban Area, 21 November 1950, translated in *Current Bulletin*, 72, Hong Kong, 1951.

17. Cited by N. B. Krishnan, *Far Eastern Economic Review*, Hong Kong, 26 May 1983, p. 46.

18. *Revolution in the Revolution?*, London, Penguin Books, 1968, p. 41.

19. 'China's economic strategy', *Monthly Review*, New York, 27/3, July–August 1975, p. 9. Others nominated proletariats according to local fashion – thus, Franz Fanon's identification in the late fifties:

> In colonial countries, the peasants alone are revolutionary, for they have nothing to lose and everything to gain. The starving peasant, outside the class system, is the first among the exploited to discover that only violence pays. For him, there is no compromise, no possible coming to terms.
> – *The Wretched of the Earth*, London, Penguin Books, 1965, p. 48.

Of course, in a different sense, the identification of 'proletariat' with almost anyone on 'our side' dates from much earlier in Soviet history.

20. 'Towards complete independence', speech to the National Council, UNIP, August 1969.

Index

FOR THE BEST IN PAPERBACKS, LOOK FOR THE 🐧

In every corner of the world, on every subject under the sun, Penguin represents quality and variety – the very best in publishing today.

For complete information about books available from Penguin – including Puffins, Penguin Classics and Arkana – and how to order them, write to us at the appropriate address below. Please note that for copyright reasons the selection of books varies from country to country.

In the United Kingdom: Please write to *Dept E.P., Penguin Books Ltd, Harmondsworth, Middlesex, UB7 0DA.*

If you have any difficulty in obtaining a title, please send your order with the correct money, plus ten per cent for postage and packaging, to *PO Box No 11, West Drayton, Middlesex*

In the United States: Please write to *Dept BA, Penguin, 299 Murray Hill Parkway, East Rutherford, New Jersey 07073*

In Canada: Please write to *Penguin Books Canada Ltd, 2801 John Street, Markham, Ontario L3R 1B4*

In Australia: Please write to the *Marketing Department, Penguin Books Australia Ltd, P.O. Box 257, Ringwood, Victoria 3134*

In New Zealand: Please write to the *Marketing Department, Penguin Books (NZ) Ltd, Private Bag, Takapuna, Auckland 9*

In India: Please write to *Penguin Overseas Ltd, 706 Eros Apartments, 56 Nehru Place, New Delhi, 110019*

In the Netherlands: Please write to *Penguin Books Netherlands B.V., Postbus 195, NL–1380AD Weesp*

In West Germany: Please write to *Penguin Books Ltd, Friedrichstrasse 10–12, D–6000 Frankfurt/Main 1*

In Spain: Please write to *Alhambra Longman S.A., Fernandez de la Hoz 9, E–28010 Madrid*

In Italy: Please write to *Penguin Italia s.r.l., Via Como 4, I-20096 Pioltello (Milano)*

In France: Please write to *Penguin Books Ltd, 39 Rue de Montmorency, F-75003 Paris*

In Japan: Please write to *Longman Penguin Japan Co Ltd, Yamaguchi Building, 2–12–9 Kanda Jimbocho, Chiyoda-Ku, Tokyo 101*

The Germans   Gordon A. Craig

An intimate study of a complex and fascinating nation by 'one of the ablest and most distinguished American historians of modern Germany' – Hugh Trevor-Roper

Imperial Spain 1469–1716   J. H. Elliot

A brilliant modern study of the sudden rise of a barren and isolated country to the greatest power on earth, and of its equally sudden decline. 'Outstandingly good' – *Daily Telegraph*

British Society 1914–1945   John Stevenson

A major contribution to the *Penguin Social History of Britain*, which 'will undoubtedly be the standard work for students of modern Britain for many years to come' – *The Times Educational Supplement*

A History of Christianity   Paul Johnson

'Masterly ... It is a huge and crowded canvas – a tremendous theme running through twenty centuries of history – a cosmic soap opera involving kings and beggars, philosophers and crackpots, scholars and illiterate *exaltés*, popes and pilgrims and wild anchorites in the wilderness' – Malcolm Muggeridge

The Penguin History of Greece   A. R. Burn

Readable, erudite, enthusiastic and balanced, this one-volume history of Hellas sweeps the reader along from the days of Mycenae and the splendours of Athens to the conquests of Alexander and the final dark decades.

A History of Latin America   George Pendle

'Ought to be compulsory reading in every sixth form ... this book is right on target' – *Sunday Times*. 'A beginner's guide to the continent ... lively, and full of anecdote' – *Financial Times*

PENGUIN HISTORY

The Penguin History of the United States Hugh Brogan

'An extraordinarily engaging book' – *The Times Literary Supplement*. 'Compelling reading ... Hugh Brogan's book will delight the general reader as much as the student' – *The Times Educational Supplement*. 'He will be welcomed by American readers no less than those in his own country' – J. K. Galbraith

The Making of the English Working Class E. P. Thompson

Probably the most imaginative – and the most famous – post-war work of English social history.

The Waning of the Middle Ages Johan Huizinga

A magnificent study of life, thought and art in 14th- and 15th-century France and the Netherlands, long established as a classic.

The City in History Lewis Mumford

Often prophetic in tone and containing a wealth of photographs, *The City in History* is among the most deeply learned and warmly human studies of man as a social creature.

The Habsburg Monarchy 1809–1918 A. J. P. Taylor

Dissolved in 1918, the Habsburg Empire 'had a unique character, out of time and out of place'. Scholarly and vividly accessible, this 'very good book indeed' (*Spectator*) elucidates the problems always inherent in the attempt to give peace, stability and a common loyalty to a heterogeneous population.

Inside Nazi Germany Conformity, Opposition and Racism in Everyday Life
Detlev J. K. Peukert

An authoritative study – and a challenging and original analysis – of the realities of daily existence under the Third Reich. 'A fascinating study ... captures the whole range of popular attitudes and the complexity of their relationship with the Nazi state' – Richard Geary

PENGUIN HISTORY

The Victorian Underworld   Kellow Chesney

A superbly evocative survey of the vast substratum of vice that lay below the respectable surface of Victorian England – the showmen, religious fakes, pickpockets and prostitutes – and of the penal methods of that 'most enlightened age'. 'Charged with nightmare detail' – *Sunday Times*

A History of Modern France   Alfred Cobban

Professor Cobban's renowned three-volume history, skilfully steering the reader through France's political and social problems from 1715 to the Third Republic, remains essential reading for anyone wishing to understand the development of a great European nation.

Stalin   Isaac Deutscher

'The Greatest Genius in History' and the 'Life-Giving Force of Socialism'? Or a tyrant more ruthless than Ivan the Terrible whose policies facilitated the rise of Nazism? An outstanding biographical study of a revolutionary despot by a great historian.

Montaillou   Cathars and Catholics in a French Village 1294–1324
Emmanuel Le Roy Ladurie

'A classic adventure in eavesdropping across time' – Michael Ratcliffe in *The Times*

The Second World War   A. J. P. Taylor

A brilliant and detailed illustrated history, enlivened by all Professor Taylor's customary iconaclasm and wit.

Industry and Empire   E. J. Hobsbawm

Volume 3 of the *Penguin Economic History of Britain* covers the period of the Industrial Revolution: 'the most fundamental transformation in the history of the world recorded in written documents.' 'A book that attracts and deserves attention ... by far the most gifted historian now writing' – John Vaizey in the *Listener*

I: The Philosophy and Psychology of Personal Identity   Jonathan Glover

From cases of split brains and multiple personalities to the importance of memory and recognition by others, the author of *Causing Death and Saving Lives* tackles the vexed questions of personal identity. 'Fascinating ... the ideas which Glover pours forth in profusion deserve more detailed consideration' – Anthony Storr

Minds, Brains and Science   John Searle

Based on Professor Searle's acclaimed series of Reith Lectures, *Minds, Brains and Science* is 'punchy and engaging ... a timely exposé of those woolly-minded computer-lovers who believe that computers can think, and indeed that the human mind is just a biological computer' – *The Times Literary Supplement*

Ethics   Inventing Right and Wrong   J. L. Mackie

Widely used as a text, Mackie's complete and clear treatise on moral theory deals with the status and content of ethics, sketches a practical moral system and examines the frontiers at which ethics touches psychology, theology, law and politics.

The Penguin History of Western Philosophy   D. W. Hamlyn

'Well-crafted and readable ... neither laden with footnotes nor weighed down with technical language ... a general guide to three millennia of philosophizing in the West' – *The Times Literary Supplement*

Science and Philosophy: Past and Present   Derek Gjertsen

Philosophy and science, once intimately connected, are today often seen as widely different disciplines. Ranging from Aristotle to Einstein, from quantum theory to renaissance magic, Confucius and parapsychology, this penetrating and original study shows such a view to be both naive and ill-informed.

The Problem of Knowledge   A. J. Ayer

How do you *know* that this is a book? How do you *know* that you know? In *The Problem of Knowledge* A. J. Ayer presented the sceptic's arguments as forcefully as possible, investigating the extent to which they can be met. 'Thorough ... penetrating, vigorous ... readable and manageable' – *Spectator*

Political Ideas   David Thomson (ed.)

From Machiavelli to Marx – a stimulating and informative introduction to the last 500 years of European political thinkers and political thought.

On Revolution   Hannah Arendt

Arendt's classic analysis of a relatively recent political phenomenon examines the underlying principles common to all revolutions, and the evolution of revolutionary theory and practice. 'Never dull, enormously erudite, always imaginative' – *Sunday Times*

Ill Fares the Land   Susan George

These twelve essays expand on one of the major themes of Susan George's work: the role of power in perpetuating world hunger. With characteristic commitment and conviction, the author of *A Fate Worse than Debt* and *How the Other Half Dies* demonstrates that just as poverty lies behind hunger, so injustice and inequality lie behind poverty.

The Social Construction of Reality   Peter Berger and Thomas Luckmann

Concerned with the sociology of 'everything that passes for knowledge in society' and particularly with that which passes for common sense, this is 'a serious, open-minded book, upon a serious subject' – *Listener*

The Care of the Self   Michel Foucault
The History of Sexuality Vol 3

Foucault examines the transformation of sexual discourse from the Hellenistic to the Roman world in an inquiry which 'bristles with provocative insights into the tangled liaison of sex and self' – *The Times Higher Education Supplement*

Silent Spring   Rachel Carson

'What we have to face is not an occasional dose of poison which has accidentally got into some article of food, but a persistent and continuous poisoning of the whole human environment.' First published in 1962, *Silent Spring* remains the classic environmental statement which founded an entire movement.

FOR THE BEST IN PAPERBACKS, LOOK FOR THE 🐧

PENGUIN POLITICS AND SOCIAL SCIENCES

Comparative Government S. E. Finer

'A considerable *tour de force* ... few teachers of politics in Britain would fail to learn a great deal from it ... Above all, it is the work of a great teacher who breathes into every page his own enthusiasm for the discipline' – Anthony King in *New Society*

Karl Marx: Selected Writings in Sociology and Social Philosophy
T. B. Bottomore and Maximilien Rubel (eds.)

'It makes available, in coherent form and lucid English, some of Marx's most important ideas. As an introduction to Marx's thought, it has very few rivals indeed' – *British Journal of Sociology*

Post-War Britain A Political History Alan Sked and Chris Cook

Major political figures from Attlee to Thatcher, the aims and achievements of governments and the changing fortunes of Britain in the period since 1945 are thoroughly scrutinized in this readable history.

Inside the Third World Paul Harrison

From climate and colonialism to land hunger, exploding cities and illiteracy, this comprehensive book brings home a wealth of facts and analysis on the often tragic realities of life for the poor people and communities of Asia, Africa and Latin America.

Housewife Ann Oakley

'A fresh and challenging account' – *Economist*. 'Informative and rational enough to deserve a serious place in any discussion on the position of women in modern society' – *The Times Educational Supplement*

The Raw and the Cooked Claude Lévi-Strauss

Deliberately, brilliantly and inimitably challenging, Lévi-Strauss's seminal work of structural anthropology cuts wide and deep into the mind of mankind, as he finds in the myths of the South American Indians a comprehensible psychological pattern.

Epilogue

Allday glanced at the rigid marine sentry posted outside the frigate's stern cabin and after a brief hesitation thrust open the door.

He had been surprised to discover that leaving England again had been so easy. There was no knowing what lay ahead, or what the war might mean to him and to his captain. But on the nine days' passage from Spithead aboard this frigate, the thirty-six-gun *Harvester*, it had felt more like a homecoming than some of the anxious moments they had shared in the past.

For a few seconds he stood by the screen door and saw Bolitho framed against the tall stern windows, with a sunlit panorama of sea and hazy coastline turning very slowly beyond as the frigate was laid on her final tack for the anchorage.

In the vivid light the Rock itself was a hint of land, rather than a solid reality; but just the sight of it made Allday tense with excitement, something else he found difficult to explain. Gibraltar was not merely the gateway to the Mediterranean this time. It opened for them a new life, another chance.

He nodded with slow approval. In his best uniform with the white lapels, and the newly adopted epaulettes gleaming on either shoulder, Bolitho was a far cry from the man in the shabby coat, facing the smugglers', then the corvette's, cannon fire with equal determination, and with a defiance which had never left him despite the setbacks, the suffering and the procession of disappointments which had taken them both to the Nore.

Bolitho turned and looked at him. 'Well? What do you see?'

Allday had served with him for eleven years. Coxswain, friend, a right arm when need be. But Bolitho could still surprise him. Like now. The post-captain, a man envied not a little by *Harvester*'s young commanding officer; and yet he was anxious, even afraid, that he would fail, and betray all the hopes he had nursed since his return to duty.

'Like the old times, Cap'n.'

Bolitho turned and gazed at the glistening water below the counter. Nine days' passage. It had given him plenty of time to think and reflect. He thought of the frigate's young captain – not even posted yet, about his own age when he had been given *Phalarope*, when his and Allday's lives had crossed and been spliced together. It could not be easy to have him as a passenger, Bolitho thought. He had spent much of his time in these borrowed quarters, alone, and cherishing that precious moment when the orders had at last arrived for him.

'*To proceed with all despatch and upon receipt of these orders, to take upon you the charge and command of His Britannic Majesty's Ship* Hyperion.'

He smiled wistfully, *The Old Hyperion*. Once something of a legend in the fleet. But what now after all those years, so many leagues sailed in the King's service?

Was he still disappointed that he had not been offered a frigate? He bit his lip and watched some Spanish fishing boats idling above their images on the clear water.

It was not that. For Bolitho it was still too easy to recall the months of illness, then his daily pleading at the Admiralty for a command, any sort of ship they might condescend to provide. No, it was not that. Failure, then?

316

The lurking fear of some weakness, or of the fever which had almost killed him with no less skill than an enemy ball or blade?

A muscle jumped in his cheek as the frigate's salute crashed across the bay, shaking the hull gun like body blows. He heard the timed response from one of the Rock's batteries, and wondered why he was not even now on the quarterdeck seeking out his new command from the many vessels moored beneath the Rock's changeless protection.

He moved to a mirror which hung above one of his sea chests and studied his reflection, dispassionately, as he might a new subordinate. The uniform coat, with its broad white lapels and gilt buttons, the gold lace and epaulettes, should have offered immediate confidence. He knew from hard experience that no matter what kind of ship lay ahead, her company would be far more concerned about their new lord and master than he should be about them. But it failed to repel the uncertainty.

He thought of his last appointment and wondered still if the thankless task of recruiting at the Nore had been the true reason behind it. Had Lord Marcuard known even then that Bolitho was his choice for the other, deeper trust? Using his desperation for an appointment, a chance, no matter what, of returning to the one life he knew, and after losing Viola, needed more than ever. Perhaps he might never learn the complete truth.

He had found himself thinking of Paice very often. *That worthy man*, as he had described him in his despatch to the Admiralty. Many hundreds would die in this war, thousands, before it was ended in victory or defeat. Names and faces wiped away; and yet there were always the solitary men like Paice, whose memory never died.

He thought too of Vice-Admiral Brennier. He had received barely a mention in the newssheets, and Bolitho guessed that Marcuard's powerful hand was in that too.

Perhaps Brennier would after all be involved in some counter-revolution.

The last gun thundered, and he heard voices calling commands as they were sponged out and prepared for the final cable or so of the frigate's entrance. Many eyes would be watching her. Letters from home – fresh orders – or simply the sight of a visitor from England to prove that Gibraltar was not entirely alone.

Allday crossed the cabin, the old sword held in his hands. 'Ready, Cap'n?' He offered a grin. 'They'll be expecting to see you on deck.'

Bolitho extended his arms and heard Allday muttering to himself as he clipped on the sword.

'You needs a bit o' fattening' up, Cap'n—'

'Damn your impertinence!'

Allday stood back and hid a smile. The fire was still there. It just needed coaxing out.

He ran his eyes over Bolitho's slim physique. Smart as paint. Only the cheekbones, and the deeper lines at his mouth betrayed the grief and the illness.

Bolitho picked up his hat and stared at it unseeingly.

It was very strange, he had often thought, that at no time since the French treasure had been landed at Dover and put under guard, had it ever been publicly mentioned. Perhaps Marcuard, or even the prime minister, Pitt, had their own ideas as to how it might be used to better advantage?

How things had changed, just as he had known they would; just as Hoblyn had so bitterly prophesied. Especially with Pitt, he thought. The man who had cursed and condemned the smuggling gangs, who had used dragoons and the gibbet to keep their 'trade' at bay if not under control, and now been quoted as paying tribute to the very same scum. 'These men are my eyes, for without them I am blind to intelligence of the enemy!' It was so incredible that it was all the harder to believe, and to stomach.

318

As Queely had remarked dourly, 'Had Delaval stayed alive he might well have held a letter of marque from the King!'

Queely: another face in memory. He had been appointed to command a sturdy fourteen-gun brig at Plymouth. Bolitho wondered if he would take all his books with him to this different ship and different war.

He turned to Allday. In his blue coat and flapping white trousers, the tarred hat in one big fist, he would stir the heart of any patriotic landsman, or woman. Bolitho thought of the song he had heard when he had boarded *Harvester* from Portsmouth. 'Britons to Arms'. How poor Hoblyn would have laughed at that.

He heard a yell from the quarterdeck, the instant creak of the rudder as the wheel was put over. He could see it in his mind, as clearly as if he had been there on deck. The cluster of figures around the cathead ready to let go one anchor. The marines lined up on the poop in neat scarlet ranks. Captain Leach, anxious that everything should be right on this fair June morning, and justifiably proud of his fast passage from Spithead.

Bolitho shrugged and said quietly, 'I can never find words to thank you, old friend.' Their eyes met and he added, 'Truly, heart of oak.'

Then he walked through the screen door, nodding to the sentry before moving out into the sunlight, the expectant seamen who were waiting to furl every sail with only seconds between them when the anchor splashed down.

Leach turned to greet him, his expression wary.

Bolitho said, 'You have a fine ship, Captain Leach. I envy you.'

Leach watched him cross to the nettings, unable to conceal his astonishment. Surely Bolitho wanted for nothing? A post-captain of distinction who was almost certain to reach flag rank before this war showed signs of

319

ending, unless he fell out of favour or was killed in battle . . .

'Ready, sir!'

Leach held up his arm. 'Let go!'

Spray burst over the beakhead as the great anchor splashed down, but Bolitho did not see it.

I am a frigate captain.

And that gentle, remembered correction. *Were – a frigate captain.*

He ignored the voice in his memory and stared at the large ships-of-war anchored astern of one which wore a vice-admiral's flag at the fore.

One of them is mine.

He looked at Allday and smiled freely for the first time.

'Not a lively frigate this time, old friend. We've much to discover!'

Allday nodded, satisfied. The smile gave light to the grey eyes once more. It was all there, he decided. Hope, determination, and a new strength which her death had once taken away.

He breathed out slowly.

The Old Hyperion. So be it then.

Also by Alexander Kent and available in Arrow

THE INSHORE SQUADRON

Alexander Kent

Copenhagen, 1778

After seven years of cruel war against France, Britain's long-standing ally, Denmark, suddenly poses a threat. The scene of battle shifts abruptly from Europe to the East where the British Navy encounters the bitter hardship of blockade duty.

Richard Bolitho, recently appointed rear-admiral, is in charge of his first squadron, and is thrown immediately into a fierce and bloody struggle with the enemy. The outcome of the crucial Battle of Copenhagen is in Bolitho's hands . . .

SIGNAL – CLOSE ACTION!

As master of France, Napoleon now turns towards the East – and the vast wealth of India. But first he mut secure the eastern Mediterranean and Egypt.

Now Commodore of a newly formed squadron, in a British fleet stretched to the limit, Richard Bolitho faces one of the toughest comissions of his carrer: to ascertain the fighting strength of the French – then seek, find and bring them to battle!

SWORD OF HONOUR

March 1814

Admiral Sir Richard Bolitho returns to England from several months' rigorous patrolling off the North American coast. War with the United States has not yet ended, but news of Napoleon's defeat and abdication has stunned a navy and a nation bled by years of European conflict. Victory has been the impossible dream and now, for Bolitho, a vision of the future and a personal peace seems attainable.

However an unsympathetic Admiralty dispatches him to Malta. Is this appointment a compliment or a malicious ploy to keep Bolitho from the woman he loves and the freedom he craves? he cannot know, but the voice of duty speaks more insistently even than the voice of the heart, and in this familiar sea where both glory and tragedy have touched his life, Bolitho must confront the future, the renaissance of a hatred tyrant, and the fulfilment of destiny.

Other titles available in Arrow

☐ Sword of Honour	Alexander Kent	£5.99
☐ Midshipman Bolitho	Alexander Kent	£5.99
☐ Stand into Danger	Alexander Kent	£5.99
☐ In Gallant Company	Alexander Kent	£5.99
☐ To Glory We Steer	Alexander Kent	£5.99
☐ Command a King's Ship	Alexander Kent	£5.99
☐ Passage to Mutiny	Alexander Kent	£5.99
☐ Form Line of Battle!	Alexander Kent	£5.99
☐ Enemy in Sight!	Alexander Kent	£5.99
☐ The Flag Captain	Alexander Kent	£5.99
☐ Signal – Close Action!	Alexander Kent	£5.99
☐ The Inshore Squadron	Alexander Kent	£5.99
☐ A Traditon of Victory	Alexander Kent	£5.99
☐ Success t the Brave	Alexander Kent	£5.99
☐ Colours Aloft!	Alexander Kent	£5.99

ALL ARROW BOOKS ARE AVAILABLE THROUGH MAIL ORDER OR FROM YOUR LOCAL BOOKSHOP.

PAYMENT MAY BE MADE USING ACCESS, VISA, MASTER-CARD, DINERS CLUB, SWITCH AND AMEX, OR CHEQUE, EUROCHEQUE AND POSTAL ORDER (STERLING ONLY).

☐☐☐☐☐☐☐☐☐☐☐☐☐☐☐☐☐☐

EXPIRY DATE .... SWITCH ISSUE NO. ☐☐

SIGNATURE ....

PLEASE ALLOW £2.50 FOR POST AND PACKING FOR THE FIRST BOOK AND £1.00 PER BOOK THEREAFTER.

ORDER TOTAL: £................................. (INCLUDING P&P)

ALL ORDERS TO:
ARROW BOOKS, BOOKS BY POST, TBS LIMITED, THE BOOK SERVICE, COLCHESTER ROAD, FRATING GREEN, COLCHESTER, ESSEX, CO7 7 DW, UK.

TELEPHONE: (01206) 256 000
FAX: (01206) 255 914

NAME ....

ADDRESS...

....

Please allow 28 days for delivery. Please tick box if you do not wish to receive any additional information. ☐
Prices and availability subject to change without notice.